The
Journey
Home

BOOKS AND AUDIOS FROM KRYON
by Lee Carroll

BOOKS

Kryon Book One: *The End Times*
Kryon Book Two: *Don't Think Like a Human*
Kryon Book Three: *Alchemy of the Human Spirit*
Kryon Book Four: *The Parables of Kryon**
Kryon Book Five: *The Journey Home**
Kryon Book Six: *Partnering with God*

AUDIO BOOKS

The End Times
Don't Think Like a Human
Alchemy of the Human Spirit
*The Parables of Kryon**
*The Journey Home**

AUDIOS

Earth Changes...Your Wake-Up Call
Past Lives, Present Fears
Changes Within You
Honoring the Only Planet of Choice
Ascension in the New Age
Nine Ways to Raise the Planet's Vibration
Gifts and Tools of the New Age
Co-Creation in the New Age
Seven Responsibilities of the New Age

MUSIC AND MEDITATION

Crystal Singer Music Meditation Tape
Guided Meditations

(All of the above are available by calling 800-352-6657. Items marked with an asterisk may also be ordered by calling Hay House at 800-654-5126 or by faxing 800-650-5115.)

Please visit the Hay House Website at: **www.hayhouse.com**

The *Journey Home*

— *A Kryon Parable* —

The Story of Michael Thomas
and the Seven Angels

LEE CARROLL

Hay House, Inc.
Carlsbad, CA

Published and distributed in the United States by:
Hay House, Inc., P.O. Box 5100, Carlsbad, CA 92018-5100 • (800) 654-5126
(800) 650-5115 (fax)

Designed by: Christy Allison

Library of Congress Cataloging-in-Publication Data

Kryon (Spirit)
    The journey home : the story of Michael Thomas and the seven
angels / Kryon ; [channeled through Lee Carroll].
        p.   cm.
    ISBN 1-56170-552-7 (tradepaper)
    1. Spirit writings.   I. Carroll, Lee.   II. Title.
PS3561.R877J6   1997
133.9'3—dc21   97-28197
                                                   CIP

ISBN 1-56170-552-7

01 00 99 98   5 4 3 2
First Printing, September 1997
Second Printing, July 1998

Printed in the United States of America

*Dedicated to those who have realized
that a human has the power to change his or her life,
and that things are not always as they seem!*

CONTENTS

Who is Kryon?

Kryon is a gentle, loving entity who is currently on the earth to help us move into the high energy of what we call our "new age." Kryon's words have changed lives and brought love and light into some of the darkest places of our inner being. The storyline for THE JOURNEY HOME was inspired by Kryon and written by Lee Carroll.

$\mathcal{I}$NTRODUCTION

On December 8, 1996, Kryon sat before more than 500 people in Laguna Hills, California, at the close of an afternoon seminar. In a storytelling session that lasted over an hour, the journey of Michael Thomas was presented—a trek borne of the desire of an earth-weary human to join his spiritual family and go "home."

The very name Michael Thomas represents the incredibly sacred and holy attributes of The Archangel Michael, and also the old energy properties of Thomas the Doubter. This combination represents many of us who feel we are spiritual beings, but often doubt our abilities to move forward into a new millennium that has increasing spiritual demands or fear-based challenges.

Michael's journey home slowly reveals an adventure through seven colorful houses, each occupied by a Grand Angel. Each house represents an attribute of the New Age and carries with it wisdom, teaching, humor, and insight into what it is God wants us to know about ourselves. We also get a glimpse of the way things work as we move through the new paradigm of our New Age.

Progressing to a moving and surprising end, Michael Thomas's journey reveals to humans a package of loving instructions coming from a spiritual source that constantly desires to "wash our feet."

If you have ever asked God, "What is it you want me to know?"—THIS MAY BE IT! Join Michael Thomas in his exciting journey. It may remind you of your own.

CHAPTER ONE

Michael Thomas

T he black plastic pieces flew in all directions as Mike pushed his "in box" a bit too hard against the cubicle wall of his sales office. It was another instance where an inanimate object bore the brunt of Mike's growing anger at his situation. Suddenly, a head popped up through the dusty leaves of a plastic plant to his left.

"Everything okay over there?" asked John from the next cubicle.

The walls of each cubicle were just high enough to allow a person to pretend he had an office of his own. Mike had placed several tall items on his desk. This had the effect of hiding the fact that his co-workers were only about four feet from him at all times—all of them sharing in the pretense that they were alone in their spaces, having "private" conversations. The glow of white fluorescent light from the myriad naked fixtures above the cubicles bathed Mike and his peers in the kind of false illumination only found in institutions and industry. It seemed to absorb all the red in the visual spectrum, turning everyone pale, even though they lived in sun-drenched California. Years without direct sunlight made Mike seem doubly pale.

"Nothing that a trip to the Bahamas wouldn't cure," replied Mike without looking at the plant that had John's head showing through it. John shrugged and returned to his phone conversation.

Even as the words escaped his mouth, Mike knew that he would never see the Bahamas on the salary of an order taker working in the "coal mine," as the employees called the sales factory they worked for. He started picking up pieces of the plastic tray that he had shattered, and he sighed—something he found himself doing a lot lately. What was he here for? Why didn't he have the energy or the incentive to make his life better? His gaze took in the dumb-looking stuffed bear that he had bought himself. It said, "Hug me." Next to it was his favorite *Far Side* cartoon—something about the "bluebird of happiness" escaping Ned, the cartoon character; instead he was being visited by the "chicken of depression."

It didn't matter how many smiling faces or cartoons he tacked up on the cubicle walls. Mike still felt stuck. He was glued to an existence that resembled the workings of an office copy machine—each day duplicated over and over again without any purpose. The frustration and helplessness that he felt made him angry and depressed, and it was beginning to show. His supervisor had even mentioned it.

Michael Thomas was in his mid-thirties. Like many others in his office, he was in "survival mode." It was the only job he could find where he didn't have to care about what he did very much. He could simply disengage for eight hours a day, go home, sleep, try to pay his bills on the weekend, and go back to work again on Mondays. Mike realized that he only knew the names of four people in this Los Angeles office of over thirty individuals. He just didn't care, and he had been at this for over a year—ever since the emotional breakup that had shattered his life forever. He never shared his memories with anyone, but they ran through his head almost nightly.

Mike lived alone, except for his solitary fish. He had wanted a cat, but the landlord wouldn't allow it. He knew he was playing "victim," but his self-esteem was at an all-time low, and he continued to massage the wound that was his life—purposefully keeping it open, hurt, and bleeding so he could recall it at will. There wasn't anything else he felt he could do, and he wasn't certain he had the energy to change things even if he had wanted to. He had named the fish "Cat" just for fun, and he would speak to it each time he came home or left for work.

"Keep the faith, Cat," Mike would say to his finned friend on the way out. Of course, the fish never said anything in return.

Over six feet tall, Mike was somewhat imposing until he smiled. His grin carried with it a charm that melted all prejudgments anyone might have had upon seeing his large frame. It was not by chance that he found himself working on the phone where customers could not see him. Rather, it was a purposeful way of denying himself his best attribute—almost like a self-imposed prison, allowing him to wallow in the melodrama of his current situation. He excelled at people skills, but he seldom used them except when necessary at work. Mike did not cultivate friends willingly, and the opposite sex didn't even exist for him in his current mind-set—although they would have liked to.

"Mike," his male co-workers would say, "when is the last time you got lucky? You need to get out there and find a good woman—get your mind off your life!"

Then they would go home to their families, dogs, and loving children—and sometimes a fish, too. But Mike couldn't fathom how to start the process of rebuilding his lost love life. It wasn't worth it, he decided. *I found my partner early*, he would say to himself. *Except that she didn't know it.* He had been very much in love, with all the expectations that go with it. She, on the other hand, had just been having fun. When that fact was finally brought home, it was as if Mike's entire future had shriveled up and disappeared. He had loved her with a singular passion that he believed he would feel only once in his life. He had spent it all on her, but she had thrown it away.

Raised by his parents on a farm in the small town of Blue Earth, Minnesota, Mike escaped what he felt was a dead-end situation—that of growing crops that were either purchased by a foreign country or were stored indefinitely in large silos due to an overabundance of grain. Very early on, he knew that farming was not for him. It didn't seem to be valued even by his own country. What good was it? Besides, he couldn't stand the smell of it all, and he wanted to work with people instead of animals or tractors. He did well in school and was absolutely stellar in anything that involved interaction with others. Ending up in sales was a natural for Mike, and he had no problem at all finding good jobs selling a multitude of products and services he could represent with honesty. People loved to buy things from Michael Thomas.

When he looked back at what his now-deceased parents had given him, he realized that the one thing that had "stuck" was his belief in God. A lot of good it was doing right now, he often thought bitterly. Mike was an only child, and his parents—his beloved mom and dad—had been killed in a car accident just before his 21st birthday. He still mourned them greatly and always kept photos around to remind him of their lives—and deaths. Through everything, even now, Mike kept going to church and at least went through the motions of worship. When asked about his spiritual health by the minister, Mike openly admitted his faith and the belief in his spiritual nature. He was certain that God was just and loving, but not really in his corner at the moment—or even for the last few years for that matter. Mike often prayed for a better situation, but he had little optimism that things would really change.

With the ruddy complexion of his father, Mike was not really handsome, but attractive in a rugged sort of way. Women found him irresistible. His flashing smile, blond hair, tall frame, square jaw, and deep blue eyes were captivating. Those who had good intuition also knew that Mike was a man of integrity, and they trusted him almost instantly. He'd had many opportunities to take inappropriate advantage of situations—both in business and in romance—but he'd never done so. Mike was a product of farm consciousness—one of the only valuable attributes that followed him from the cold country of his upbringing.

He couldn't lie. He understood intuitively when others needed assistance. He opened doors for people coming into and out of the supermarket, respected and spoke to elders, and always gave the down-and-out men and women in the street the dollar bills they asked for, even if he suspected it might be wasted on alcohol. He felt that everyone should work together to make things better, and he never understood why people didn't speak to each other in his adopted town or seldom even met their own neighbors. Perhaps it was because the weather was so nice that people never needed help. *How ironic*, he thought.

Mike's only female role model was his mom; therefore, he treated all women with the kind of respect he had known for the wonderful, sensitive woman whom he missed greatly. Part of his misery now was the seeming betrayal of this respect in the only "real" relationship he had ever had. Actually, Mike's experience had only been a result of culture clash; what was expected from one person was not what was given, and vice versa. The California girl who had broken his heart was only following what she believed was her cultural truth about love, but Mike hadn't seen it that way. He had been taught differently, and he didn't have tolerance for other ideas about love.

AND SO IT IS that our story really begins. Here was Michael Thomas at his lowest ebb, coming home on a Friday night ready to greet his studio-style two-room apartment (two rooms that included the bathroom!). Mike had stopped at the store to pick up the meager groceries he needed to exist for the next few days. Long ago he had found that he could make his money go very far indeed if he bought the generic brands and used his coupons wisely. But his real key to frugality? Don't eat much!

Mike purchased packaged items that didn't need to be cooked. Then he didn't have to use the stove or pay for the electricity. This practice left him unfulfilled, somewhat hungry, and always without a dessert to look forward to—which seemed to fit his self-imposed role of victim just fine. He also found that if he ate everything right from the package over the sink, he didn't have to wash any dishes! He hated washing dishes and often bragged to John, his co-worker and only friend, about how he had solved the problem. Knowing Mike's habits, John commented in jest that before long Mike might find a way to do everything—even going without an apartment—by living at the nearest homeless shelter. John had laughed and slapped Mike on the back when he said it. Mike, however, had actually considered it.

By the time Mike got home from the store, it was dark. A heavy mist had been trying to turn into rain most of the day and was still at it, turning everything slick and shiny in the artificial yellow rays of the streetlight reflected on the apartment steps. Glad to be living in Southern California, Mike often remembered the hardships of the winters in Minnesota where he had grown up.

All during his youth, he'd had a passion for anything from California. He swore to himself that he had to escape the punishment of weather that everyone else simply took for granted. *Why would anyone choose to live where you could die in ten minutes from exposure?* he would ask his mom. She would smile and just look at him, then say, *"Families stay where their roots are, you know. Besides, it's safe here."* That was her familiar sermon about how dangerous Los Angeles was and how nice Minnesota was. That only made sense if you didn't add *death by freezing*! Mike couldn't convince her that the danger of earthquakes was like a lottery. It might happen in your lifetime—and it might not. Grueling Minnesota winters, however, were the norm every year—a cyclical occurrence that you could absolutely count on!

Needless to say, Mike escaped his country home as soon as he was done with high school, moving to California for his college years. He had used his sales abilities to personally finance everything he did. Now, he wished he had stayed home for a while—to be with his mom and dad during the years before the accident. He had lost precious times with his parents in his quest to escape the cold, or so he thought. He felt selfish in retrospect.

In the dim light, Mike trudged up the front steps to his ground-floor apartment and fiddled around with his key chain. He balanced his grocery bag and slid the key into the lock. The key went in normally, but that's when, on that Friday night, "normal" stopped for Michael Thomas. On the other side of the door was a gift—potentially a part of Mike's destiny—something that would change his life forever.

Due to a warped door frame, Mike had learned to use his body weight to help open the stubborn entrance to his lodgings. The result was that the door always burst open forcefully. Mike had perfected the method of balancing a bag of groceries on one hip, slipping the key into the lock, turning it, and pushing with his foot all at the same time. This maneuver required an awkward hip movement, and although it got the job done, his friend John had commented that it looked very funny indeed!

The obstinate door flew open with the impact of Mike's hip, startling the thief who was busy in the darkened room. With the swiftness of a frightened cat, and years of experience with the unex-pected, the uninvited man, a good foot smaller than Mike, instantly darted forward, grabbed Mike's arm, and yanked him into the room. Since Mike's balance was in the "funny" mode of opening his sticky door, he was already in full forward motion. The thief's action easily tumbled Mike into the apartment and smashed his large frame to the floor, where the groceries were launched against the far wall with enough force to break the seals on the packages. Just before he hit the floor, a shocked Mike, with all his bodily alarms going off at once, heard the door slam behind him—with the thief still inside! Mike caught a quick glimpse of the broken glass his face was headed for, a result of the shattered window that had allowed the smaller man to enter.

These are often the times, recounted after the fact, when people say that things slowed down in their minds. This was not the case for Michael Thomas. The seconds screamed by in a blur, compressing time and creating overwhelming panic! The man who had broken into the apartment was determined to continue his quest to remove the apartment's television and stereo, and he certainly didn't care what happened to his victim. Hardly had Mike fallen to the floor, when the man was on top of him with hands like a sweaty vise grip-ping Mike's throat. The man's eyes were wide and inches from his own. Mike could feel and smell the hot, foul breath in his face, and the weight of the man's rump on his stomach. He instinctively reacted as any person would who was about to die, and mustered up a move one might witness in a "B" movie. Despite his disorienta-tion, and with all his force, he quickly threw his head forward, smashing against the thief's head. It worked. The assailant, sur-prised by the force of the move, released his grasp long enough for Mike to violently roll to the side and try to stand up. Before he could right himself, however, the thief again attacked, this time with a strong blow to Mike's midsection. Mike was actually lifted up by the impact, then fell back and to the left, brutally connecting with something big that he dimly realized was his aquarium. With a hell-ish noise, the cabinet, the aquarium, and the solitary fish joined the groceries against the back wall of the small room.

Mike was in pain, and without breath. He gasped—his lungs on fire from oxygen deprivation—as his widening eyes watched a boot that seemed as big as Montana descend upon him. His assailant was grinning now. It happened too fast! The boot found its mark. Mike felt and heard the few bones in his throat and neck crunch in a horrible way. He gasped in horror, knowing absolutely that his air passage was gone—and perhaps his spine, too. His entire body reacted to the snapping and popping of his mutilated neck. Shock tore through his consciousness as the reality of the situation began to sink in. This was it—death was near! He tried to cry out, but his voice box wouldn't work. There was no more air for Mike, and things quickly went dark. All was quiet. The thief hurried to conclude his night's work, unconcerned about the very still man on the floor, when he was again startled by a racket at the much-abused apartment door.

"What's going on in there? Is everything all right?!" A neighbor was frantically pounding his fist on the uncompromising wood.

The thief cursed his luck and grudgingly moved toward the broken window. He punched out some remaining glass shards to clear his way and easily slipped through.

Mike's neighbor, who had never actually met Mike, heard the sound of more glass breaking inside and decided to try the doorknob. Finding the door unlocked, he entered to find the apartment trashed and a man fleeing through the broken window. Moving silently in the near dark to avoid the TV and stereo oddly stacked in the middle of the room, the neighbor snapped on a light switch, and a bare bulb came to life on the ceiling.

"Oh my God!" He heard his voice break in shock.

In a split second, the man was on the phone dialing for help. An unconscious and critically injured Michael Thomas lay on the floor. The room was quiet now—the only sound being that of a flopping fish two feet from Mike's head. "Cat" was wriggling among the lettuce and precooked noodles from the spilled groceries—an unsavory mix now beginning to redden from the slowly growing puddle of Mike's blood.

✤ ✤ ✤ ✤ ✤ ✤

CHAPTER TWO

The Vision

Mike woke up in unfamiliar surroundings. Then, with a flash of returning consciousness, he remembered everything. His eyes darted around, only to discern that he was not in his apartment—or a local hospital. Everything was quiet. In fact, the silence was so overwhelming that it unnerved him. There was simply no sound other than his own breathing! No cars passing by, no hum of an air conditioner—no anything! Mike managed to sit up slightly.

He looked down to find himself lying on a strange-looking white cotlike bed. There were no covers, but he was wearing exactly what he'd had on at the time of the attack. He reached up and touched his neck. His last conscious thought was that it had been mangled, but to his relief, he could detect no sign of injury. Mike actually felt good! He gently poked himself in several places. Strangely enough, there was no injury or soreness at all. But that silence! It was driving him crazy that there was no other stimulus to his ears. The lighting was odd, too. It seemed to come from nowhere and everywhere at the same time. It was brilliant white—a white so void of color that it hurt his eyes. He decided to examine his surroundings more closely.

This was spooky. He wasn't in a room—and he wasn't outside! There was only him, the cot, and a white floor that extended as far as he could see. Mike lay back down. He knew what had happened. He was dead. It didn't take a rocket scientist to understand that what he was observing and feeling didn't add up correctly in the real world. But why did he still have his body?

Mike decided to try something silly. He pinched himself to see if there was pain. He flinched and uttered a loud "Ow!"

"How do you feel, Mike?" asked a soothing male voice.

Mike instantly looked in the direction of the voice and saw a sight he would not forget for the rest of his life. Mike felt an angelic presence, a feeling of great love. He always went for how he FELT first, then on to what he SAW. It was his habit to describe his experiences in this manner when asked, and at this moment, he saw a figure in white that was in some way ominous, but splendorous at the same time. Were those wings, he wondered? How trite! Mike smiled at the vision in front of him, having difficulty believing it was real.

"Am I dead?" Mike inquired stoically, but with respect to the being before him.

"Not at all," said the figure, who approached Mike. "It's just a dream, Michael Thomas." The apparition came closer, seemingly without walking. Mike saw a veiled, blurred face on the giant "man" in front of his bed, but somehow it made him feel comforted, safe, and cared for. It was all he could do to continue speaking—the feeling was wonderful!

The figure was dressed in white, but he wasn't wearing a robe, exactly, or a suit. The garment seemed somehow to be alive, and it moved with the man as though it were skin. His face was the same— indistinct. Mike couldn't see any folds, buttons, or creases where clothing ended and skin began, yet the odd apparel was not tight. It was gossamer, flowing—sometimes actually glowing and indistinct. Adding to the vision was that Mike's eyes tended to blend the white of the man's attire into the incredibly white background of his surroundings. It was actually hard to see where the figure ended and the background started.

"'Where am I?' sounds like a stupid question, but I guess I am entitled to ask that," Mike said in a very small voice.

"You are in a sacred place," the figure replied. "A place of your own making, and a place that is filled with great love. That is what you are feeling right now." The angelic figure bowed to Mike, and it seemed to fill the area with even more light than was already there.

"And you are...?" Mike asked respectfully, his voice shaking.

"You probably guessed. I'm an angel."

Mike didn't blink an eye. He knew that the vision in front of him was telling the absolute truth. The situation, however odd, was extremely real. Mike felt all of it clearly.

"Are all angels male?" Mike regretted the question as soon as it had left his lips. What a dumb thing to ask! This was obviously a very special time. If it was a dream, then it was as real as anything he had ever experienced.

"I'm only what you wish to see, Michael Thomas. I am not of human form, so what you see before you has been presented in order to make you comfortable. But no—all angels are not male. We are actually neither gender. We don't all have wings, either."

Mike smiled again, realizing that perhaps what he was seeing was of his own making. "What do you really look like?" asked Mike, who was feeling a bit more free to speak normally to this loving being. "And why is your face hidden?" It was a valid question under the circumstances.

"My shape would astound you, and at the same time you would feel an odd remembrance upon seeing it, for it is the way *you* look, also, when you are not on Earth. It simply is beyond description, so I will continue to look like this for now. As for my face, you shall see it soon enough."

"When *I'm not on Earth*?" Mike probed.

"Earth existence is temporary, but you know that, don't you? I know who you are, Michael Thomas. You are a spiritual man, and you understand the eternal nature of humans. Many times you have given thanks for your spiritual nature, and those of us on my side have heard every word."

Mike was silent. Yes, he had prayed in church and at home, but to really think it all was heard clearly was just a bit too startling to grasp. This entity in his dream knew him?

"Where do you come from?" asked Mike.

"Home."

The loving entity now seemed to be glowing directly in front of Mike's small cot. The figure cocked its head to the side—and was patient while Mike took it all in. Mike felt tingles go up and down his spine. He had the strong sense that there was great truth standing here before him and that he had only to ask and wonderful knowledge would pour out.

"You are right!" the angel responded to Mike's inner musings. "What you do right now will change your future. You are feeling it, aren't you?"

"You can read my thoughts?" Mike inquired somewhat sheepishly.

"No. We can feel them. Your heart is linked to the whole, you know, and we respond when you need us."

"We?" This was getting spooky. "I only see *you*."

The angel laughed, and the sound was spectacular. What energy that laughter had! Mike felt every cell in his body resound with the humor the angel expressed. Everything the angel did was fresh, larger than life, and somehow there a wonderful remembrance of something deep within Michael's subconscious. Mike was stunned at the sound but said nothing.

"I speak to you with the voice of one, but I represent the voices of many," stated the angel as he held out his arms, letting the odd garment/skin flow and undulate from the move. "There are many in service to each human, Michael. This will become obvious to you, if you choose it to be."

"I DO CHOOSE!" Mike shouted the words. How could an invitation like that be ignored? Then Mike felt a little embarrassed, as if he were acting like a child in front of a matinee star. He was silent for some time and watched the angel move slightly up and down, as if he were on some kind of a mini-hydraulic lift. He again mused to himself how much of what he was seeing might be the result of his desire to perceive things a certain way from watching movies, attending church, or looking at great works of art. Things were silent again— oh, that silence! The angel was obviously not going to impart information unless Mike started asking questions.

"May I ask you about my situation?" Mike asked respectfully. "Is this really a dream? It seems so real."

"What is a human dream, Michael Thomas?" The angel moved slightly closer. "It is a visit into your biological and spiritual mind that enables you to receive information from my side of things—sometimes metaphorically. Did you know that? A dream may not seem like your reality, but it is actually closer to God's reality than anything you experience regularly! Those times your father and mother came to you in your dreams—how did that make you feel? Did it seem real? It was. Remember the week after the accident when they visited you? You wept for days in response. It was THEIR reality. Their messages to you were real. They continue to share love with you even to this day, Michael, because, like you, they are eternal, also. As far as questions about your situation, why do you think you are having this dream? It is the sole purpose for this visit, and it is timely and appropriate." Mike was pleased by the long stream of conversation from this beautiful one, who seemed increasingly familiar to him.

"Will I come out of this situation okay? I believe I am horribly injured and that I am unconscious somewhere, perhaps dying."

"Depends," said the angel.

"On what?" inquired Michael.

"What is it you really want, Michael?" asked the angel in a loving manner. "Tell us what it is you REALLY want. Be careful with your answer, Michael Thomas, for the energy of God is often literal. Besides, we know what you know. You cannot fool your own nature."

Michael wanted to be honest with his answer. The situation was becoming more real with each passing moment. He indeed remembered the vivid dreams he had about his parents right after their accident. They had come to him together in the few times he could sleep in that horrible week, and they had hugged and loved him. They told him that it was their appropriate time to leave—whatever that meant. Mike hadn't accepted that it was.

His parents had also told him that part of the arrangement of death was to give him a gift in their passing. He always wondered what the gift was, but then again, it was only a dream, or was it? The angel said it was real. This current experience certainly seemed real to Mike, so perhaps the parental messages were, too, just like this angel was, or is. This dream or vision is confusing, he thought with frustration!

What is it I want? Mike asked himself. He thought about his life ˙ ɪd all the things that had happened to him in the past year. He knew ɪat he wanted, but he felt it was wrong to ask for it.

"It does not suit your magnificence to withhold your innermost desires," mused the angel to Michael.

Drat! Mike said to himself. *The angel again knows what I am about. There is nothing I can hide.*

"If you already know, then why are you here to ask me?" Mike asked. "And what's this about me being magnificent?" For the very first time, the angel showed something other than a smile. It was a feeling of honor, of respect!

"You have no idea what and who you are, Michael Thomas" the angel said seriously. "You think I am beautiful? You should see what *you* look like! Someday you will. As far as me knowing your thoughts and feelings, of course I do. I am here as part of your support, and therefore I am with you in many very personal ways. It is my honor to appear before you, but it is your intent that will bring change at this time. You have the choice to tell me, or to not tell me, what it is you desire most at this moment as a human. The answer has to come from your own heart, spoken out loud for all to hear—even for YOU to hear. What you do at this point will make a difference for many." Mike took it all in. He would have to speak his truth even though it might not be what the angel wanted to hear. Mike contemplated for a moment, then he spoke.

"I want to go HOME! I'm tired of this life as a human." There! He had said it. He wanted out. "But I don't want to bail out of something important to God's plan." Mike was passionate. "Life seems so meaningless, but I was taught that I was created in the image of God for a purpose. What can I do?"

The angel moved to the side of the cot so that Mike could see him better. It was amazing, this vision, dream, or whatever it was. He swore he could smell violets—or was that lilac? Why flowers? The angel actually had a smell! It—he—was more beautiful the closer he got. Michael was also aware that the angel was pleased with the dialogue. He could feel it, even though he could not discern any expression on the angel's face.

"Tell me, Michael Thomas: Is your intent pure? Do you really want what God wants? You want to go home, but you are also somehow aware of a greater plan—so you don't wish to disappoint us, or act spiritually inappropriate?"

"Yes," said Mike. "That's it exactly. I want to leave my situation, but my desire seems like it is at odds with itself—it seems selfish."

"What if I told you that you might be able to have both?" asked the angel with a smile. "And that your wish for home is not selfish, but natural, and it is not in conflict with the desire to honor your purpose for being human."

"How? Please tell me how I can do this," an excited Mike now verbalized.

The angel had seen Mike's heart, and now he honored him spiritually for the first time. "Michael Thomas of Pure Intent, in order to determine if this can be your quest, I must ask you one more question before I tell you more." The angel moved away slightly. "What is it that you expect to gain by going home?"

Mike thought this through. His silence would have been awkward during a normal human conversation, but the angel understood him completely, knowing that this was a sacred time for the soul of Michael Thomas. As time is measured on earth, Michael was still for ten minutes or more, but the angel never moved or said a word. No feeling of impatience or weariness was displayed. Mike was beginning to realize that this entity was indeed timeless, without feeling the impatience that humans would, whose only reality was that of linear time.

"I want to be loved, and to be around love," was Mike's reply. "I want to feel peaceful in my existence." He paused. "I don't want to be subject to the concerns and trivial interactions of those around me I don't want to worry about money. I want to feel RELEASE! I'r tired of being alone. I want to mean something to other entities in th Universe. I want to know that I exist for a reason, and do my part in heaven—or whatever you call it—to be a correct and appropriate part of God's plan. I don't really want to be a human as I have been. I want to be like *you!*" He paused again. "That's what going home is about for me." The angel once again moved to the foot of the cot.

"Then, Michael Thomas of Pure Intent, you indeed shall have what you strive for!" The angel seemed to be taking on still more light, if that were possible! He absolutely glowed with white, which was now starting to be mixed with a golden hue. "But you must follow a path that is predetermined, and you must do it voluntarily with intent and choice. Then, you will be rewarded with a trip home. Will you do this?"

"I will," replied Mike. He felt the beginnings of a wonderful feeling that could only be described as a wash of love. The air was starting to feel thick. The glow of the angel was starting to creep into the cot and surround Mike's feet. Chills began to go up his spine, and he involuntarily started to shake with a fast vibration, the likes of which he had never felt before. It was almost a buzz; it was so fast. It traveled right up his body and into his head. His vision started changing, with momentary flashes of blue and violet showing up with great contrast against the intense white that he had been looking at since this had all started.

"What is happening?" asked Mike fearfully.

"Your intent is changing your reality."

"I don't understand." Mike was terrified.

"I know," replied the angel in a very compassionate tone. "Do not ?ar the integration of God into your being. It is a meld that you have requested, and it will suit your journey home."

The angel backed away from Mike's narrow bed as if to give him room.

"Please don't leave yet!" exclaimed a still overwhelmed and fearful Mike.

"I'm just adjusting myself to accommodate your new size," said the angel in a slightly amused way. "I'll leave only when we are complete."

"I still don't understand, but I'm not afraid," Mike lied. Again the angel laughed and filled the space with a resonance that surprised Mike with its wonderful mirth and intensity of love. Mike realized that there were no secrets here, so he continued to speak. He had to know what this feeling was. Then the angel laughed.

"What is it that happens when you laugh? It affects me inside somehow, and it's something I haven't felt before." The angel was pleased by the question.

"What you hear and feel is an attribute that is purely from the God source," said the angel. "Humor is one of the only qualities that passes untouched from our side to your side. Did you ever wonder why humans are the only biological entities on Earth that laugh? You might think the animals laugh, but they are responding only to stimulus. You are the only ones who have the real spark of spiritual awareness that supports this full property; the only ones who can create humor from an abstract thought or an idea. Therefore, your consciousness is the key. Believe me, it is sacred. That is why it is so healing, Michael Thomas of Pure Intent."

This was more explanation than the angel had provided up until this point. Mike felt that he might squeeze out some more gems of truth before this time passed. He eagerly tried.

"What is your name?"

"I don't have one." There was the silence again. A long pause. Oops, Mike thought. We are back to short answers.

"How are you known?" Mike continued to probe.

"I AM known by all, Michael Thomas—and THAT I AM known by all; therefore, I exist."

"I don't understand," Mike replied.

"I know." Again the angel mused, but not at the expense of Mike. It was an honoring of Mike's naïveté in a situation where he was not expected to know more—the way in which a parent might indulge a child who asked probing questions about life. There was love in everything the angel did or said. Mike knew he had to stop pressing and get to the point.

"What is the path you speak of, dear angel?" Mike felt uncomfortable for a moment with his salutation of "dear," but somehow it fit the personality before him. The angel was parental, brotherly, sisterly, yet had the personal feeling of a lover all at the same time. This was a feeling Mike would not soon forget. He longed to stay in this energy, and he dreaded the thought that it might come to an end.

"When you return to your reality, Michael, prepare your things an adventure of many days. When you are ready, the beginning of the path will be shown to you. You will be required to journey to seven houses of Spirit, and in each house you will meet an entity somewhat like me, each with a different purpose. The path may contain surprises and even danger, but you can stop anytime you wish, and there will be no judgment about this. You will change along the way and learn many things. You will be required to study the attributes of God. If you traverse all seven houses, then the door will be shown for you to go home. And Michael Thomas of Pure Intent," the angel paused and smiled, "there will be great celebration when you open that door."

Mike had no idea what to say. He felt a sense of release, but also a nervousness about journeying into the unknown. What would he find? Should he do this? Perhaps this was simply a dream that was all nonsense! What was real, anyway?

"What you have before you now is real, Michael Thomas of Pure Intent," said the angel, again reading Mike's emotions. "What you will return to is a temporary reality built just for humans to learn within."

All Michael had to do was feel his doubt, and the angel knew it. Once again, Mike felt that he was in some way being violated by this new way of communicating, and in another way he was being honored! In a dream, Mike thought, you are in contact with your own brain. Therefore, there can be no secrets from yourself. Perhaps that is why it seemed appropriate to have such a conversation with this entity who knew what he was thinking. Besides, Mike was experiencing just what that angel said. He was beginning to feel quite comfortable in this "dream reality," and he was not looking forward to going back to anything short of it.

"What now?" asked Mike hesitantly.

"You have given intent for the journey. So it is that you will return to your conscious human state. There are some points to remember along the way, however: Things will not always be as they seem, Michael. As you progress, you will become closer to the reality that you experience now with me. Therefore, you may have to develop a new way of being—perhaps a bit more..." The angel paused. "...CURRENT than what you are used to, as you approach the door to home." Mike didn't understand what the angel was talking about, but he listened intently, anyway.

The angel continued. "There is another question that I must now ask you, Michael Thomas of Pure Intent."

"I'm ready," replied Mike, feeling less than confident, but honestly ready to move ahead. "What is the question?" The angel moved closer to the end of the cot.

"Michael Thomas of Pure Intent, do you love God?" Mike was startled by the question. Of course he did, he thought. Why was this being asked?

Mike answered quickly. "As you can see my heart and know my feelings, you must know that I love God." There was silence, and Mike could tell that the angel was pleased.

"Indeed!" It was the last word that Mike heard from the hidden lips of this beautiful creature who obviously loved Mike a great deal. The angel reached out to Mike and moved his hand in such a fashion that it intersected Mike's throat. How could he reach that far? Immediately, Mike felt as though hundreds of fireflies had flown into his neck and were altering his persona. Mike felt no pain, but suddenly he vomited.

CHAPTER THREE

Preparation
(THE JOURNEY BEGINS)

"Hold his head to the left next to the tray!" cried the nurse to the orderly. "He's vomiting."

The emergency ward was crowded that night, as is often the case on a Friday. This time the full moon also complicated matters. Although they might not possess a shred of belief in astrology or anything metaphysical, most hospitals had a tendency to put more personnel in the ER at this time of the month. Things seem to occur that never happen at any other time. The nurse rushed out of the room to tend to another urgent matter.

"Is he awake?" asked the neighbor who had accompanied Mike into the ward. The white-coated orderly bent down to closely examine Mike's eyes.

"Yeah. He's coming out of it," the orderly replied. "When you can speak to him, don't let him up. He's not only got a nasty head bump with a few stitches, but his jaw is going to be real sore for a while. The x-rays show that it was almost fractured. Good thing we were able to set the dislocation while he was out."

The orderly moved out of the cubicle, an area separated by a curtain on a semicircular rod. On the way out, he pulled the curtain so that Mike and his neighbor were again alone. The many sounds of the emergency ward were subtle, but the neighbor could hear people and activities in the cubicles on each side of the one he was in. There was a female stab-wound victim in the cubicle to the left; and to the right, an elderly man suffering from shortness of breath and a numb arm. They had been there almost as long as Mike had—about an hour and a half.

Mike opened his eyes and felt a searing pain in his lower jaw. He knew immediately that he was awake. *No more angel dreams*, he thought, as the reality of the pain and the entire situation slowly became his reality. The fluorescent fixtures that bathed the emergency area in a bright, sterile light made Mike wince and close his eyes. The temperature in the room was cold, and Mike instantly felt the need for a blanket—none was offered.

"You've been out for a while, buddy," said the neighbor, feeling a bit embarrassed that he didn't even know Mike's name. "They dressed your head and set your jaw. Don't try to talk."

Mike looked appreciatively at the man who was bending over him. Although still in a daze, he analyzed the features of the man's face. Mike recognized him as the tenant in the unit adjacent to his. The man took a seat to the side of Mike, who fell into a very deep sleep.

WHEN HE AWOKE next, Mike knew he was in a different area. It was still and quiet, and he was in a bed. As he opened his eyes and tried to clear his foggy mind, he realized he was still in the hospital, but this time he was in a private room. It was well appointed for a hospital, Mike thought. His dreary gaze took him to the pictures on the wall, and the ornate chair by the side of the bed. There was expensive sound-absorbent material on the ceiling, crisscrossing the room in small, elegant squares made slightly oblong by Mike's fuzziness. The fluorescent fixtures were still there, but turned off and semi-hidden within the pattern of the soft design. Most of the light was coming from a bay-view window and a couple of incandescent lamps within the room. Instead of a bare shelf on the facing wall holding up a television set, as in most hospital rooms, there was a finely finished armoire. The doors of the exquisite cabinet were closed now. The lamps had shades, much like in a fine hotel, and the shades matched the wallpaper! What kind of place was this? A private residence? Further examination with his eyes only, however, revealed the standard hospital air, gas, and electrical outlets available at various points in the room. Mike could also tell that there were a number of diagnostic tools behind him—one that was attached to his arm with some medical tape. It was beeping softly every few moments.

With no one apparently around him, Mike started to analyze what had happened. Did they operate on his throat? Could he talk? Slowly, he brought his hand up to his throat, expecting to find massive bandages or even a plaster cast. Instead, Mike found smooth skin! He moved his fingers all over his neck, only to discover that all was as it should be. Mike gradually tried to clear his throat and was surprised to find his voice immediately. It was when he opened his mouth, however, that he realized where the problem was. Stinging red pain, enough to cause nausea, instantly stabbed Mike down behind his mouth and below his ears. *That's pain you can hear*, thought Mike as he mentally made a note not to open his mouth so fast again.

"Oh, we're awake I see. We can give you anything you need for the pain, Mr. Thomas," said a whining but kindly female voice from the doorway of the room. "But you will recover faster if you find your own level of tolerance without the pills. Nothing is broken, you know. Your jaw just needs to be exercised back to normal." The nurse, wearing what could only be called a designer nurse's outfit, approached the bed. Not only was her outfit pressed and perfect, but it was obvious that she was very experienced. Above her pocket were several awards and experience badges. Mike spoke carefully through his clenched teeth, moving his jaw only slightly with each word.

"Where am I?" he mumbled.

"You're at a private hospital in Beverly Hills, Mr. Thomas." The nurse moved next to him. "You spent the night here after they brought you over from the emergency room recovery area. You are also scheduled to leave shortly, you know." Mike's eyes opened wide, and his face wrinkled with worry. He had heard stories of two- and three-thousand-dollar-a-day bills for a stay in a place such as this. His heart began to race as he wondered how he'd pay for it all.

"It's okay, Mr. Thomas," the nurse said reassuringly, reading Mike's expression. "It's all taken care of. Your father made all the arrangements, you know. Oh, yeah, he paid for it all."

Mike was quiet for a moment, contemplating how his dead father could have made any arrangements. Perhaps she only *assumed* it was his father, and it was really his neighbor? Mike mustered up the strength to speak through his barely moving mouth.

"Did you see him?" Mike grunted.

"See him? Oh, yeah! Some looker, your dad! Tall and blond like you, with the voice of a saint. Had all the nurses a-twitter, you know." Just listening to the nurse, Mike knew she was from his home state in Minnesota. They all seemed to talk backwards there, often placing the subject of the sentence last—an odd thing that he had overcome shortly after moving to California. It made them sound like the character Yoda from *Star Wars.*

She continued. "Paid for everything, he did, in cash no less. Don't you worry now, Mr. Thomas—and, oh yes—he left a message for you, you know."

Mike felt his heart leap even though he suspected that the so-called father was just his neighbor; the nurse's description didn't fit either one. The nurse had left the room to fetch the message. Not more than five minutes went by before she returned with a piece of paper that obviously had a typewritten message on it.

"Dictated it, you know," said the nurse, as she took a piece of folded paper out of a hospital envelope. "Said that his handwriting wasn't very good, so we typed it at the desk for you. Kind of hard to understand, if you ask me. Did he used to call you *Opee* when you were a kid?" The nurse handed the paper to Mike, and he read it.

> *Dear Michael-Opi,*
>
> *Not everything is as it seems. Your quest begins now. Heal quickly and prepare your things for the journey. I have prepared the way home. Accept this gift and move forward. You will be shown the way.*

Mike felt chills run up and down his spine. He looked at the nurse with grateful eyes and held the paper to his chest. He then closed his eyes as if asking to be left alone. The nurse got the point and left the room.

Mike's mind raced with possibilities. *"Not everything is as it seems,"* the note said. That's an understatement! He knew that his throat had been mangled and stomped on yesterday by a criminal who almost did him in on the floor of his apartment. He had felt every bone-crunching second of that horrible event! Yet, now there was no injury except a badly dislocated and reset jaw to contend with, along with some cuts and bruises on his face and head. These things would be sore for a while, but they were not incapacitating. Was this the *gift*?

The idea that the angel vision could have been an actual event was not part of Mike's reality until he had read the note. If this wasn't the angel, then who? He simply didn't know anyone who had the money or who knew him well enough to give him anything, much less pay his substantial medical bill. Who else could know of the journey he promised to take? His body was vibrating with questions, and he was still reeling with doubt over the note and what it meant, when he received the final validation and smiled.

The nurse had asked about being called Opee? On the note it was spelled Opi, like a name— undoubtedly dictated letter by letter by the "angel" who had paid his bill. It wasn't a nickname. The letters were initials! O-P-I—*Of Pure Intent!* Therefore, the salutation was, *Dear Michael of Pure Intent.* Mike's smile turned into a laugh. It hurt a lot, but he continued to laugh, and his whole body shook with the mirth of the moment, until he was quiet and let the tears of joy also come. He was going home!

THE NEXT FEW DAYS were special. Mike left the hospital with some pills that would help him with the pain, but he found that he didn't need them. His jaw seemed to be healing with incredible speed, and he was able to exercise it gently. His speech was coming along fine.

Eating, although a chore at first, came back to normal within a day or two. Through the process, pain simply wasn't a concern. There was stiffness, but it was bearable under the circumstances. Mike didn't want any pain pills to interrupt the "high" he was feeling about going on his spiritual quest. The cuts and bruises slowly vanished with time, although Mike was again astonished by how fast it was all happening.

Mike quit his job over the phone. He had practiced doing it so many times in his mind; he really savored the act of terminating his connection with that awful job. He then called his friend John and explained as best he could that he would be leaving for an extended vacation and might not be back. John wished him well, but he expressed concern over Mike's secrecy regarding his plans.

"Buddy," John had said persuasively, "you can tell me! I'm not going to do anything. What's going on?" Mike knew very well that John would not understand if he told him that an angel had appeared and had given Mike instructions—so he kept quiet.

"I have a private journey to take," he told John. "It's meaningful for me." And he left it at that.

Mike gave notice at his apartment and packed his things. He carefully separated his very personal belongings from his clothing and appliances. He didn't have much, but the things he cherished the most—the photos and the few books—he packed into two special cases. Mike realized that he could not take many clothes, so he packed the bare minimum for a very light journey, which also fit in the cases along with the photos and books.

Mike invited his neighbor over—the one who had saved him—and gave the man some clothes, his television set, the bike he used to pedal to work, and various other meager belongings that he had accumulated over the past year or so.

"If you don't want these," Mike had said, "then give them to charity."

The neighbor seemed overwhelmed by the gesture, and he smiled broadly while pumping Mike's hand. Mike got the impression that the man had indeed needed much of what was offered. "Cat" the fish had been saved by the neighbor after calling 911, and it only seemed fitting that it should also go to him, seeing as how it was now in the man's aquarium anyway.

"Good-bye, Cat!" Mike had said with a smile, while in the man's apartment. "Keep the faith." Cat didn't even look at him. He was busy with his new fish friends.

It was the fifth day after Mike returned home from the hospital that he realized that he was approaching the end of his preparations. He didn't know exactly how to proceed, and he didn't know where precisely where he was going. It was evening and all was quiet. He knew that the angel would be aware when he was ready and that tomorrow would be the start of something new. Mike felt that the reality of his journey was absolute. He "owned" the belief that he would be shown what to do. Everything that had happened in the last week justified the logic of his faith. Mike decided to review the precious belongings in the cases he was hauling along his spiritual trek.

He opened them and painstakingly examined the items that he felt needed to be taken along. The first group of items consisted of the photos. The photo album was fairly tattered with time, and many of the aged pictures had been originally attached with the old-fashioned gummed corner mounts from the '50s. He opened the book carefully so as not to disturb the weaker mounts, and once again he felt the familiar feeling of melancholy when he gazed upon the wedding photo of his parents—the first photo in the book. He had found this and other personal photos of them after the accident, and he'd barely had the strength to look on them back then.

There they were—very much in love—smiling at the camera—beginning their lives together. Their clothes looked funny to Mike, and it's the only time he remembered seeing his dad in a tie. Later Mike found Mom's old wedding dress in the attic. He had asked a neighbor to pack it for him, since it was too painful. Mike was just a glimmer in their eye when the photo was taken, and their future was filled with expectation of good things. Mike stared at the photo for a very long time, finally speaking softly to it:

"Mom and Dad, I am your only child. I hope what I am about to do will not disappoint you in any way. I love both of you and wish to see you soon."

Precious moments went by as Mike turned the pages of the book that contained the lineage of his boyhood. He smiled often. There was the old farm, the occasional pictures of his friends along the way. He loved the photo of himself on the tractor when he was six. What a treasure this album was! Mike felt that God would be happy to have him honor his parents and his upbringing by taking the photos on this special trip. What would eventually become of the album was unknown, but for now Mike felt that he could not leave these items behind.

Then, there were his books. He loved them! His Bible was worn thin with many readings, and it had comforted him so many times. Even if he didn't understand all of it, he felt its spiritual energy. It was carefully packed, and Mike could never leave it behind. Then, there were his boyhood books that meant so much—*The Hardy Boys*, *Charlotte's Web*. These were just a few paperbacks that he continued to read periodically, each time remembering what he was doing at the age he first experienced those great stories and characters. Finally, the great adventure of *Moby Dick* when he got older, and the *Sherlock Homes* series; and then some of his favorite poetry by obscure writers.

All the books and the photos fit nicely into two satchels, and they could be carried easily, allowing him to also carry a medium-sized sack that could hold a snack or two. Mike felt he was ready, so he lay down on the floor of his now bare apartment for the final time. He had a pillow, and that was enough. He was ready for the next day, and the excitement of starting his spiritual quest made sleep almost impossible as he turned over in his mind the things that had happened, and the promise of things yet to come. Tomorrow would be the beginning of his journey home.

❧

Chapter Four

❧

The First House

T he next morning dawned a bit dreary, but Mike's spirits were high. With some meager funds that he had saved, Michael purchased a large breakfast, which he ate on the patio of a local bistro. It felt odd to be outside at this time of day. Normally, he was working by now, used to toiling all day, eating a sack lunch at his desk, and having the sun go down out of his eyesight while he was still in the confines of the building.

With satchels in hand, and the bag over his shoulder, Mike stood outside the diner wondering exactly which way to go. He knew that he could not head west, since the ocean would soon intervene. East it was, then, until he was shown another route. Appropriately, Mike felt pretty good about beginning a trip built on faith, but he still wished he had a more clear destination.

If only I had some sense of direction—a map, perhaps, or an indication of my current position, Mike said to himself as he plodded eastward, passing very slowly through the suburbs of Los Angeles toward the foothills of yet another endless neighborhood. *It's going to take weeks to walk out of here*, thought Mike.

Mike didn't really know where he was going, but he just kept heading east. At lunchtime he sat down on a curb and consumed the leftovers he had saved from breakfast, and again wondered if he was on the right path.

"If you're there, I need you now!" said Mike out loud to the sky. "Where is the gate to the path?"

"*A current map it shall be!*" Mike heard a familiar voice speaking in his ear. He stood up and looked around but saw no one. He recognized the voice of the original angel.

"Did I hear that, or feel it?" muttered Mike under his breath with a sense of relief. At least there was some communication!

"What took you so long?" asked Mike with some humor.

"*You only asked for help a moment ago,*" replied the voice.

"But I've been wandering for hours!"

"*That's your choice,*" stated the voice. "*What took you so long to verbalize YOUR request to us?*" The voice was obviously having fun, turning Mike's objection back at him.

"You mean that I only get help when I ask?"

"*Yes. What a concept!*" replied the voice. "*You are a free spirit, honored and powerful and able to make your own way if that's your choice. It's what you have been doing all your life. We are always here, but only active when you ask. Is that so odd?*" Mike was momentarily irritated by the absolute logic of the angel's words.

"Okay, where do I go? It's past noon, and I feel that I have been guessing all morning about which direction to walk."

"*Good guessing,*" replied the voice, with an implied wink. "*The gate to the path is just ahead.*"

"You mean I was headed for it all along?"

"*Don't be so shocked that you went right to it. You are a piece of the whole, Michael Thomas of Pure Intent. With practice, your intuition will serve you well. I am here today only to help steer you in small ways.*" The voice hesitated. "*Look ahead, you're already at the gate!*"

Michael stood in front of a large hedge that led into a canyon between rows of houses.

"I don't see anything."

"*Look again, Michael Thomas.*"

Mike stared at the bush and slowly realized that there was an outline of a gate. It had been hidden by the fact that it blended in, and looked like part of the overall structure of the plant. Now it seemed that he couldn't NOT see the gate even if he wanted to. It was so obvious! He turned away for a moment, then looked at it again with a new perception. There it was, now even clearer than it was a moment ago.

"What is happening?" asked Mike, aware that his perception was changing.

"When unseen things become obvious," the gentle voice said, *"you can't go backwards into ignorance. You will now see all gates clearly, since you gave intent for this one."*

Although Mike didn't fully understand the significance of what was being given him, he was all too ready to move onto the main path of his journey. The hedge stopped resembling a gate and actually became one! Right before Mike's eyes it was changing and growing in its definition.

"This is a miracle!" whispered Mike as he continued to watch the tall hedge transform into a tangible gate. He even backed up slightly to allow room for the phenomenon to occur.

"Not really," replied the voice. *"Your spiritual intent just shifted YOU slightly, and the items that vibrate at your new level simply have snapped into view—no miracle. It's just the way it works."*

"You mean my consciousness can change reality?" questioned Mike.

"Semantics," replied the voice. *"Reality is the essence of God and is constant. Your human consciousness only reveals the new parts of it you wish to experience. As you change, more of it comes into view, and you may experience and use the many new revelations as you wish, but you cannot go backwards."*

Mike was beginning to understand, but he had an additional question before he started down the path through the newly exposed gate before him. He was always ready to test everything for truth—even the angelic voice he was hearing in his mind. Mike formed his question and stated it.

"You said I was a creature of free choice. Why can't I go backwards if I choose to? What if I want to ignore the new reality and return to a simpler one? Isn't that free choice?"

"It is the physics of spirituality that creates an axiom that states you will never be able to return to a less-aware state," replied the voice. *"If you actively choose to try, however, then you are denying the enlightenment you have been given, and you will become unbalanced. Indeed, you are able to try to move backwards. It is your free will. However, sad indeed are those humans who try to ignore what they know is truth, for they will not last long with a dual vibratory rate."*

Mike did not understand all the new spiritual information that the voice was imparting to him. He did receive the answer, however, to his question. He knew he could turn around right now and go back to the city. It was his choice. But every time he stood here he would see the gate, and knowing it was there, but ignoring it, would make him unbalanced and no doubt sick. Somehow it all made sense, and it was his desire to move forward, not backward—so Mike picked up his satchels and bag and moved forward through the gate, onto the path that was the beginning of his journey. It was a plain dirt path, like any other in any canyon. Mike was excited and moved right on, quickly leaving the gate behind.

Mike had just gone through the gate when a dark, shadowy greenish figure also slipped through. The shrubbery wilted where IT walked, and had Michael not moved on, the stench would have alerted him to ITs presence. IT quickly took up position behind Michael Thomas, staying just out of sight but keeping up with him in his exuberance. Like a swift and cunning phantom, IT shadowed Mike's excitement and his glee with an equal amount of hatred and dark purpose. Mike had no idea that IT was there.

Shortly after setting off on the path, the scenery, even the feeling of the land changed greatly for Michael Thomas. Nowhere could he see the sprawling city of Los Angeles or the myriad suburban homes. In fact, there was no hint of civilization—no telephone poles, no airplanes, and no freeways. He had eagerly embarked upon the new dirt path before him like a kid opening gifts at Christmas—plowing ahead without really thinking—and now he realized that with each step he was going deeper into another world. This journey was taking him into a reality that was far removed indeed from the one he had just experienced. Mike wondered if he was now in some kind of place

between earth and heaven where he might start his spiritual school-
ing—something he assumed would be taking place soon to prepare
him for the honor of going home. The trail-like path had slowly
become wider, and now was almost the width of a road. It was about
three to four feet wide, without footprints of any kind, and very easy
to follow.

Mike turned around suddenly. What was that? Something dark
green and quick caught his eye as it darted to the left behind a boul-
der. *Must be the wildlife*, Mike thought. The road behind was now a
mirror image of where he was heading—a long path that twisted and
turned, disappearing over hill after hill in the distance, all within a
gloriously lush countryside of green trees, meadows, and rocky out-
crops. Flowers dotted the landscape like so many blips of color precisely in the right places on the perfect canvas of nature.

Mike stopped to rest. He didn't have a watch, but by looking at
the sun's position he estimated that it was about 2:00 P.M.—time for
food. Mike sat down next to the road and ate the final crumbs from
the large breakfast that he had partially hoarded for his last two
snacks. He looked around and felt the stillness.

No birds, he thought. He looked even closer at the dirt at his feet.
No insects, either. This really is a strange place. Mike contemplated
it all. He felt the sudden breeze in his hair. *At least there is air!* He
looked up at the sky and saw the pure blue of a refreshing, grand day.

Mike realized that there were no more snacks in his bag, but he
also knew that he was not alone and that he would be afforded sustenance from God somehow. He remembered the stories about
Moses in the desert, roaming for 40 years with the tribes of Israel.
He remembered how those nomads were fed from the sky, and he
mused at this story, wondering if it was true. *All those families following Moses probably had headstrong teenagers just like we do
today,* he thought. He could just see them turning to their parents,
complaining, "Hey! We've been by this same rock eight times since
I was a kid! Why are you trusting that guy, Moses? He's taking us in
circles! The desert just isn't that big! Hello?"

Mike laughed as he thought about it all, then wondered if he was
going to see the same rock shortly, indicating that he also was going

in circles! He had no idea where he was going, either, just like the Israelites in the desert—and without food, too! This made him laugh even harder at the similarities.

Perhaps the laughter was honored, or it was simply time, but around the next bend in the widening dirt road Mike saw it. It was the first house—and it was bright blue! *Good grief,* Mike thought. *If Frank Lloyd Wright could see this, he would scream!* Mike inwardly chuckled to himself. *I hope this is not irreverent,* he thought, *but I've never seen a blue house before.* The path actually led up to its door, so he knew that it was supposed to be his first stop. It was also obvious in that there were no other structures anywhere.

As Mike approached the small cottage, he could see that it was more of a cobalt blue, and it softly glowed from within somehow. As he turned to go up the path to the door, Mike saw a small sign that identified the house as the "HOUSE OF MAPS." Mike realized that this is what he had asked for! Now he was getting somewhere. Perhaps the rest of the journey would not be so filled with uncertainty. A current local map would be a valuable commodity in this strange land.

The door to the house opened suddenly, and out strolled a beautiful large blue creature that exactly matched the color of the house! It was obviously an angelic entity, for like the original angel in the vision, it was larger than life—bigger than a human. Its presence filled the air with a feeling of splendor and a flowery essence. Again, Michael could actually smell the fragrance of the entity! The large blue one faced him.

"Greetings, Michael Thomas of Pure Intent! We have been expecting you."

Unlike the angel of the vision, this angel's face was clearly visible, and Mike could see the expression of well-being and mirth that seemed to be constant, no matter what the entity said. Mike was appreciative of the company and was respectful of the situation. He greeted the angel.

"Greetings also to you, oh great blue one." Michael swallowed hard right away. What if the angel didn't want to be called blue? What if his blueness was only a human perception and he really wasn't blue at all? Maybe he doesn't even like blue! Mike sighed at the stream of *what ifs* that ran through his human mind.

"I'm blue to every entity, Michael Thomas of Pure Intent," mused the angel, "and I accept your greeting with joy. Please enter the House of Maps and prepare to stay the night."

This time Mike was glad an angel had read his thoughts—or what was it the original angel had said? He could *feel* them? In any case, Mike was glad that he had not offended the keeper of the first house.

Mike and the blue angel, two unevenly matched entities, turned and entered the blue house. Even as the door shut behind them, two huge, intense, angry, beet-red eyes peered from the ample brush slightly to the left of the house entrance. They were very alert. They didn't get weary. They were silent and very patient. They wouldn't move or blink again until they saw that Michael Thomas was ready to continue.

As Mike entered, he was astounded by what he saw. The inside of the structure was immense! It seemed to go on forever, yet the outside was humble and modest. He remembered that the original angel had said that *all might not be as it seemed*, and this was obviously part of the strange new reality of his awareness. Mike wondered about this new perception. Did it have a greater meaning?

Mike wandered the huge halls of the House of Maps while following the angel. The interior resembled a library of the highest order, perhaps like some illustrious one you would visit in Europe, where important historical books of every kind would be stored. Instead of books on shelves, however, there were seemingly tens of thousands of small wooden holes lining the walls, each containing what Mike felt might be a scroll. The walls seemed to go up forever, and there were holes on both sides of every hall they entered, several stories high. He couldn't see the holes up close yet, but contained in them might be maps, since the name of the house implied such. But why so many of them? The journey around the giant rooms seemed endless, and in the process not one other living soul was encountered.

"Are we alone?" Mike asked. The angel turned and chuckled.

"Depends what you mean by 'alone,' I suppose. You are looking at the contracts of every human being on the planet." The angel casually continued walking forward.

Mike stopped and stared, reacting with amazement to what the blue entity had just said. The distance between them widened as the angel continued forward without Mike. Sensing that he was not being followed, the angel stopped, turned, and waited patiently for Mike. He said nothing.

Mike saw the ladders leaning up against the high walls of the multistory racks of endless wooden cubbyholes that contained scroll after scroll. Contracts, the angel had called them. What could that mean?

"I don't understand this at all!" exclaimed Michael as he caught up to the angel.

"Before your journey is over, you will," replied the angel with a comforting voice. "There is nothing here that is frightening, Michael. All is in order, and your visit was expected and is honored. Your intent is pure, and we can all see that. Relax, and enjoy being loved by us."

The blue one's words really impacted Mike. There was nothing that any entity could say in the Universe that was better than what had just been said to him. Was he starting to feel more? The original angel had given Mike some of the same loving vibrations, but he now felt a great deal more of an emotional reaction than he had before.

"It's a grand feeling to be loved, isn't it, Michael?" The blue angel had returned to Mike's side and was towering over him.

"What is this feeling?" Mike asked softly. "I feel almost teary."

"You are shifting into another vibration, Michael."

"I don't understand what that means. Uh...do you have a name, sir?" Michael again wondered if he had offended the entity. What if it was a *she* angel? Mike had no idea about those kinds of things, but the angel's demeanor and appearance could easily have been feminine.

"Just call me Blue," said the angel as it winked at Mike. "I'm genderless, but my size and voice tell your mind that I'm male. Call me a HE. It's okay." The angel paused to let Mike take it all in. Blue continued, "Your cellular structure as a human may exist in many vibratory rates, Michael. The one you have grown used to is, let's say, rate number one. You are familiar with it, and it has served you well. On this trip, however, it will be necessary for you to move forward to rate six or seven in order to move toward your goal. Right now you are passing into what I will call rate two, for want of a better name. Each vibratory rate brings more awareness of the actual reality of God, as you have been told. What you are feeling now is the awareness of love. Love is thick, Michael. It has physical properties and is powerful. Your new vibratory rate is letting you feel it more than you ever have before. It is the essence of home and will intensify with each house you visit."

Michael loved listening to Blue. This was more explanation than he had received up till now.

"Are you a teacher?" asked Mike.

"Yes. Each of the House angels are here for that very purpose, except the last one. I will have truths to reveal to you that are part of my house, and the others will as well. When you are finished, you will have a far larger overview of how things work in the Universe than you do now. My job is to dispense something to you that you have earned through your expression of intent. You are here in my house to receive your contract map. Early tomorrow I will present it to you and answer a few questions before you continue on your path. It is important that this house is first, for it will help with your journey. For now, I encourage you to enjoy our gifts of sustenance and rest."

Mike again followed Blue, who was starting to feel like a very familiar friend—but a very blue one. He was taken into a wonderful interior garden, where every possible fruit and vegetable was being grown in row after row of carefully cultivated agriculture. The light, as in every other room, was streaming in through ports in the roof. It filled each area with a natural outdoor essence. He could also smell the aroma of baking bread coming from another area of the complex.

"Who takes care of all this?" Mike asked. "I only see you...and do you eat?"

"Each house has rooms like this, Michael, and no, I don't eat. This garden exists totally for the humans who are on the same path you are, spending time suspended in this learning experience, passing through here. The garden is attended by many—you just don't see them now. You will not be without sustenance, health, and shelter while you walk your path of knowledge. It is our way of honoring you and your intent."

Mike started to feel the overwhelming sense of being cared for as the two continued on into the other rooms—the human following the large blue entity. Finally, they reached a quaint sleeping area—private quarters with a wonderful canopied bed and pristine white lace sheets, inviting Mike to plop his weary body down. Overstuffed pillows beckoned to him, offering the comfort and security of a deep sleep. Mike was astounded by the degree of preparation.

"All of this is for me?" Mike was impressed.

"You and others, Michael. It is prepared for any who have the kind of intent you do."

In the adjacent room was a feast that Mike could not even begin to consume! There was more succulent food than he had ever seen— much more than just one person could eat.

"Eat what you wish, Michael," suggested Blue. "None will be wasted. But do not hoard the extra. Resist the temptation to carry it with you. This is a test of your process—something you will understand fully later."

Blue left Mike alone and exited the area. Mike dropped his bags, immediately sat down, and ate like he had seldom done before. He took care not to be gluttonlike, but he filled his belly fully with the luscious cuisine. His eyelids were starting to droop, and the surroundings created a degree of comfort that Mike hadn't experienced since he had been a child in the care of his loving parents.

Oh, that I could sustain this feeling! Mike thought. It made being a human all worth it. Mike got up from his meal, feeling that he would somehow address the issue of the dirty dishes in the morning. He was tired! He was barely able to get out of his clothes, which he hung on provided hooks on the wall. He fell into bed, and the warm cocoon of peaceful sleep came fast.

In the morning stillness, Mike arose feeling incredibly refreshed. He washed up and made his way to the dining area, only to find that all the dishes from the night before had been removed and a wonderfully prepared breakfast spread was in its place! Part of his awakening that morning had come from the smell of fresh eggs, potatoes, and delicious bread. Mike enjoyed his solitary breakfast alone, and in his solitude he again wondered about the appropriateness of his request to go home.

Is it wrong to want out of the earth experience? he asked himself. *What about those left behind? They won't be able to experience the levels of vibratory enhancement that he would. Was it fair?* A feeling of melancholy began to wash over him as he thought about his friends and the people he worked with. He was even concerned about his former lover!

What is happening? wondered Mike. *I'm starting to feel empathy for everyone. This is not like the me I have always been. This is actually painful! I'm starting to regret having something that others don't have. Does this mean I'm in the wrong? Should I go back?*

"It is inevitable that you ask yourself that question, Michael," said Blue, who had suddenly appeared in the doorway and had once again tuned into Mike's feelings. Although startled, Mike was delighted to see Blue and greeted him with a nod.

"Speak to me of these things, Blue," said Michael. "I honestly need direction. I'm beginning to wonder if I have done the correct thing."

"The workings of Spirit are marvelous, Michael Thomas of Pure Intent," said Blue. "And the postulate of human enlightenment is this: Take care of yourself first, and the honor of your journey will be passed to those around you in a synchronous way, for the intent of the one will always affect the many."

"Again, I don't fully understand, Blue," replied a confused Mike.

"Even though you do not understand at the moment, Michael, your actions will affect others—giving them opportunities for their own decisions—something they would not have had without your decision to be right here, right now. Trust that these things are true, and do not be reproachful with yourself."

Mike felt a burden lifted from his soul. Blue hadn't been able to fully make him understand why things work spiritually, but the assurance was enough, and he felt much better about continuing.

Mike picked up his belongings and left the private dining and sleeping quarters. He stepped back into the great hallway that led to the door he had originally entered yesterday from the outside. Blue walked slowly behind him as Mike marveled at the immensity of it all. Blue said nothing as he noticed the bagel and other bread sticks protruding from Mike's sack.

"Where are we going?" asked Mike. "Should I continue in this direction?" He knew that he was about to receive his very own map, and he wanted Blue to take the lead.

"You may stop now," said Blue. The two paused in the middle of a huge blue ornate hall where Blue silently walked over to a far wall near a ladder. "Come over here, Michael."

Mike did as he was told, and before long, Blue had him climbing a very tall ladder on a quest to find a specific cubicle where his map resided. As Mike clawed his way up the ladder, he noticed that each cubicle hole had a name on it. There were actually two names for each compartment. One name looked like it was in an Arabic lettering, and one was in Roman lettering. Rather than being placed alphabetically, the boxes were arranged into some other system unknown to Mike, but no doubt understood by Blue. Blue had told him exactly where to look, and he was now just a few feet from the place Blue had indicated.

Finally, he saw it. The box marked "Michael Thomas," along with the other strange lettering that was on all the others—*probably angel language*, Michael thought to himself. His instructions were to not look around, but to retrieve the scroll from the selected box and return it to the floor for examination. Mike had just pulled out the scroll and was starting down the ladder when his eye caught another group of names, and his heart stopped. His mom and dad were also here! The arrangement was in family groups! That was the spiritual system used in the great hall. Mike knew he was absolutely forbidden to touch another's scroll, but he lingered a bit too long as he examined some of the names that made no sense to him. *Why were these other names with his family?* he wondered.

"Michael?" Blue inquired from below.

"Coming, sir," said a sheepish Mike. Blue knew what he was thinking, but Mike would not ask the kind of question that might violate the protocol of this sacred place. Pensively, Mike made his way down the long blue ladder and presented the scroll to Blue. Blue looked at Mike for a long moment, and in that steady gaze there were no secrets. Instead, there was a transmittal of gratitude from Blue that Mike had honored the anointed ways of the system, and Mike felt the love of God permeate his very being. Both Mike and Blue smiled broadly at the wordless communication. Mike was starting to feel that words were no longer necessary! It seemed that he could communicate anything he wanted to Blue without saying it out loud. *This is weird!* thought Mike.

"Not as strange as what you are about to see," replied Blue to Mike's thoughts. *Rats!* thought Mike. *I can't get away with anything in here.* Blue ignored Mike's latest thoughts and placed the small scroll on a table. He then turned and faced Mike.

"Michael Thomas of Pure Intent," Blue formally stated, "this is your life map. In some form, you will have it with you from this point on. It is given in love and will be one of the most valuable items you will own." Mike suddenly remembered the original angel's words about the new energy being far more current than before. Mike asked the obvious question.

"Is the map current?"

"More so than you might desire," was the whimsical answer from the tall blue one. Mike actually thought he heard Blue snicker.

Blue handed the map to Mike and wordlessly invited him to examine it for himself. Mike took it and held it to his chest for a moment, savoring the gift as a child would. He felt the sacredness of the moment and opened the map with a ceremonial flare that made Blue smile. Blue knew what was coming.

All sense of wonderment and expectation disappeared as Mike uncoiled the small scroll. It was blank! Or was it? Right in the middle of the scroll, visible only by careful examination, was a group of letters and symbols. Mike bent over and peered at the grouping. An arrow pointed to a small red dot. Next to the dot were the words "YOU ARE HERE." A small symbol for the cottage labeled "House of Maps" was next to the dot. A small but richly detailed area was drawn around the dot for about an inch or so on the paper, including the path Mike had followed, then it stopped, incomplete! The map showed Mike only where he was and detailed a small area extending only a hundred yards or so in every direction.

"What is this?" asked Michael, not too respectfully. "Is this an angel joke, Blue? I have come all this way to the House of Maps to receive a wonderful sacred scroll that tells me that...I'm in the House of Maps?"

"Things are not always as they seem, Michael Thomas of Pure Intent. Take this gift and keep it with you." Blue didn't really answer the question at all.

Mike knew intuitively that it wouldn't do any good to ask again, so he rolled up the seemingly useless map and placed it in his sack. He was clearly disappointed. Blue led the way back to the front door and stepped outside into the fresh air, with Mike following him. The angel faced Mike.

"Michael Thomas of Pure Intent, there is one question that I must ask before you continue on your journey home."

"What is the question, my Blue friend?" asked Mike.

"Michael Thomas of Pure Intent, do you love God?" Blue was very serious.

Mike found it strange that the original angel had asked the same question—in almost the same tone. He wondered what the significance of such repetition was.

"Dear magnificent blue teacher, since you can see my heart, you know that I indeed love God." Mike stood and faced the angel as he delivered his honest answer.

"So it is," said Blue, and with that he stepped into the small blue cottage and closed the door firmly. Michael had a feeling of sudden disconnection. *Do these guys ever say good-bye?* he wondered.

THE WEATHER WAS balmy and pleasant. Mike picked up his bag and his sack of supplies, including the bread he had removed from the blue house, and he started down the dirt road in a direction he knew would bring him to yet another house of lessons. He started to review all of the humorous elements in the events that had occurred while in the House of Maps. *Imagine a map that only tells you where you are at the moment! How useless. Of course I know where I am! What a funny place this is,* thought Mike.

Peals of laughter echoed from the hills as Michael Thomas of Pure Intent bellowed his enjoyment of his situation to the rocks and trees as he continued on his path home. His laughter also fell on the wart-covered green ears of a very dark entity lurking just 200 yards behind him. Mike had no idea that this dark shape had patiently waited for him to resume his journey and was once again following his every step. This thing didn't belong in this realm. It didn't need to eat or sleep. It had no joy—only the determination that Michael Thomas would never, ever reach the last house. Its agenda was set, and it was closing the distance between itself and Michael Thomas of Pure Intent.

CHAPTER FIVE

The Second House

It wasn't long before Mike realized that there was a change at hand from what he was used to up to this point in this journey. Easily moving forward on this path, he never considered that there would be any kind of choice presented to him as to which way to go. In addition, he was perplexed by what he intuitively perceived was a feeling of being watched.

In the distance up ahead, he could clearly see a troubling situation developing—there was a fork in the road that would require him to choose the path that would take him to the next house. Mike shrugged his shoulders and stopped, staring at what was up ahead.

What is this? he thought to himself. *How am I supposed to know my way around in this strange land of colored houses and angels?* Mike didn't expect any answers, since the questions were rhetorical and only for his own mind to hear, but he was bothered. Then he remembered the map.

He sat down along the side of the road. Mike had placed the map in the same bag with the bread and was about to retrieve it when he was almost knocked over by the smell emanating from the bag. *What died in there?* Mike said out loud to himself.

It smelled so bad that Mike almost didn't want to see what was causing it. It was definitely an organic smell, so he guessed that the bread was responsible. He was right.

Mike gently removed the map from the bag, treating it as the pre-cious gift that it was, and hoping that the smell had not somehow damaged the sacred but seemingly useless object. It came out in one piece but the bread did not. He emptied the contents of the bag on the ground and winced at what he saw.

There on the ground were the rotten remains of a bagel and bread sticks that looked like they had spent months hanging outside in a tropical rain forest. The putrid pieces were black with mold, and Mike saw the first and only insects of this truly strange land—and there were thousands of them. It looked like maggot city! Mike dropped the bag and stood up quickly. *Bread isn't carrion!* Mike thought to himself. *There is no dead flesh here! How can this be? In addition, I just left the blue house a few hours ago! Even rotting meat wouldn't do this. What's happening?*

Holding his nose, Mike stooped and came in for a closer look. The black seething mass on the ground was continuing to age before his eyes. He watched as the small, disgusting creatures ate the rest of the abhorrent decomposing mess—and then each other! Mike was revolted by the sight and turned his head away from the loathsome vision when something caught his eye from behind.

Yes, there is something there! He knew he had seen something green and indistinct flee his gaze and take cover within the brush. Mike felt chills go up and down his spine. Intuitively, he knew the danger in going back to see what it was, so he remained. A fork in the road? An animal or creature or something perhaps following him? What is happening in this sacred place? And what about the bread?

Mike turned to again gape at the detestable mess he had dumped on the road and realized he was now looking at a pile of dust! No maggots, no bread, no smell. It had completely reverted to its basic origins, which were beginning to blow away with the gentle wind.

What was the meaning of this? Mike remembered that the angel had admonished him not to take any food, but he didn't think it meant snacks for the road! Perhaps the items within the houses were some-how different and could not survive long on the path? He looked at the map with concern, picking it up carefully so as not to touch any lingering maggots. The map was pristine, just like when he had placed it in the bag. Mike didn't understand. It had been resting alongside the food, yet it was unaffected. Mike attempted another test. He picked up the bag and hesitantly smelled it. There was no residue from the horrible odor that had permeated his senses a few minutes ago. He had no idea what had truly taken place, but he had learned a valuable lesson: He would never again remove food from any house along the path.

There was movement behind him again! Alarms were starting to go off in his head. Get moving! Mike felt desperate. He instinctively unrolled the map in the hopes that it would give him a hint as to which way to turn at the fork. There it was again on the map—the red YOU ARE HERE dot with nothing around it but his current status. The fork didn't even show on the useless thing!

"Damn!" Mike exploded out loud.

Somehow the expletive was completely out of place in this land, but it reflected Mike's frustration.

"Some map, Blue!"

Again, he detected movement in back of him. Was it getting closer? Why couldn't he see it? How could it be so quick? What was it? By now, the sensors in Mike's brain were on PANIC ALARM, and he quickly rose and walked forward, looking over his shoulder about every other step. The fleeting shape didn't show itself when Mike's eyes were looking behind him. How could it know exactly when Mike was going to look forward? Each time he did so, his pace quickened until he was actually speed walking. The presence behind him matched his pace. The quarter mile to the fork was covered faster than he had yet traveled in this puzzling land. Mike was afraid.

He quickly arrived at the fork, panting from the exertion of his fast pace—and his fear. He arrived at the crossroads without any inkling as to the direction he was to going to take, but now he was distraught with indecision. Mike stood motionless at the junction, heaving with panic, and he shouted to the clouds in desperation.

"Blue! Which way?"

Mike didn't really expect to hear from Blue, so the gentle voice that seemed to emanate from within his head was a shock.

"*Use the map, Michael. Quickly!*"

Mike was in no mood to question either the strangeness of the request or the illogicality of it, since he had just done exactly that only moments earlier. With practiced speed, Mike again unfurled the map. The red YOU ARE HERE dot was seemingly right where it used to be. It never moved, remaining always in the center of the map. But what was this? Mike peered closer, with drops of sweat falling on the parchment.

The dot now showed the fork! Since he was actually standing at the crossroads, the map was now *current.* Mike's mind didn't stop to take in the humor of the angel's meaning of the word. He looked closer. In addition to the fork, there was now an arrow clearly pointing to the right!

Mike didn't hesitate. While rolling up the map, he scampered to the right and made his way up a small hill. He continued looking backward at almost every opportunity, sensing, knowing, that there was a pursuer just out of sight. The green blur flitted between rock and bush, keeping pace with Mike's increase in speed. Just over the rise, Mike sighed in relief. In the distance, he saw another house! He felt that salvation was at hand. While his eyes continually darted behind him, Mike picked up the pace and ran down the path to where he knew he would find safety, refuge—and food.

The dark and vile entity behind Mike was mad! Had Mike hesitated much longer on the road, IT would have caught him! IT seethed with rage at the missed opportunity and took ITs place high in the trees just outside a brightly colored orange house that Michael Thomas had just entered. There, the repugnant entity patiently waited. It would be a long wait. IT didn't care.

JUST INSIDE THE DOOR of the orange house stood the expected angel. Michael was practically bowled over when "Orange," as Mike decided to call him, spoke his first words.

"Greetings, Michael Thomas of Pure Intent! We have been expecting you."

"Greetings back to you!" Michael hoped he didn't sound as relieved and out of breath as he actually was. His voice had quivered. He had to restrain himself from hugging the huge orange entity that now stood in front of him. He was so glad to be protected again.

"Come this way," stated his orange host, as he turned and led Mike into the "HOUSE OF GIFTS AND TOOLS." Mike made certain the door was closed. He followed, still shaking and out of breath from the experience he'd had only moments before. He was still frightened and filled with more questions than ever about this land of perplexing contrasts.

As before, this angel was magnificent. Again, Mike was impressed by how large the being was, and by the kindness he felt. This entity made him feel as welcomed and loved as the others he had so far encountered. *I guess they're all made of the same stuff*, he mused to himself.

"Actually, we are all in the same family," said the angel.

Mike was mortified that he had so quickly forgotten how the communication worked around these spiritual creatures.

"I'm sorry," was the only thing that Mike could blurt out. Orange turned and stopped. He cocked his head to one side in a quizzical manner. Mike looked into his face.

"Sorry?" He paused. "For complimenting me on my magnificence? For feeling loved? For wondering who we are?" The angel smiled. "We get many guests, Michael Thomas. Of the many who visit this second house, so far you have asked the fewest questions."

"The day is young," Mike replied, sighing. He wanted to ask the angel about the fear and panic of the last few moments. What was following him? The angel knew the question was coming.

"I cannot tell you what you wish to know, Michael," the angel stated.

"Can't, or won't?" asked Mike respectfully. He knew the question was rhetorical and continued, "I know that you know." Mike hesitated and then tried posing questions at a rapid-fire rate.

"Why can't you tell me about it?" he queried.

"You know more about it than I do," the angel replied.

"How can that be?"

"Not all is as it seems here."

"Will it be there when I exit?"

"Yes."

"Does it belong here? It seems out of place in this spiritual setting."

"It has the same right to be here as you do."

"Can it hurt me?"

"Yes."

"Is there a defense?"

"Yes."

"Will you help me?"

"That is why I am here." The angel stood quietly as Mike suddenly stopped his inquiry.

The angel's answers confirmed to Mike that Orange knew everything. He began to relax. *If he knows, then there is potentially more for me to know*, Mike thought to himself. *I will be patient. I'm certain more will be shown as I go. It seems to be the way of things here.* Michael suddenly remembered how useless he thought the map was not more than an hour ago, and how it had saved him at the moment he needed it.

"God is very current, you know," said the angel, almost laughing. He was once again tuning in to the thoughts of Michael Thomas. The orange one turned and began to lead Michael into the inner areas of the house. Michael followed.

"I'm getting used to it," said Mike as he walked. "It's what you need only at the point you need it?"

"Something like that," replied the angel. "The lower vibrational human time frame is linear, Michael." The angel was a obviously another teacher. "Angelic time is not."

"So how do YOU perceive time?" As they spoke, Michael was being led through a warehouse. A warehouse? Like the previous house, the internal portion of this one was titanic. Mike's jaw dropped as he observed dozens of rows of stacked crates within a room with a ceiling that had to be 50 feet high.

"We don't have a past or future," replied the angel. "Your concept of time travels on a straight track, and ours is a turntable rotating clockwise with the engine at rest. We can always see the full extent of our track, since it is always beneath us, and therefore we are always in the 'now' of our time. Our motion is always around a known center. Because your track is straight, and you are in forward motion, you never get to fully experience the present. You look behind you and see where you have been. You look forward and see where you are going. You are never allowed to experience a BEING type of existence. Instead, you experience a DOING existence. It is part of your lower vibration, and it is appropriate for your dimension."

"That would explain your map," said Michael, remembering that the red YOU ARE HERE dot was always in the middle, and that the events of his new existence seemed to move in and out of one spot. Mike thought to himself, *It's exactly the opposite of a human map.*

"Correct!" said Orange over his shoulder as he continued to lead. "In your time frame, the map is known, and the human moves. That's because you perceive time and reality as a constant, and the human is the variable. When you move closer to our vibration and time frame, the human entity is the known constant and the map, or reality, is the variable."

Mike had to really think about this one. It was confusing, but somehow familiar. His experience at the fork outside the orange house had shown him the value of his spiritual map, even if it was different from what he had expected. He knew that the next time he had a choice of that nature, he wouldn't worry about it until he actually got to the fork—then the map would work.

As Blue had, Orange led Mike in and out of many beautiful and ornate areas on their way to a place of refuge, sustenance, and rest. This grand house, however, contained crates with names on them instead of cubbyholes with names on them as was the case in the House of Maps. Again, the names were mostly in that strange Arabic lettering and unreadable to Mike, but he assumed correctly that somewhere there was a crate with his name on it and that he would know soon enough.

"These are your quarters," stated Orange. "Tomorrow we will begin. Your meals will be served in the room to the left. You may wash in the room to the right. A meal has been prepared for you." With that statement, Orange closed the door to Mike's room and left.

Mike stared at the closed door. *You might be an angel, but your social graces leave a lot to be desired,* Mike thought to himself regarding the lack of a farewell gesture. *I guess I can't expect them to understand human nature completely.*

Mike dined sumptuously, as before. He wolfed down the delicious food and marveled at the handcrafted wooden utensils. He felt odd to be leaving his dirty dishes for someone else to clean, but then he remembered how much he hated that task. He knew that even though he could not see them, there had to be other entities here with the angel to take care of such things. *What an odd combination,* Mike contemplated. *A place that is angelic, but which had to cater to those on a lower human vibration as well.*

Mike started to wonder about the sewer system, and then was struck by an amazing revelation: He hadn't been to the bathroom for days! There WAS no toilet! There had been areas of water for bathing, but nothing else. He realized that he hadn't felt the human "call of nature" since he had passed through the gate! Something was happening to his body in this surprising land. He didn't mind eliminating...elimination, but it was an odd feeling indeed.

IN THE MORNING Mike felt invigorated. He dined alone on a breakfast of fresh fruit and breads and savored the awesome taste of this wonderful meal. He examined the angelic food and realized that it was somehow different. He would ask Orange about it, he thought.

"It's in our time frame," said a cheerful Orange from the open door of his room. The angel had just arrived and had overheard Mike's thoughts. The angel continued, "It cannot exist in a lower vibration and contains spiritual attributes that are interdimensional. That is why there is no human waste, Michael, and that is why it cannot be stored. It knows no future or past. It was created moments before you ate it and will not survive if you try to take it from this place."

"So I discovered," said Mike, remembering the disgusting mess on the road to the Orange house that almost got him into trouble.

The angel led Mike out of the living quarters and into a large circular well-lit arena. Several crates were laid open, and a few orange benches were available for humans to rest upon. There were other preparations as well: what appeared to be an altar, some incense, and some odd-looking packages.

"Welcome to the House of Gifts and Tools, Michael Thomas of Pure Intent," said the angel as he faced Mike. "Please take a seat. You will spend much time here."

This was the beginning of a long series of teaching sessions. It was to be followed by an even longer period spent on practice/testing sessions with respect to the use of the gifts and tools on a new spiritual vibration. Before Mike was finished, he would spend more than three weeks in this orange house.

"You are slowly raising your vibration, Michael Thomas," Orange repeatedly stated throughout the learning process. "These are the promised gifts and tools to help you accomplish that task. They are yours due to your intent. You cannot enter the next houses without knowledge of how all of these work, and you absolutely cannot go home unless you are skilled in their use."

Mike paid attention. He knew this was preparation for home, and he remembered being told that this training would be coming. Orange unwrapped many gifts as Michael watched. Some were seemingly made of magnificent crystal, and through ceremony and intent, they were magically placed into Mike's body to complement his spiritual power. Each was explained thoroughly, and Mike was given time to digest what each one meant. He was then asked to explain to Orange what they were for. This was not easy, for much of the testing required speaking about concepts and using words that were brand new to Mike.

Orange spoke of how humans came into the planet carrying certain qualities that pertained to different realms of existence—other lifetimes in the past. Mike had heard of this, but he was not prepared to hear it from an angel! He expected that some day a longhaired Indian guru might broach the subject, but an angel? Past lives were a staple of humanism, Orange would tell him, and the instructions from a past life were carried in to a new one as lessons at birth. These lessons were called "karma," or, as some called it, "remembrance" and "experience." The karma allowed for human learning, and also somehow helped the planet. This was the way things worked for humans life after life. Orange told Mike that in order to move into a new vibration, he had to remove some of the older qualities, such as the karmic lessons he had been born with. The path home would not allow for them—any more than they did for the rotten food he had experienced on the road.

Mike instantly thought of himself as a pile of rotting flesh on the road—one that didn't pay attention to the teacher. He intensified his interest so he would not create that condition. Ugh!

Orange saw Mike's thoughts. He laughed out loud and shared much wonderful mirth with him. Mike was astounded by how close he felt to Orange. He was a wonderful teacher. He was a great companion—even if he didn't know how to say hello or good-bye.

Mike was shown how to shape thoughts that would actually create energy. "This is how you control your reality," Orange told him. "Use your internal spiritual feeling and knowingness to propel you into situations that you deserve and that you've planned for." Mike had no idea what that meant, but he did as he was told and apparently passed all the tests. The spiritual empowerment gift of co-creation was imbedded into his being, as well as the gift to clear all his karmic attributes from past incarnations. Each gift was celebrated with ceremony and verbalization. Also, each one seemed to transmute from the physical to the spiritual as it was absorbed by his body under the direction and careful tutelage of the great orange angel.

Mike felt as if he were studying for some holy priesthood! Each time he would verbalize what Orange taught him, he could see Orange actually looking at his heart! Orange could be intense, and during these times when Mike made promises and verbalized intent for this or that gift to be implanted into his spiritual power center, Orange seemed to be reading Mike's soul. It was uncomfortable at first, but then Mike realized that Orange was doing an integrity check on what Mike was saying out loud. If Mike had been faking it, Orange would have known it instantly, and he would not have let Mike go further.

Eventually, over a two-week period, the small packages were all opened, explained, and integrated into Mike's spiritual self, and tests were given along the way. One test was especially hard. Mike was afraid of small spaces; he didn't know why, but early in life he realized that he would have a panic attack if closely confined in any manner. One of the gifts from Orange was the power to overcome this phobia. Mike gave the intent and did the ceremony. Orange told him that the feeling of panic in enclosed spaces was a KARMIC OVER-LAY, and that clearing it represented the clearing of many other past-life experiences that Mike had brought into his humanness this time around.

Days later, a large crate was opened during the training period. Instead of something coming out, Mike was asked by a very loving Orange to step in! The lid was closed, and darkness was all around Mike as he crouched in the container. He heard the ominous, loud pounding of each nail as the cover of the lid was secured by Orange. Then silence and more darkness.

He could clearly hear his breath in the enclosed space, and he was very aware of his cramped position. He could even hear his heart. Orange gave no explanation. He didn't have to. It was another test that Mike could not fake.

For about ten seconds, Mike's heart raced with the remembrance of his problem. Then, when his entire body should have turned into a fit of shaking panic, the claustrophobic feeling fizzled completely, and he relaxed. Mike realized, much to his joy, that the gift had worked, and that his body had first reacted as in the old days, but his new spirit had stopped it. Peace took over, and Mike sang some songs to himself and finally dozed off. A delighted Orange opened the box and let Mike out about an hour later.

"You are remarkable, Michael Thomas of Pure Intent," said the broadly smiling angelic being. Mike could actually see pride in the eyes of Orange. "Not all make it this far."

This was the first time Mike actually realized that he was among others who had also asked for the path home. This fact had come up several times before, but he had not seen the implication of it. He thought about this for many a night as Orange finally progressed through the gifts and started to bring out the big tools. It was the during the third week of training that Orange brought out the big case.

"There are three tools you will need on your journey," Orange said with great emphasis. He went over to a special crate and opened it. Each time Orange opened a package or crate, Mike would sit expectantly on the bench provided, wondering what magic item was next that would increase his spiritual awareness, knowledge, or power. He was not prepared for what Orange had to give him.

Orange's back was toward Mike, so he couldn't see what the angel had drawn from the crate. As the angel turned to present the first tool, Mike caught a flash of something silver. NO! It couldn't be—Orange was holding an immense sword!

"Behold the sword of truth," stated the orange angel as he presented the weapon to Michael Thomas. If it looked big when the angel held it, it looked huge when Mike did. It was heavy beyond belief, and unwieldy. Mike couldn't believe this was happening.

"This is a real sword!" Mike exclaimed to Orange.

"As real as the other gifts," reminded Orange. "Only this is one of three that you will carry with you on the outside of your body as you travel to the next four houses."

Michael held the sword for some time, examining its beauty. Yes, it had his name on it—he guessed. The weapon was intricately embossed with designs, which all had great spiritual meaning. Its handle was large, and the grip was a bright cobalt blue stone of some kind. It was breathtaking—and very sharp on both of its edges.

"Try to swing it." The angel stepped back.

Michael did as he was told, and the sword almost swung itself! The unexpected power of the weapon toppled Mike over! He felt stupid and clumsy as he arose to try again. Orange held up his hand to stop Mike from continuing.

"Here, see if this helps." The angel approached the crate again and brought out something else. Again, the new object flashed a silver color upon being retrieved. It was a huge shield! Mike shook his head in disbelief. What was this all about? This was odd indeed. Spiritual gifts? Weapons of war? Am I being prepared for a past life in Camelot?

"Everything is not as it seems, Michael Thomas of Pure Intent." Orange stood before him with the shield in his hands, answering the thoughts of a confused student. "Try this."

Orange showed Mike how to strap the shield to his arm and gave him a few tips on how the shield and the sword balanced each other in weight so that it was possible to swing the sword without falling over—a good thing to learn.

"Michael," said the angel, "the shield is the knowledge of Spirit. Together with truth, the balance is all-powerful! Darkness cannot exist where there is knowledge. No secrets can survive in the light, and light will be created when truth is revealed from examination of knowledge. There is no greater combination than this. They must be used together."

"Anything else in that crate?" asked Mike in a joking way as he staggered with the weight of the new sword and shield.

"Funny you should ask!" Orange again went to the crate with a disbelieving Mike staring after him. The angel reached down and picked up on object that was even larger than the rest, and again silver in color.

"Behold the armor!" exclaimed a very amuscd Orange angel, almost laughing at the expression of disbelief on Mike's face.

"I don't understand!" Mike sat down dejectedly on the bench. "How can I ever be expected to carry all this?"

"With practice," replied Orange. "Here, let me show you."

Orange took the sword and shield. He helped Mike put on the heavy, ornate armor. It was like a vest, and covered Mike's upper torso. As it was accepted arm by arm, it went on like a body mold— a perfect fit! The snaps were secured, and Orange belted Mike with a special scabbard to sheath the sword of truth; then, he showed him how to stow the heavy shield with a special fastener on his back for traveling. When all was complete, the angel again stood back.

"Michael Thomas of Pure Intent, you now possess the triad of tools that will allow passage into the new vibration. You have the sword of truth, the shield of knowledge, and finally—the armor of Spirit. The armor is called the "mantle of God." It represents the wisdom necessary to use the other two tools appropriately. Tomorrow you will begin your training as a warrior of the light. There is great power in the triad. Never use them separately!"

Orange took the weapons from Michael and led him back to his room, where Mike washed, ate, and went to sleep. He lay in bed for a very long time wondering about the many inconsistencies that he perceived in this great land. He dozed off to sleep with many conflicting thoughts in his mind.

In the morning, Mike again found himself in the hall of training. It was during the next few days that Orange began to show Mike how to use the old weapons with some skill. The first practice was balance. He made Mike run up and down stairs in full battle dress—sword out and shield at the ready. He showed him how to fall and get up quickly by using the shield as a counterweight. Through all of this, Mike noticed that the tools never got dirty, and they never became dented or scarred.

He ran with the tools, walked with them, twirled with them, did everything but fight with them. Mike was slowly getting a feeling of balance. With time, an odd thing developed. At night when he took the battle dress off, there was no feeling of relief in discarding the heavy weapons. Instead, he felt small and defenseless and much too light!

Many days went by before Orange began the final training on how to actually use the sword of truth. Mike expected Orange to turn into some kind of samurai master and teach Mike how to fight. Instead, Mike got an entirely different training.

"You are now ready to learn how to use the weapons, Michael Thomas," Orange said. "Draw your sword."

With a flourish that would have made any knight proud, Mike easily produced the massive sword of great length. The angel watched approvingly.

"Now raise it to God." Michael did as he was told. "Before you speak your truth, Michael Thomas, feel the sword."

Mike didn't have any idea what Orange meant. Feel the sword? It was in his hands. How could he not feel the sword?

"Michael Thomas of Pure Intent," said the intense Orange one, "hold the sword up high and speak your truth. Do you love God?"

Michael was beginning to get the picture. There was that question again! Only this time, he was holding a massive spiritual weapon pointed toward heaven, and he was expected to give some kind of speech? Michael began his now-standard reply.

"Yes, I do, Orange. As you can examine my heart—" Mike was stunned and could not finish. The sword was starting to vibrate! It was almost singing as it seemed to sweep an intense vibratory warmth down his arm and into his chest. The shield was humming in response—he was certain of it. And the armor was growing warm as well! The tools he had grown so used to carrying with ease were somehow alive with his intent! He was being overtaken by the feeling of power within these elements that he was holding and wearing. He remembered that he was speaking.

"I do most certainly love God!" Mike held the sword up high and was able to FEEL it vibrate with his truthful intent. He felt empowered. He felt enlightened. He felt as if he could stand there for another hour with the heavy, vibrating weapon at the ready, intending his purpose to go HOME where he belonged. He FELT the three units vibrate and sing with a musical *F* note that resounded within his heart. Tears began to stream down his face as he felt and saw the appropriateness of the ceremony at hand. The units were accepting Mike's biology. They were integrating themselves into his Spirit, and his truthful intent was the catalyst for the ceremony! So this was the reason for the sword, shield, and armor? It was a metaphor. What else could it be? This explanation was good enough for Michael Thomas, for it had taken him to a new level of commitment and awareness.

Orange and Michael Thomas exchanged loving feelings that night. Mike knew it was almost time to leave. Orange never did show Mike how to fight, and Mike knew that it was due to the fact that the weapons were only symbols. Mike asked Orange about home and the path. He repeatedly wondered why weapons of Earth war were being taught in a sacred, spiritual land. Orange successfully dodged all the questions except the ones that Mike was allowed to have answered— and then even those answers were vague.

"Orange, you would have made a wonderful Earth politician," kidded Mike.

"What did I do that would cause you to insult me like that?" Orange kidded back.

"I feel a genuine bond with you." Mike realized he was choking up. He really didn't want to leave this great master angel.

"Say no more, Michael Thomas of Pure Intent. I will share a secret of angeldom with you." Orange had made up a word just for Mike. He bent down so that he was at eye level with him and continued. "You and I—we are of the same family. We don't say good-bye because we never leave one another. I am always with you, and available. You will see...now it is time for you to retire."

Mike was shocked by the forthright nature of this communication with Orange. The same family? How could that be? Then Mike felt foolish, for he realized that Orange had indeed overheard him the first night when he complained that angels never say good-bye. What an answer! What a great revelation! What a thought! They never leave me?

Mike remembered for the first time since he'd arrived three weeks ago that at the fork in the road, Blue had somehow given him advice on how to use the map. He had actually heard Blue's voice in his head.

"Do you know Blue?" asked Mike on a whim.

"As I do myself," was the reply from the Orange one.

Mike said nothing and retired to the room he was growing very fond of, the place where he ate and slept. Although nothing had been said about leaving, Mike found himself packing his things into the bags that he had almost forgotten about—readying himself to continue his journey in the morning. He took a few looks at the books and photos and sighed again at his Earth experiences and the preciousness of his few possessions. Somehow they were beginning to seem out of place.

It was a pensive Michael Thomas who appeared at the door of the Orange house that morning after his meal. Orange had silently led him in that direction, with Michael following behind. This time, however, Mike had some extra burdens to carry—the bag with his map, the new tools swinging and clanking as he walked, and the two suitcases of books and photos.

"Michael, are you certain you wish to take all those items on the journey?" asked the orange one. "It would be better if you didn't have them."

"They represent all my earthly possessions," replied Mike. "I need them."

"For what?"

Mike thought about that question, but to leave his bags was not an option.

"For remembrance and honor of my former life," said Mike.

"For connection to the old ways, Michael?"

Mike was getting irritated by the line of questioning. The angel spoke again.

"Why don't you leave your bags with me, Michael. I love you, and I will keep them safe for you if you ever should return here."

"No!" Mike didn't want to hear any more about his bags. It was his stuff, and he would keep it as long as possible. He needed something in this odd place to remind him of who he really was.

The angel nodded. Mike always got his way. He noticed that all the angels had honored his choices and never argued with his final decisions.

Michael Thomas didn't say good-bye to Orange that morning. Standing on the steps facing the angel he had been with for weeks, he remembered the explanation from Orange about such things.

"See you shortly," said Michael, not believing it.

Orange simply went inside and shut the door. *I don't know how they do that*, thought Mike to himself. *Never any closure—except doors.*

Mike started down the path in a direction he had not yet been. It was all he could do to hold everything together, for he was overburdened with his load. The addition of the sword, shield, and armor, along with his bags and map pouch were almost too much. He lamented the fact that these heavy symbols of the New Age actually had to be physically carried around! *What a dumb deal*, Mike secretly thought. *I must look very silly. Are these weapons really necessary? I'll never use them in any battle. I really don't know how! Orange never taught me. They are only for looks and ceremony, so wouldn't it have been enough to acknowledge them?*

As he was preoccupied trying to balance all his new gear and the old bags, he had forgotten about his trouble on the path before. He had forgotten that something was waiting for him. As Mike noisily clanked off down the path, dragging his bags and balancing his tools, a dark green ominous force was watching him from the trees. The thing examined Mike with new interest. Gone was the old Mike. It had been replaced with one who had weapons and power! This was no longer going to be easy. A new strategy would be called for—one that would confront Michael Thomas with great power and directness. Time will make the difference, but until then, the dark one would continue to follow Michael at a distance, waiting for the opportunity to strike. IT took up ITs chase just out of sight and detection, following the journey of Michael Thomas of Pure Intent. IT was confident that this human would never make it to the final door marked "home."

CHAPTER SIX

The Great Storm

Mike had been on the road for no more than two hours when he noticed that the wind was picking up and the sky was darkening. *Oh, great!* thought Mike. *Storms in paradise.*

For the last hour or so, he had indeed been struggling with his load and had been stopping at increasing intervals to rest. Not only was all this stuff heavy, but it was awkward as well! This irritated Mike at a deep level and made him feel out of balance—now a storm, too! He would need to find some shelter shortly if it was going to rain. He didn't want his bags to get wet and didn't know whether the new battle gear would rust or not.

He stopped again for a moment and looked behind him for the first time. IT WAS THERE! The green blur darted at lightning speed behind an outcropping of boulders. This time Mike had seen it. It had substance and was huge! Feelings of apprehension swept over Mike's tired body as he realized that this apparition had not gone away since he had visited the last house. He remembered Orange telling him that it was dangerous and could hurt him. As he rested, he positioned himself to face the rear so that he could observe the path behind him at all times. He knew that he must stay alert. He had no idea how alert.

The wind picked up, making it more difficult to walk. An unencumbered person would have had no difficulty at this point, but the new battle shield acted almost as a sail, strapped to his back as it was. If he hadn't had all the baggage, he would have simply held it in the balancing position he had practiced and would have probably moved much faster—holding it against the wind to stabilize himself. But that was not possible while carrying his satchels. Mike knew that he would have to find a place soon that would protect him until this unusual weather calmed down and returned to the balmy conditions he had been used to so far.

Mike had never seen anything like it. The weather was changing drastically within a very short period of time! Constantly on the alert for his pursuer, Mike noted to his horror that the thing was gaining on him despite the wind and the driving rain. It was quick! *How could it move so fast in this wind?*

The increasingly inclement weather prodded Mike to take action. Things were changing too fast! Mike plodded forward in a crouch, trying to present a smaller profile to the wind. Finally, he stopped and huddled on the ground—forward motion becoming utterly impossible.

The storm was starting to take on a personality of its own as it began to groan and wail with the increased wind velocity. Where he was not protected by his armor, the rain felt like so many needles drilling into his flesh, as it was propelled horizontally with hurricane force. Mike knew he was in grave trouble. He sneaked a peek at the path behind, which was now practically obscured by the driving rain and fog. But he could clearly see the dark green figure, now standing tall, its eyes appearing to glow red. It was starting to move forward! It wasn't affected by the storm. *How could this be?* Mike was fearful.

Blue's voice was unmistakable as once again it prompted Michael from within.

"USE THE MAP!" The voice was so clear, Mike thought! He is indeed with me. The storm's fury was beginning to rival anything that this Minnesota boy had ever witnessed. He felt like he was inside the funnel of a twister. He was now flat on the ground and was still trying his best not to be swept up by the incredible force of the storm. The flatter he could get, the better. The screaming of the elemental bombardment had grown—the noise was deafening! Mike's fear

could have been destabilizing and might have gripped him with terror, but somehow there was sense in all of this. If only he could reach his map!

Unfortunately, Mike didn't have the ability to retrieve his map; he was too preoccupied with just staying alive. The fierceness of the elements was like an attack on his very being, and he was literally hanging on to the plants of the earth with one hand and his precious cargo of books and photos with the other. The map bag had been slung around his neck and was crumpled beneath him—safe, but completely out of reach. Momentarily, he felt his body lifted by the driving, howling wind and the sail-like qualities of the shield on his back. Like a bullying personality, the fierce storm poked and prodded him to action. Mike forced his body closer to the ground, and by sheer will, he anchored it by driving the toes of his feet into the mud and hanging on to an especially obstinate weed with one hand.

It was completely dark now; the billows of black clouds that had developed in the sky had descended to the very area where Mike was lying—making sight a thing of the past. His eyes were barely slits, trying to protect themselves from the attacking wind and rain, but there was nothing to see. He was even having difficulty seeing the ground beneath him! Where was the dark thing? Was IT coming to get him? Did he dare move, or would the storm blow him to his death? Like bells in a fire drill, Mike's every cell vibrated with an alertness he had never experienced before. Fear? No! His will to survive and fight the situation was dominant. He was committed. He had to find a way to get to the map!

Orange's voice inside Mike's head was an incredibly welcome sound. *How could a soft sound be heard when there is so much noise?* Mike thought.

"Michael Thomas, let go of the baggage!"

Mike knew it was either that or he would die. His clothing, even beneath the armor, was thoroughly soaked now, and he was starting to shiver. Through the shriek of the attacking wind, Mike heard and felt a tremendous, percussive wallop. What was that new sound? He felt its vibration through the ground. Was it coming closer now? He had to do as Orange advised. He knew it was coming!

One by one, Mike slowly but methodically let go of the bags that he had so carefully packed with his precious cargo of memories. First went the books. By uncurling two fingers, he released the strap of the first bag. The satchel was snatched by the storm like an angry power tool just waiting to shred it. Mike felt it being ripped from his hand as he let go. He wondered if his finger was broken. He could hear the tearing of the bag's seams and the heart-wrenching flipping sound of hundreds of pages being torn to tiny pieces only feet from his head. It was the most awful sound he had ever heard. His precious books! Without thinking too much about it, he let go of the other bag by opening the thumb of the same hand. This was even worse! The storm had the violence of a mad prize fighter standing over him, wrenching the case from his tentative grip and pummeling him to the ground. He actually wondered at that point if the dark thing had finally arrived and had begun to overwhelm him and tear him apart. The battering from the storm was like a team of drill sergeants jumping up and down on his back!

Unlike the books, the photos disappeared without a sound. They were simply gone in an instant—and it made Michael Thomas angry. His entire lineage and the priceless, beloved memories of his dead parents were being scattered over the landscape by an uncaring force of nature, while he continued to be hammered by the same wrathful force.

The pandemonium around Mike was fierce. He tried to raise up slightly so that he could slip his now-free hand under him to grasp the map. He almost lost his grip as he was again lifted slightly by the force of the wind and the battle shield still strapped on his back, but he timed it well and was able at last to grasp the scroll beneath him. Using forefinger and thumb, he managed to gradually unroll the map so he could see the spot where the red dot was. Working on instinct alone, he slowly inched the parchment up his chest, pulling with it the wet earth and dirt that was being scraped along between the hard metal of his armor and the wet ground. It was an interesting balance—pressing his body down as hard as he could against the dirt, yet allowing his hand and the map to travel up his torso. He scraped his hand on a small rock, trying to bring the map up to eye level. But how was he going to be able to see the map once it was high enough? It was pitch black—he couldn't see anything! Even if he could see it, would the writing be washed off? The deathlike grip of his other hand on the weed was beginning to loosen against the bombardment of rain and wind. His arm was growing numb. Michael was losing his grip.

IT WAS NOT AFFECTED by the storm. As a low-vibration visitor in a high-vibrational land, the wretched creature was not touched by the wind, rain, and turmoil that pounded the earth around IT. IT easily stood up to full height and slowly made ITs filthy, dark way to the middle of the path, striding toward a prone and groveling Michael Thomas, who was barely hanging on against the elements—elements that had no influence whatsoever on IT.

IT was not swayed by the incredible force of the howling wind. Nothing the weather did seemed to affect the dark figure, except the lack of visibility. As IT approached Michael, with the casual ease of a stroll in the park, IT began to feel that fate had indeed presented a gift this day. But the darkness of the storm was having an effect, and soon IT could not see any better than ITs prey. Nevertheless, as IT moved closer to Michael Thomas, IT was prepared to finish what the odd storm had started. IT was prepared to scatter the various parts of Mike's body to the farthest corners of this nonsensical fairyland that IT despised so much.

Mike's intuition was correct, for IT was close now. Darkness had raced in as if the entities there had requested a personal blindfold. But IT was moving on instinct, sensing where Mike was on the ground. IT attacked with great purpose and power—only to find itself tearing apart a section of the earth very close to where Mike was lying. Mike had heard IT, but IT had also heard something else—the flipping of pages and the tearing of fabric as Mike lost his books. IT quickly turned to face the new sound. Now IT knew where Michael was! IT was pleased.

IT came closer, and finally in the dimness of the great raging storm that IT could not participate in, IT barely made out the shape of a helpless Michael Thomas with one hand under him and one hand grasping a small resolute weed. If IT could have smiled, IT would have at that moment.

IT descended on Michael Thomas's back with a vengeance, slamming down with the force of 12 grown, muscular men. Instantly, IT felt a million darts pierce ITs wart-covered carcass. In a blinding flash of pure white light and a gleam of silver, IT was repelled by a tremendous force. Like being shot from a cannon, IT traveled a long trajectory and landed unceremoniously in almost the exact place where IT had started. With ITs exterior smoking from contact with something extremely hot, IT tried to take stock of what had happened. IT was dazed, to say the least, and was momentarily weakened by the force that had thrust IT away with such power.

Michael Thomas's shield had been firmly strapped to his back, and it covered most of his body. The item that Mike thought was going to be his undoing—his shield—had suddenly became his protection. It had done its work even without Mike's direction. It was part of him. The intermingling of the dark creature's low vibration with the high vibratory rate of the shield had immediately caused a powerful physical reaction. Like two powerful forces of opposite polarity, the shield of knowledge had repelled the attack.

MICHAEL THOMAS HAD managed to bring the map up to throat level. He peered down into the darkness of that small pocket, hoping he might be able to see something in the blackness. Suddenly, there was light! To Michael it seemed like an especially violent blast of wind had hit him, but with it came a miracle—a light so bright that it didn't matter that his eyes were almost closed as protection against the wailing wind and rain. It was a light so intense that it illuminated everything around him long enough for him to clearly see through the slits that were his eyes. The section of map he had so carefully unwrapped while the storm had raged was indeed there! His eyes danced over the map and quickly found the YOU ARE HERE dot. Michael ignored the sudden smell of smoke and ozone around him. The map showed his path, and right around the corner was a cave. A few yards east, and he would be safe!

In retrospect, Michael Thomas thought that God had brought him a close lightning strike in that needful moment. He never understood that it was a negative force bent on undoing him that synchronistically was responsible for his miracle of illumination at the exact point he needed it most. Michael Thomas of Pure Intent had experienced his first co-creation, and he didn't even know it. Orange had instructed him on the use of the gift that would help him be "in the right place at the right time," but Michael never dreamed that this could have been the right place that day.

It was an act of sheer strength and will that allowed Mike to crawl at a snail's pace from weed to weed and rock to rock—planting his toes firmly every few inches to maintain stability and direction. It took almost 20 minutes to accomplish this task, as he hugged the soggy earth and was flattened against the dirt by the fierceness of the storm. All this effort just to travel a few yards eastward—but Michael had to do it. Even in almost total blackness, he found the entrance to the small cave that would be his respite from certain death had he remained in the elements. With each agonizing pull of his body along the ground, he thanked God that the dark entity behind him had not come closer. Even as he slowly pulled himself into the opening, he heard the storm intensify. He was astounded by what he heard going on around him. *This magic place is not immune to trouble*, thought Michael.

All seemed quiet in the cave, but Mike was a mess. His hand was bleeding where he had scraped it on the rock. His clothes were soaked with mud and dirt, but it was still too cold in the cave to remove them. Slowly he arose and took stock of the situation.

You might think at this point that Michael Thomas would have felt overwhelmingly grateful to have escaped the storm—and the mysterious enemy that came so close to claiming its prey. Instead, Mike was angry! He shook, not from the cold, but from his sudden anger and fury at the situation. His precious belongings had been ripped from him. He knew who controlled the elements, and he blurted out his rage to anyone who would listen.

"You have tricked me!" He went to the mouth of the cave and yelled at the still-howling wind. "Do you hear me?" His face was twisted with fury. His indignation at being forced to give up his priceless objects were paramount in his thoughts. He had been victimized by those who controlled this seemingly sacred place.

"Now I see how it works!" he continued to angrily shout to anyone who could hear him. "If I don't take a suggestion from one of the angels, then they just DO IT TO ME ANYWAY!" Mike shook uncontrollably from both his rage and the cold as he continued to face the mouth of the cave. He felt the sting of grief at the loss of his parents' photos. He began to sob uncontrollably—wracked by emotional pain—until there were no tears left. He felt violated and robbed.

Mike felt a sensation of warmth behind him and could see the subtle flickering of a small fire on the walls of the cave. He turned to look as a gentle voice spoke.

"I gave you good advice, Michael Thomas of Pure Intent."

Orange was standing in the back of the cave. In front of him was a small fire, inviting Mike to feel its warmth. Mike had calmed down now, and slowly came over to the fire and sat before it with his head down in resolve. In time, still with tears in his eyes, he finally looked at Orange and asked the questions.

"Was all this necessary?"

"No," said Orange. "That's the whole point."

"Why did you take away my things?"

"This is still a land of free choice, Michael Thomas. Despite what you think, the human is the focal point, and the human is honored above all creatures in this place."

"Free choice!" exclaimed Mike. "If I hadn't let go of my bags, I would have died!"

"Exactly," stated Orange. "You chose not to relinquish the bags at a point when you had the chance. Had you taken my suggestion, you could have learned more about these things. The bags would have been safe. You cannot understand the overview of this place. That is why we are here, and why the new gifts and tools were given to you."

"I still don't understand," countered Mike. "Why couldn't I simply keep a few things I loved? They wouldn't have hurt anyone here. They meant a great deal to me!"

"They were inappropriate for your journey, Michael." Orange sat down on a rock on the other side of the fire. "These things that you carried represented the earthly part of you. They pull on your old self and keep you in a place that is not comfortable with the new vibration that you are studying and accepting. All of you is changing, Michael, and we know you feel it."

"Why didn't you simply tell me this? It would have saved so much trouble." Mike looked at his bleeding hand and ruined clothing.

"You rejected the opportunity, Michael Thomas; and so your lesson had to be personal." Mike knew there was wisdom in what Orange said.

"If I hadn't let go, what would have happened?"

"You could not have gone forward on the path carrying the old energy objects," Orange answered. "The wind would have carried you back to a place of old consciousness. You would have eventually been safe, but you would have lost all that you have learned and gained so far on this sacred path. It would have been the death of the new Michael Thomas, and you would have left this place." Orange paused for a moment for effect, then continued.

"This is important, Michael Thomas of Pure Intent. You cannot embrace any part of the old energy—even the seemingly precious things—and move forward into the new. The two are not compatible. You are actually moving into a new dimension, and the physics of the old do not mix with the physics of the new. Let me ask you this." Orange came closer to Mike. "Does part of you still hold love and remembrance for your parents even though the physical items are gone? Or did you lose that too in the storm?"

"I still have it," replied Mike, knowing where this conversation was going.

"Then where is the loss?" Orange inquired.

Mike was silent. He realized what was being taught. Orange continued, like a wise father imparting simple wisdom to an inquisitive child.

"The memories of your loved ones are in the energy of your life experience—and not from any old object. When you wish to remember, then do so using the love consciousness and gifts of the new Michael Thomas. When you start doing this, you will even find that your perceptions are different from what you thought was there in the past. You are gaining new wisdom about who your parents were...and who you are. The new tools and gifts will actually enhance your memory of these things. Old memorabilia simply draws you backward to a time when you could not understand the overview."

Mike still didn't understand all this new language and Spirit talk. Orange knew his thoughts and spoke again.

"When you have finished with the seventh house," Orange smiled, "there will be full understanding."

Mike understood only a portion of what Orange was saying, but he was beginning to get the picture. Much like the rotting food explanation, he realized that he could carry nothing of the old Mike to the place called home. He lamented the loss and still felt somewhat betrayed by his angel friends because they had not been more specific. But he was starting to see the metamorphosis that was being asked of him, and he also realized that he had now been given two suggestions along the way; one by Blue not to take food, and one by Orange to leave his baggage. In both cases, he had ignored the advice, and both times it had gotten him into trouble.

Michael vowed to himself to start listening closer to what the angels along the way told him. This was a strange place with multiple-dimensional facets, and he realized that HE had the biological information, and the ANGELS had the spiritual information. If he would listen more and assume less, his journey would be far smoother. Even if he didn't yet understand all the language and many of the concepts, he still had to trust the angels' overview of a land they knew, and yet he had to do the work of traversing the path himself.

"Orange!" Michael wanted to get the angel's attention. "Why are there storms here?"

"Michael Thomas of Pure Intent, I will give you still another answer that is true, but that you will not understand." Orange retreated to the mouth of the cave, turned, and delivered the answer. "When the human is not here, there are no storms." Orange was right. Mike had no idea why that should be. Mike stood up to ask about the dark thing that he had seen chasing him...and realized that Orange was gone!

"Good-bye, again, my brightly colored orange friend," said Mike to the vacant space where the Orange Spirit had been a moment before. For the first time, there was a response to his farewell. In his mind, he clearly heard the voice of Orange, soothing and loving and wise.

"It is when you realize why we never say good-bye that you will know you are part of our dimension." More confusing talk, thought Mike—but somehow comforting.

Mike used the fire that Orange had somehow provided to warm himself and dry his clothes, which he removed and laid on rocks next to the warm blaze. He noticed that the armor and shield had suffered no damage as he carefully laid the pieces next to his clothes. Gradually, he fell into a slumber, not knowing if it was day or night outside, and slept several hours. The storm continued for a while but had totally cleared up by the time Michael awakened.

Michael peered out of the cave and could see that it was now dusk of the same day. He had slept the afternoon away during the remainder of the storm and was now feeling energetic. Slowly and cautiously, he assembled his battle gear, put it on as he had been told, lifted the map bag over his neck, and stepped into the roadway. All seemed so peaceful! He looked backward but could sense no danger, nor could he detect any wisp of a dark shape scurrying to hide behind a rock or tree. Mike felt good!

Even though it was almost dark, Mike felt that the next house would present itself shortly, and he was right. He strode off down the path with another house just out of sight over a hill. He felt light! Both hands were free, and without the bags there was no irritating clanking of his battle gear. He almost forgot he had it on. His step was nimble. Michael Thomas had accepted his physical loss as being appropriate for his journey and had put the experience behind him. He practiced seeing the photos of his parents in his mind and was rewarded with full memory. He still felt their love, and he had all the feelings he used to experience when gazing at their photos. Orange was right. What was really his was in his mind. It was all he really needed.

✤ ✤ ✤

SEVERAL HUNDRED YARDS behind, a revolting dark green shape was recovering from a painful experience. Each time IT moved, there was a painful reminder of the burn it had received. IT didn't know it, but that wound would never heal. IT was perplexed, but still determined to thwart Michael Thomas's path. As if life itself were in the balance, IT knew that even if IT had to completely sacrifice itself in battle, there would come a time soon where Michael Thomas would look into ITs searing red eyes, feel ITs hot breath, and know what ultimate fear was, before he could take another step toward home.

CHAPTER SEVEN

The Third House

Mike paused at the footpath before he entered the third house. This one had a sign on the lawn that read, "House of Biology." The entire house and the sign were all one hue, just as the other houses had been. This cottage-style structure was a beautiful Kelly green that seemed to blend in with the surrounding natural color of the luxurious grass and trees, tempered by the subdued lighting of dusk. Mike knew that he was about to meet still another angel who would undoubtedly become his friend. He took stock of where he had been so far and guessed correctly that the first two houses had both been preparation oriented, helping him prepare for his journey. Now came the beginning of substance and training. *After what he had been through so far, this had to be easier,* Mike thought.

As he approached the house, an enormous green angel stepped out on the porch, watched him approach, and gave Mike the standard salutation.

"Greetings, Michael Thomas of Pure Intent!" This angel, whom Mike would automatically call Green, seemed especially stout and filled with mirth. Mike felt that all the angels had a great humorous streak in them, but Green always seemed to be smiling. The angel looked Mike up and down and winked.

"Nice sword!"

"Good evening to you, Green," Mike replied, ignoring the comment about the sword. *I'll bet he did that just to make me feel more comfortable about carrying something so seemingly out of place in this spiritual quest*, thought Mike.

"Nope," replied the angel, reading Mike's thoughts. "Not all swords are as grand as the one you have. I know. I see a lot of them."

"What makes the difference?" Mike asked.

"We named you for a reason, Michael. Your intent is indeed pure, and your heart literally rings with your quest. Your tools therefore reflect something that all such as I can see. Please, come in." Mike followed Green into the house, continuing the conversation.

"Does that make me different?—special?—better?"

"It makes your potential huge, Michael! Remember that as a human you have choice. We never grade humans or compartmentalize them. We view each of you as a level of energy potential."

"Potential for what?"

"Change!" exclaimed Green.

"Why?"

Green stopped and faced Mike. They had just passed through a number of small, green rooms and were now in what seemed to be the entrance to another of Mike's temporary quarters. The angel spoke softly and with a tremendous sense of patience and honor for the human he was standing before.

"Why are you here, Michael Thomas?"

"To allow for my journey home," Mike stated quickly and honestly.

"And what must you do to allow for that?" The angel was creating a space for Mike to define his current situation.

"Travel on the road of seven houses?"

"And?" Green wanted more.

"Become a different dimensional being?" Mike sheepishly parroted what he remembered Orange had told him. Green smiled broadly and spoke.

"Eventually, Michael of Pure Intent, you will actually understand some of the words and concepts you are reflecting now. Did Orange tell you that?" Mike knew he'd been found out.

"Yes, he did. I really don't know what it means yet."

"I know," mused the large green one. "So—back to the question. What are you doing about getting home?"

"Changing!" Mike stated triumphantly.

"Why?" Green asked. Now the question had gone full circle, and Mike was about to answer his own inquiry.

"I can't go there unless I change?" stated Mike quizzically.

"Exactly! The journey home has several parts, my human friend. First, there is intent to go. Next, there is preparation. This is always followed by self-discovery, and understanding that the changes you must undergo are necessary for you to get there. You are already feeling that. And, finally, you study how things work so you will be able to be comfortable with the overview. Opening that final door marked 'home' is like a graduation, Michael. There is nothing like it!"

This was the very first time an angel had begun to discuss the goal and the final door. Mike was very excited.

"Tell me more about what to expect, Green." This is what Mike was really interested in—the final goal—what to expect when he opened that door.

"When you initially asked, you defined it yourself," Green answered.

"When was that?" Mike didn't remember.

"When you first asked for this journey," answered Green.

Mike suddenly remembered the conversation that had started all this, with the great white faceless one, when he was asked to describe home.

"You know about that?" Mike was shocked.

"We are all part of the family, Michael." Green glided into the room where Mike was to stay. "This should all look familiar to you," said Green.

Mike looked around. It was much the same as the other houses and was extremely inviting for rest and sleep. He smelled the meal that was already prepared in the adjacent room.

"There are also clothes this time, Michael." The angel pointed toward the closet.

Mike suddenly realized what a sight he must be, with blood and dried mud on his torn clothes, a product of the life-threatening storm he had just experienced. Mike looked into the area where Green had pointed. There indeed were clothes! He took a closer look and discovered fine traveling clothes just his size, and a grand green robe. He turned to ask Green how his exact size was known, but Green was nowhere to be seen. Mike smiled to himself and spoke out loud, knowing that Green would hear him.

"Good night, my green angelic friend. See you in the morning."

Mike ate and slept soundly that night until about 5 A.M., when he was visited by a nightmare. In his dream, he again saw the horrible dark thing approaching during his helplessness in the storm. He again felt the forewarning that his life was about to be ended by this menace, and he was terrified. He awoke with a start, sweating profusely. Green was standing by the bed!

"Ready?" he asked.

"Do you guys ever sleep?" asked Mike rubbing his eyes.

"Of course not."

"It isn't even light outside yet!" Mike still felt weary from the seeming lack of sleep and the frightening dream.

"Get used to it in the House of Biology, Michael Thomas." Green smiled again and continued to stand there. "I will be here each morning at 5:30 to begin the lessons. Before we are finished, you will understand all about sleep patterns and biological energy—and bad dreams."

"You know my dreams?" Mike was amazed.

"Michael, you still don't realize our connection to you. We know all about you, and we honor your process greatly!" Green took a few steps back from the bed and gestured for Mike to get ready and join him. Mike felt a bit shy.

"Green, I'm not wearing clothes."

"That's how you are going to start the lessons, Michael. Don't be shy. Put on the green robe that's in the closet."

Mike did as he was asked and went into the next room to enjoy his breakfast. Green was like an attentive dog! He sat with Mike and watched everything he ate, but he said nothing. This was the first time any angelic teacher had shown him this kind of attention. Something was different.

After the meal, Green led Mike to a special teaching area. The other houses had all been enormous, with large rooms and high ceilings. In this one, all the rooms were small, and most of the teaching took place in only one of them. Green started right in. He asked Mike to take off his robe.

"Michael Thomas of Pure Intent—point to your enlightenment."

"I don't understand," said Mike.

"Where is your pure intent? Where is your love? Where is that part of you that knows God?" Green was intent, and continued, "Go ahead; point to that part of your biology that has those attributes."

Mike didn't have to think very hard about this. He now understood that Green, who was not human, wanted Mike to show him where in his body those values were present.

"Some are here." Mike pointed to his forehead. "And some are here." Mike placed the palm of his hand over his chest. "That is where I sense what you are asking."

"Wrong!" stated Green in a loud voice that startled Mike. "Care to try again?"

Slowly Mike began a tour of his body, asking Green if it should be here or there as he continued to point. Each time Green gave a negative answer.

"I give up, Green," said Mike, exasperated after having pointed to almost every part he had. "Where is it?"

"Let me tell you a joke, Michael Thomas. Then you may try again."

Mike thought this was very funny. Here he was—naked with a green angel in a land that really didn't exist in his former life—and the angel was about to tell a joke! Who would ever believe this? Was this a great place or what?

"Once there was a man who felt very enlightened," Green began, enjoying every minute of this joke-telling experience. "When the man felt he had reached a level of enlightenment to continue on his journey, he found a taxi." Green smiled broadly and paused, looking for Michael's reaction to an angel's knowledge of the word *taxi*. Mike didn't give Green the satisfaction of expressing the surprise that he wanted, suppressing his sudden desire to laugh. Mike smirked a bit. Green continued anyway.

"When the man found the taxi, he stuck his head into the window and said to the driver, 'I'm ready. Let's go!' The driver, in reaction to the instruction, immediately took off in the direction the man wanted—taking only the man's head with him!" Green was very funny in his storytelling and again looked at Mike for a reaction. Mike was deadpan and looked at Green, turning his head to the side and twisting his face into an expression that said— "And?" Green got to the punch line.

"Blessed is the man who places his whole body into the taxi before announcing that he is ready to go!" Green was proud of his storytelling, despite Mike's obviously stifled reaction, and he gloated in the silence that followed.

"Don't quit your day job," Mike announced, barely containing his desire to laugh out loud at this funny angel's antics. "So what exactly does your joke mean, Green?"

"Michael Thomas of Pure Intent, each and every cell of your human body contains a consciousness that knows about God. Each cell therefore has the potential for enlightenment, love, and the pursuit of vibratory change. Here, let me show you." With that, Green did something that shocked and dismayed Mike. He quickly approached, and with a lightning move, he stomped on Mike's toe!

"OW!" yelled Mike in disgust at such a violation of trust. "What is that about?" Mike's toe was throbbing with pain. He grabbed it and tried to soothe it, as any human would, hopping around on the floor in the process. "That hurt!" Mike shouted at Green. The toe was turning red, then black. "That hurt a lot! I think you broke it!"

"What hurts, Michael?" asked Green casually as he watched Mike move around the room while grimacing at every step.

"My toe, you slime-colored sadist!" Mike didn't know what he was saying, but he was angry. Green was unaffected by Mike's outburst and came closer to him.

"Stay away!" said Mike, holding out his hands defensively. "I don't want to sample another angelic foot massage, or your idea of sole therapy. Don't come any closer!"

"What hurts, Michael?" Green asked again, also stating, "It's not your toe."

"It's not?" Mike asked incredulously as he found himself on the floor in the lotus position, blowing on his foot, trying not to tip over. "Then you tell me, your Holy greenness. What is it that hurts?" Mike was being sarcastic, but the angel didn't mind.

"WE do, Michael," Green stated. "Every cell in your body is feeling your discomfort right now. Say it, Michael: Say, 'WE HURT.'" Mike did as he was told.

"WE hurt," he repeated not too enthusiastically.

"Do you give permission for a healing?" Green inquired.

"Yes." Mike was interested now.

"State your permission," stated Green.

"I give you permission to heal my toe," said Mike.

"WRONG!" stated Green in another loud voice. Mike didn't need a map to get this one right. He tried again.

"I give you permission to heal," Mike paused. "WE—er—I mean, US." Green was still unsatisfied, and said so.

"Michael, give permission for the event, don't give ME permission to do it." Mike thought about this and rephrased his statement.

"I give permission for this healing. WE hurt, and WE will all benefit from this cure."

"And so it is!" shouted an enthusiastic Green, as he clapped his hands in glee. "You have it correct, Michael Thomas of Pure Intent! You have just healed your toe!"

Almost immediately, Mike's toe stopped throbbing. The redness turned a healthy pink, and his entire body felt relief from the pain. Green came closer, and this time Mike did not ask him to stop.

"Michael, do you know what just happened?" Green's voice was soft and gentle.

"I think I do, but I need you to elaborate." Mike was feeling weak from the lesson. The pain had exhausted him. Green continued.

"I will never again cause you pain, my dear friend. You have my promise. From now on, you will learn from experiences other than pain. What you just learned was that the pain of the one part affects the many. It was a community experience. You feel tired now, don't you? If this experience had just involved your toe, why then would your entire countenance feel the effect? Why was there anger? Did your toe shout at me? No. Your entire body shouted at me! Your toe knew of the pain, but all of you participated. The toe was the source of the problem, but I guarantee that all the cells knew of the event. The same is true of joy, pleasure, passion, and the inner pride of truth. Each cell feels everything and has an awareness of the whole." Green paused for effect. "So it is with spiritual enlightenment and a Godly quest."

"Then where exactly is my enlightenment, Green?" Mike wanted a straight answer this time, without jokes or toe-stompings.

"It resides equally in each cell of your body, Michael Thomas. Each and every cell has a consciousness of the whole. Each cell absolutely knows about the others. Each one participates in the vibration of the complete human." Green was quiet a moment, then turned for emphasis and sat down and faced Mike. "Your time here will be to learn the characteristics of vibrational increase. Before we can begin, you must accept yourself as a group of cells that all know everything—not as a bunch of parts."

"I think I can do that." Michael spoke with serious intent.

"So do I." Green smiled his great big smile and got up from his sitting position. "Are you ready?" Still smarting from the toe experience, Mike felt himself involuntarily brought to his feet from the floor as he replied.

"Yes, sir."

The next few hours were filled with instructions about human anatomy and health. Not the medical kind of training, but advice about plain living and practical applications for good health. There seemed to be a constant stream of profound information about everything! What to eat, how to have energy, when to exercise and why—and how to know when it should be done. All through the lessons, Green constantly expressed concern that Mike understand the "WE" of his being. Mike was beginning to feel as if he wasn't allowed to have parts, and Green agreed with him.

Mike slept extremely well that night and had no more nightmares. In the morning, Green was again at his bed and watched him eat breakfast. This time Green began to explain about each type of food that Mike was eating. Green didn't seem to care what Mike ate from his magnificent selection, but gave a tour of each food group as Mike chewed away, trying to remember everything that Green was saying.

In the days that followed, Mike began an exercise program. On certain days, Green required him to again put on his battle dress so as not to forget what it felt like. Those were the days Mike enjoyed best. He didn't realize how much he had missed his sword, shield, and armor until he placed it on his body and again marveled at how well it fit.

Green instructed Mike on food, plants, herbs, and how the body balanced itself naturally. Mike marveled at how the cells worked together as if they somehow "knew" something that Mike did not. It was all so wonderful! Green told Mike that there was a fine magnetic polarity for each organ and for each cell. Again, the cells all "knew" what it was, and by themselves worked to achieve perfect balance. When in balance, each cell could rejuvenate itself perfectly, and Mike learned how the body renewed itself constantly. Finally, he asked Green a funny question.

"It seems that my cells—I mean, WE—are very smart when it comes to balancing the biology. How is it that I am seemingly in the dark in the process? Can't I contribute something to the situation? My mind really doesn't have the knowledge that the cells do. Where do I, as Mike, come in?"

"Funny you should ask, Michael Thomas of *Pure Intent!*" Green emphasized the pure intent part, and Mike knew what was coming.

Green continued, "Your body only needs you to honor it with proper intake, environmental wisdom, and maintenance, and it will do the rest. So far you have learned how to make it comfortable, feed it properly, and give it physical practice. Your systems are happy and busy without you doing anything else. Now, it's time for you to understand the test of your spirit, for you have something to give your body that it could never do for itself. Do you know what that is?"

Mike thought he did.

"Yes, I do, Green." Mike was feeling healthier than he had ever been in his life. He wasn't ashamed of his nakedness anymore, especially in front of Green, who admired the slow changes in Mike's appearance and told him so. Green was like a loving father who was also a world-class trainer. "It's time for me to make a choice," Mike blurted out.

Green almost exploded with glee. "Never before has a human realized this in such a short time!"

Mike understood that he had finally said something right and was amazed at Green's reaction. The angelic presence shot around the room, showing off for the first time its ability to defy gravity and change shape. Mike might have been afraid if it hadn't been that the show was exclusively for him. When Green calmed down, he again came and stood in front of Mike. He looked like his green angelic self again, but he was still wide-eyed with merriment.

He smiled and said, "Michael Thomas of Pure Intent, what is your choice?"

"I choose to use the new gifts of Spirit and increase my vibration." Again Mike knew he had spoken correctly. Green backed up a few paces as if to allow Mike's increased wisdom to swell around him. Green was obviously impressed.

"So it shall be this very day, Michael Thomas!" Green exclaimed. "You got it right. The thing that your cells cannot do is use the piece of God you carry with you that has the power to choose to enlighten itself. Only your spirit can do that, and although only your spirit can make the choice, each cell will know that you gave permission. Just like when your toe hurt, your spirit knew it. So it is that when you ask for a higher vibration, your toe will know it. The WE-ness of you is celebrating right now, Michael. They all know what you have given intent for. It's time you retired."

It had been a grand day, and Mike was beginning to feel that he was understanding more about spiritual matters. Evidently what he had done was very special. Green told him on the way to the bedchamber that Mike had given intent for a sacred pursuit—the first of many that Mike would have to ask for. Each time it was appropriate to move to another level, Mike was told that the biology would have to be balanced, with permission given. Green was proud of Mike and was treating him with even more respect than usual. When he came to the door of the bedchamber, Green asked Mike again to face him.

"Michael Thomas of Pure Intent, normally I just disappear now and come back in the morning. You know the routine. I am here to tell you that I love you dearly. The attributes of a vibrational change have consequences that you must learn about and get used to. I told you that I would not hurt you, and I will not. Everything to follow will unfold at a pace you control. Any hurt you feel will be from you. Nothing will ever be the same for you. This night you will go to bed as one kind of human, but tomorrow you will be another—with all the tests and properties that go with a vibrational shift."

Green looked at Mike a very long time, and Mike felt the amazing sense of honor that Green had for him. Mike knew this was different. He longed to ask Green to elaborate. *What's different? Will I know tomorrow? What's tomorrow's lesson? Tell me now!*

Mike didn't ask any of these things, and Green pretended he could not *hear* Mike. Instead, Green slowly backed out of the room—a very unusual procedure for Green. Something was changing, and Mike had an ominous feeling about it all. He spoke out loud to the walls.

"I guess I have to expect something fairly drastic in order to move across the veil toward home." Mike sat on the bed. "Perhaps I will even become an angel before I get there. I might even turn a special color!" Mike almost laughed at the thought of this, and as before, he expected to hear a retort from one of the listening angels, but there was only silence. Something inside him was already starting to change. He felt a vibration in the pit of his stomach. He was having chills. He knew he had to get to bed.

Mike did not sleep well that night. He found himself wishing it were 5:30, for he realized that he missed and needed Green. He felt suddenly insecure. Each time he fell asleep, he had the same dream. IT was there, glaring at him, and each time the gruesome thing caught him, it destroyed him! As he was being dismembered, he awoke in a pool of sweat and anxiety—hearing his own screams abruptly cut off, then absolute silence. When he got back to sleep, he'd have the dream again. How many times could he be killed? Five? Six? It seemed endless. His death was repeated over and over, each time a bit differently. Each time his dream seemed more vivid. Finally, he couldn't take it anymore and began sobbing. He continued this, realizing that he was emptying his very soul into the pillow. He could not remember feeling such deep sorrow in his life! Even his parents' deaths hadn't caused such an emotional drain. He wept loudly, his weeping became wailing, and Mike was out of control.

Mike cried for himself and for his parents. He cried for lost love and for lost opportunity. He felt IT had killed him, and Mike finally cried for his own death. He convulsed with sorrow, and could not stop the upheavals of his body in its search for new areas of hurt to ponder and react to.

Mike finally slumbered a few hours in deep exhaustion before he awoke. Something was wrong. It was almost light out. *Where was Green? Why had he been allowed to oversleep?* Mike arose and instantly felt the pain in his stomach muscles from the night of gut-wrenching, convulsive crying. He held his side.

"Boy, do WE hurt!" he heard himself say to his body.

Mike went into the room normally reserved for his meals. There was no food. He put on his green robe and began to search for Green. He noticed that the rooms he was familiar with had somehow begun to turn a brownish green—or was that just the light? Speaking of light, it seemed to be failing. *Where was Green? What's happening here?*

"Green, where are you?" No response.

Mike toured the house, but he didn't find the angel anywhere. Finally, hungry and tired, Mike sat down alone in the room where Green had lectured him many times. He was puzzled and felt a blackness begin to overtake him that was very uncharacteristic of his journey. He recognized it. It was the same depression that he had experienced for so long in Los Angeles, before all this had begun to happen.

"What's happening?" Mike wondered aloud. There was only silence. "Where is everyone? Blue? Orange? Green? Hey guys, I need you!" Silence.

Mike realized that his depression was starting to take over his personality. It wouldn't be long before he was in that same hole where he didn't care about anything or anyone. He refused to let that happen.

"Okay, guys, if you won't help me, then I'll do it the hard way!" Whatever that meant. Mike was grasping at straws for a reaction from anyone! He went back to his bedchamber and looked around. When he opened his closet, he remembered the map! Perhaps it would give him some insight. It always did when something went wrong in this odd spiritual "current" land. Mike easily found the scroll and unrolled it.

Mike wasn't prepared for what he saw. He stared in disbelief and slowly put away the map. He got back into bed, robe and all, and pulled the covers up around him. It was only one in the afternoon. Mike didn't care. He stared at the wall.

On the parchment where the "YOU ARE HERE" indicator always was, there was only a black smudge—no words. There were no markings on it. The map was dead. It had lost its magic.

Had IT invaded the house and actually killed Mike during the night? Had Mike experienced dreams, or reality, during his sleep? Had IT also killed the angels? How could all this be? Mike was fighting depression and blackness. He tried to make sense of it all and stretched his mind, trying to remember anything that Green said that would explain this. In the approaching black haze of his consciousness, Mike remembered Green telling him: *"Any pain from now on will be from you. Nothing will ever be the same; I love you dearly."* Had this been Green's good-bye? Mike again remembered what the great white one had said at the beginning: *"Everything is not as it seems...."* Mike had to hang on. He believed in God, and this was all a trick—a test!

Mike did the only thing he could think of. He got up and put on his armor. It didn't feel good. It was heavier than he remembered, and the sword felt stupid. He didn't care. Mike wore it with pride, and spoke aloud.

"Nothing will defeat my spirit! I claim victory over my depression!"

Nothing. Silence. Empty words. No feeling of love or honor, or that anyone, or anything, cared about Michael Thomas. This land was completely empty. Michael Thomas was the only one there.

Mike was fighting for his very sanity. He would not give up! He went to the learning room and took his place in full battle dress in the student's chair. There he stayed until the sun went down, waiting and watching in the absolute silence of a land without sound. Even then, he continued to sit there, alert and waiting. He didn't know what to expect, but he would not give in to the darkness of the depression that he had conquered so completely before he entered this beautiful land.

Finally, in the darkened room he dozed off. His sleep was not fitful this time. He was beginning to create peace where peace had not been before. His power to do so was beginning to show. As he slept, his sword gently oscillated and "sang" to itself, responding to the new vibratory rate of the precious human who owned it—but Michael Thomas was unaware of it. His shield glowed slightly, reacting to a new set of instructions from a changing biology—but Michael Thomas was unaware of it. His armor kept him warm, replying to spiritual instructions from a newly awakened source within Michael's DNA—but Michael Thomas was unaware of it. All the cells in Michael Thomas's body were being changed, and the metamorphosis was almost complete. Mike slept very well indeed.

THINGS WERE DIFFERENT when Michael woke up in the morning. He was still in the chair that he had spent the night in, but it was somehow brighter and more cheerful in the room. He arose and tested his mind. Odd that his first thought was not to see if he was still alone, but instead if HE was okay. The depression was gone! Mike realized that he was wearing his battle dress, but somehow he didn't even feel it. As he briskly walked toward the area where food had previously been served in order to see if he was going to starve again that day, he was greeted halfway by the wonderful aroma of a fine breakfast. Mike knew all was going to be well again.

Mike ate like he had never eaten before. He was famished, almost ravenous in his attack upon the meal before him. He reveled in his feeling of well-being. He found himself singing out loud—with his mouth full!

"Mom should see me now!" Mike mused aloud, egg yolk dripping from the corner of his mouth. "She would be so ashamed at my manners."

"She is actually very proud of you, Mike." Green was standing in the doorway. "We all are."

Mike stood up in respect for his green friend. He was overjoyed to see the angel.

"Green!" Mike yelled in delight. "I wondered if I had lost you. Please, come and sit with me!" Mike sat back down and continued eating.

The large angel moved to the table and sat before Mike, but waited for Mike to speak first. He knew that his friend must have dozens of questions about what had happened the day before, but Green wanted to see when he would ask. There was silence while Mike continued eating and humming at the same time, smiling foolishly and looking at Green with sparkling eyes. Green took it all in, scanning Michael's body, obviously noticing the battle dress. He couldn't contain himself any longer.

"Nice sword," said the smirking green one.

Mike burst out laughing at the remark, remembering that this was Green's first remark to him when he had arrived. Food spewed everywhere, and the great green one joined Mike in his laughter. They embraced for the first time, hugging each other affectionately. It was the first time Mike had been allowed to touch any of the angels of the land, but he knew intuitively that it was somehow appropriate now. Neither could stop laughing. Michael found himself actually dancing with the great green angel to the music of his very soul, trudging on bagels and other delightful breads that were knocked off the table during the ruckus. He realized that now there would be pieces of blueberry muffin stuck between his toes. The room was a mess, but he didn't care.

Mike's chest was still heaving from the exertion and hilarity as he again sat down, trying to recover from his joyful antics. He finally spoke to Green, who stood before him.

"I knew you would come back, you know."

"How did you know?"

"Because you told me you loved me."

"I do," replied Green, smiling again. Mike took another bite of the now decimated meal before him. He paused.

"Can my mother and father really see me, Green?" This was the most important question to him. He remembered Green's comment when he had entered the room a few moments ago.

"It is a measure of your new awareness that you ask this question first, Michael Thomas of Pure Intent. Sometimes the angels of the land take wagers about which question will be asked first after the challenge of the change. The one that is normally asked, you have not yet voiced. We have been together again in this room for some time— yet you have still not asked it. Instead, you ask about your parents. Truly, I stand before a special human being!"

Mike wasn't certain, but he thought that Green was getting emo-tional—if that was possible for an angel. There was a pause until Green spoke again.

"Yes, Michael Thomas, your parents can see you, and they are indeed proud." Green waited for more questions.

Mike thought about what Green had said. He spoke again. "I think I know what yesterday was all about."

Green cocked his head to one side. "Really? Tell me, then." Green was all ears. Normally, at this point in a human's lessons in the House of Biology, the angel spent all his time trying to explain to a puzzled human where in the world everyone had gone the day before and the reason for the horrible, lonely journey into apparent black-ness of spirit.

"I've changed, Green, just like you said I would. I feel different. I feel..." Mike paused for a moment. "...WE feel empowered. I have an awareness about you, Green, that I did not have before. You have somehow moved from being my teacher into a role of—" Mike thought about the right word, but paused a bit too long. Green inter-rupted him.

"Family?"

"Yes!" Mike quickly agreed. He was becoming introspective, but continued. "What happened yesterday—I thought it was a test, but it wasn't." Green continued to listen, letting Mike pour out his ideas of what had taken place. "I know you will eventually give me the details of what took place, but I think I know the WHY." Mike spoke slowly and deliberately, as an instructor would. "Green, every cell in my body felt a withdrawal. It's like I turned off a switch and died. There was no solace anywhere; not even my own mind could come up with any reason to exist. I was somehow a neutral human being. That's when I knew what was happening—when I looked at the map. It was a signal to my mind, and I knew what was happening."

Green was impressed. Never before had a student in the green house been so accurate and aware of the characteristics of vibrational shift. Usually it took a very long time to explain. Green knew he sat before a special entity—this Michael Thomas. Green was proud of his student and loved him even more. Mike continued.

"The map died, too. I was in limbo; then, I knew what was taking place. In order to receive this spiritual gift of intent, I had to go through a rebirth of sorts. Almost like the power was turned off of my existence for a day, and then it was restarted with new circuitry. I knew that if I could somehow keep my sanity through it all, I would eventually be okay. I used a visualization of you telling me that you loved me, Green. It's the only thing that worked. When I thought about you, then I could focus on why I was here." Mike looked at Green and smiled. He tried to hide the fact that his eyes were tearing. "Am I right?"

"There is almost nothing I can add, Michael Thomas of Pure Intent." Green stood up for emphasis. "What I will tell you is this: When you were thinking of my love for you, it wasn't just me. I am part of a collective, Michael. When you speak to me, you are speaking to the whole. You are part of it, too, but you don't feel it as I do. As you vibrate higher, these things will come into focus. When you felt the love of the one you call Green, you were also feeling the love of Blue, Orange, and even of your parents—as well as the ones you are going to meet next along this path. You don't know them yet, but they know you. We are all one, Michael, and you felt it at the moment of your greatest need. Your intuition won! What a gift you already have!"

Mike knew there was more, so he kept quiet, waiting for Green to gather his thoughts. Green continued.

"Everything you said is correct, my wise human friend. In order for you to move to a higher level, there is a time of challenge. It is a time when all of us in the collective must move away and let you change. We can do nothing for you during this time, and our energy will actually disturb your process. You are enabled spiritually to move through it. You felt the loss of your family, Michael. You felt abandonment and emptiness during the brief time that you had to remain alone. The only thing that centered you was love, and I, as an instructor in this house, could never have given you that solution. You found it in the blackness for yourself. I congratulate you for your awareness and maturity in this place." Green again paused to let Mike absorb the compliment. "Do you have any other questions?"

"Yes, I do. Will it happen again?"

"Yes, it will, each time you shift into a new vibratory state."

"What can I do to make it better the next time?"

Green faced Mike and spoke seriously. "Recognize what it is and busy yourself with other things. Don't dwell on it, and remember that it is temporary. Hold ceremony around it! Honor the process in the midst of the blackness! Do exactly as you did, Michael Thomas of Pure Intent—feel the love that is involved in the gift!"

Mike understood and took it all in.

SLOWLY, THROUGH THE DAYS that followed, the lessons resumed. Because of Mike's new vibratory rate, there was even more to impart. Subtleties of awareness regarding the body were taught, and he was shown ways to tell if there was imbalance present. Green told Mike about new sleep patterns and food desires that would accompany each vibrational shift. There was so much to remember!

The last days in the green house were approaching when Green broached a new subject, one that had never before come up. "Are you ready to talk about sex?" inquired Green.

Mike almost fell over. He eyed his great green friend to see if this was another joke. "You have to be kidding!" Mike was embarrassed.

"Not kidding," said Green.

Mike spoke softly, as if someone might overhear him. "Green, that's not angel stuff. That's something humans do in the dark. It's a lowly lust thing. I'm surprised you even used the word!" Mike turned his face away and spoke to the corner of the room. "I don't think we should discuss it in such a sacred place."

Green was unyielding. "It's not what you think, Michael. Your reaction to it is only what humans have made of it. It's biological, and that's why you are here." Green was silent, letting Mike have his space while he thought about what Green had just said.

Mike was resigned. He knew that he could not escape something that Green was supposed to teach him. He had visions of high school sex-education class, where some unlucky male teacher was given the task of explaining to a group of guys what they already knew. They giggled like girls the whole time, giving each other those knowing looks— and wishing they were somewhere else. It was just too personal.

"Green, do we have to?"

"Yes."

What followed would forever change Michael Thomas's view of the physical relationship between human beings. Green spoke eloquently as though from personal experience, but Green was genderless! He told Mike that sex was one of the greatest spiritual aspects of biology. He described to an astounded Mike what the real purpose was, what males and females were supposed to get from the experience—besides children. He spoke of the elegance of raising the consciousness of two individuals simultaneously through the bringing together of emotion in a specific way. Green even gave Michael examples of how things worked in the spiritual realm of the body when passion was controlled and channeled in specific ways. Sex was an actual catalyst to enlightenment! When he finished, Mike was silent.

"I just can't believe it," Mike said, holding his face in his hands. "All this time, and I thought it was dirty. Something you didn't bring into the light. Something carnal that we brought with us through the evolutionary chain—and now you tell me it is spiritual? Wow, what a concept. Wait till the priests hear about this!" Mike was being funny, but the concept was overwhelming to a farm boy who had only learned about such things by watching animals and, later, in bits and pieces of misinformation from his adolescent friends. Mike suddenly lifted his head in realization.

"Green, I've missed so much! I wish I could have had this experience with a woman I loved. Now it's too late."

"Don't be harsh with your path, Michael. Not everything is as it seems. This information, although delivered late, will have its purpose as you proceed. The information is the important thing, even though its application might seem out of place where you are headed. The key is to change your attitude. See the process as sacred. It will help you to honor your biology even more than you do now."

Green was right. As a male human, Mike still had his imaginings and his dreams—even in a place like this. He would have to start honoring them now, instead of feeling that they were somehow wrong or corrupt. It meant a great deal to him. He understood how it all fit into the picture, and he felt more complete because of it. Now there were even private parts of his body that could join the "WE" with more respect! Mike laughed at this thought. Green saw his process and grinned in response.

The next day, it was time to go. Mike dressed himself in his new clothing, somehow magically supplied by those in the green house. This had been the most profound experience in Mike's life. As he stood on the doorstep of the green cottage in the warm sun next to Green, he didn't know what to say. Mike felt good. His battle gear looked great over his new clothes, and the materials chosen for him felt wonderful on his body. Everything fit perfectly, and he marveled at how those who tailored the garments would have known his new size due to the workouts he had been through in the past weeks.

Green looked him over carefully, his eyes pausing momentarily on Mike's weapon, and was about to speak. Mike interrupted him.

"I know, I know—nice sword!"

It was Green's turn to burst out laughing, and he did. "You took the words right out of my green angel mouth." There was awkward silence while the two stood in the warm sunlight. Mike spoke first.

"Promise me that I will see you again."

"I promise," replied Green instantly, without reservation.

"Do you have a question for me?" Mike spoke the words, remembering the protocol as in the houses before, when he was asked each time if he loved God before he departed.

"Yes, I have a question, and you know what it is." Green looked intensely at Michael Thomas. "Do you wish to answer it before I ask?"

"Yes, I do," spoke a ceremonial Michael Thomas. "I love God with all my heart. My intent is pure, and my body is one with the Spirit of all of you. I am closer to your vibration than ever before, and with that closeness comes a feeling of purpose, sacredness, and belonging. I am on my way home."

There was nothing Green could say. Whereas before, the angel had simply gone inside the house without a word, this time it was Mike who departed without saying good-bye. He confidently strode down the pathway, heading north toward the hills where the next house would be. Green stayed on the porch until Mike was out of sight and hearing range. Then, he spoke aloud, seemingly to himself.

"Michael Thomas of Pure Intent. If you survive the next house, you indeed will be the warrior I think you are." Green remained on the porch, waiting.

It wasn't long before a detestable, ugly green creature silently passed the house on ITs dark quest, following Mike and looking directly at Green. The angel said nothing and gave IT no recognition or acknowledgment. Green knew all about IT. Green also knew that Michael would know shortly. Green smiled at the thought.

"What a meeting that will be!" he spoke. Then, he turned and reentered the Green house.

CHAPTER EIGHT

The Fourth House

A s Mike casually continued on the path, he felt better than he had so far on this journey. His new custom-tailored clothes and battle gear fit together in a package that seemed to belong to this great place. He had an odd sense of familiarity regarding his surroundings. Although he had spent most of his time actually *in* the various houses, his trek on the pathway seemed somehow commonplace to him. He was beginning to recognize the smell of things and the way they looked. It was as if memories of Mike's former life were beginning to fade, and the unusual characteristics of this new land were becoming his home. In addition, Mike kept having the feeling that he "remembered" these things, although he consciously knew better since he had never been here before.

Mike also had a keen sense of new power. He actually felt as if he belonged to this land. He knew that much of this feeling came from the recent events in the House of Biology, and he smiled broadly each time he remembered Green. As he walked, he reflected that he had truly moved to a new level while he had been there. What more could there be? He had been through only three houses of seven, and he wondered what other lessons awaited him.

There was a sound behind him.

Like lightning, Mike spun around automatically, taking a position of alert defense. He even surprised himself at how instinctive his reaction was. He found himself leaning forward, his hand gripping the ornate handle of his fine sword of truth. Was he imagining it, or was the handle vibrating? His ears became the focus of all his concentration, and he stood poised like a statue waiting to spring into some unknown but perfect action.

Nothing.

It could have been the wind, but Mike noticed there were no leaves moving in the surrounding trees. Moving only his eyes, keeping the rest of his body absolutely still, Michael scanned the area. What keen vision he had in this place! He did not remember having such wonderful acuity before on the path. It was almost as if someone had turned on a bright light that had not previously been there.

Mike willed the focus of his concentration from his ears to his eyes, and he slowly looked at every large rock and bluff in sight.

Nothing.

Mike began to realize that as comfortable as he now felt with his newly found country of colored houses, it was a dangerous place for him. The dark apparition that had been so present in his dreams while in the House of Biology might still be here. He had to be careful. Oddly, Mike felt no fear. He remained motionless, watchful, straining his senses to the limit.

In this state of heightened awareness, Mike was discovering something new about his abilities. Although he could neither hear nor see anything unusual, he FELT that something was there. There was a feeling of discomfort in his very soul—a feeling of danger and of warning for his very being, yet...

Nothing.

Slowly, he turned and continued along the sunny path, his head turning slightly from left to right in order to hear behind him, straining for early detection of anything unusual. As he continued, he again contemplated the puzzle. *What could it be? In a land dripping with so much love and spiritual discovery, how could such a dark entity exist? And why was it chasing him? Why hadn't any angel been willing to speak of it?* It was a great mystery indeed, but Mike felt forewarned, and he wasn't about to let this evil dark thing sneak up on him again. He remained alert, with the feeling of danger always present.

Michael walked well into the afternoon. With dusk approaching and the next house not yet in sight, Mike stopped his brisk pace, turned around to face the way he had come, and slowly removed his map. He continued to scan the area behind him for motion or sound. He was relieved to see that indeed his precious map was active again, and it again showed the "currentness" of his situation. The YOU ARE HERE dot appeared as before, and just on the edge of the small area around the dot was the next house. It was just around the bend. Mike smiled to himself, put his map away, and continued.

The journey to the next house had taken almost a day. Mike realized that the houses were placed just far enough apart to require a person to make an effort to get to them, but none required that you spend the night in the elements. Mike was glad of that. He was feeling a bit tired and knew that it wasn't all physical. The state of alertness that he had been in for hours had taken its toll on his energy.

In that mysterious time of twilight, where everything seems to turn all one warm color, Mike saw the next house as he rounded the curve in the path. Although everything around it was reflecting the orange and red of the dwindling day, the country-style house seemed to glow a pure violet color, as if the surroundings had no effect on it. Mike stopped and gaped in awe. Never had he seen such a beautiful hue! The violet was intense, serene, and powerful all at the same time. He had the feeling that the structure was entirely translucent and somehow lit from within. He continued, remembering that to stop for too long wasn't prudent, even at this seemingly safe distance from his goal.

In the beauty department, Mike had only gotten the first taste of what was to come, for when the angel appeared at the door to greet him, he was speechless. Never had he beheld such a beautiful creature as this! He almost felt he should kneel in respect for the sight before him. What was happening? Did he somehow have increased color receptors in his eyes? He couldn't remember ever seeing such a color! He stood silently in awe of the sight, like a child seeing a sunset for the first time, wondering if there was magic involved. Then he heard the voice—and oh, what a voice!

From the depths of tranquility seemed to come a silky smooth voice that calmed the very air that carried its vibration—and the voice was obviously female!

"Greetings, Michael Thomas of Pure Intent," the serene voice said. "You have been expected."

Mike was stunned and said nothing. He didn't even have a coherent thought for the angel to read! He was dumbfounded. He realized that he had stopped breathing. She smiled and continued.

"I'm no more female than Green was, Michael. Angels are genderless, but they contain all attributes of both your biological genders. My voice and appearance are for your comfort in this house."

Mike understood almost nothing of what Violet was saying. He could breath now, but didn't know what to say. He tried, but was embarrassed by the croaking sound that accompanied his words.

"You're quite a sight!" Not only did he croak out his message, but he knew it was an incredibly stupid greeting. What a thing to say to such a beautiful entity! Mike experienced the awkwardness he had felt as a boy, the first time he was actually required to say something intelligent to an adult—and didn't. Mike's stupor was in part induced by the incongruity of what stood before him. Here was an enormous angelic presence with what seemed to him the countenance of female gentleness, although there was no body distinction between Violet and any other angel. All wore indistinct flowing garments of the color of their respective houses that would hide or disguise any gender. All were very large—but this face! Violet's face was definitely female. It had the gentleness of his mother and his grandmother and the beauty of a saint. Mike sighed and tried again.

"Please, forgive me...uh...Violet." Mike even found that calling her by the color name somehow violated his sense of proper etiquette since it sounded like the familiar first name of a woman. He continued. "I didn't expect—I mean I didn't know that angels could be women." Mike was immediately sorry he had opened his mouth again. How stupid that was! Of course angels were female! Hadn't almost every painting he had ever seen of an angel been female? Violet just stood there. He tried again.

"What I mean is, that...none of the others so far...they seemed to be guys...I mean men—er—male." Mike wanted to rewind the episode and start over. His communication skills and any eloquence of speech were completely gone. He had failed miserably to greet this entity properly. He sighed again and simply shrugged. Violet now smiled at Mike.

"I understand fully, Michael Thomas."

The look she gave Mike could have melted his armor. There was no romance here. The feeling was an incredible love of pure maternal essence. This is what had taken Mike by surprise. It was as though he had suddenly met his mother again; he had the sense of being reunited with long-lost family, with the accompanying joy and disbelief. It had been so long since he had been looked at like that! He wanted to snuggle up and be held. He was immediately embarrassed by his thoughts, knowing that Violet could somehow feel them as well. She continued.

"You'll get used to it very soon, Michael. There are reasons why I look this way to you. It's not this way with all those who travel this path, but for you it is different."

Mike got the idea. Violet's appearance and demeanor were for his benefit. He accepted this, but wondered why he needed to "see" a motherly angel.

"Because you earned it!" said a wise Violet. "Not everything here is just for lessons, Michael. Much of it is given in the form of gifts for your growth. You have only been through three houses, and already you stand out as one of the most special who has ever joined us here."

Michael took that all in, but before he could think of something to say in response to the obvious compliment, Violet did something that Mike would never forget.

"Michael Thomas of Pure Intent," she spoke softly. "Please remove your shoes."

Mike did as he was asked. In addition, he saw that there was an area prepared at the door for one pair of shoes, and he placed his there. They fit perfectly.

"Michael, do you know why I have asked this?" inquired Violet.

Michael thought about it. "Because it's sacred ground inside?" He remembered Moses and the burning bush, and the dialogue of that story.

"If that were the case, why didn't the others ask the same of you?"

Mike continued to think about it; he tried again. "Because you are a very special angel?"

Violet was amused at this game and began to chuckle. Mike was perplexed. He knew he hadn't given the right answer.

"Please come inside," Violet said as she turned and entered the house.

Mike followed but was bothered by their conversation's lack of closure. He called after her as he followed her inside.

"Violet, tell me. Why did you ask me to remove my shoes?"

"You indeed will tell ME, Michael, before you leave this place." Violet continued, leading the way.

Mike didn't like it when the angels made him wait for answers, especially when he was required to somehow figure it out for himself. Too much work, Mike thought.

"That's why you're here," said Violet as she led him farther into the violet house. Mike again felt silly at his thoughts.

The violet house was very plain—unlike its host. Mike realized that in his awe of the new angel's appearance, he had neglected to read the sign naming the house.

"Violet, what is the name of this house?" Mike asked. Violet stopped, turned, and faced Mike.

"It is the House of Responsibility, Michael Thomas." She waited for Michael's response, her beautiful expression one of expectation. Mike immediately knew there was trouble ahead.

"Oh," he said, with little expression. He didn't give Violet the reaction she wanted. She turned and continued the tour.

Mike was disturbed at hearing the name of the house. In his mind, he had conjured up many scenarios that might take place here. Responsibility had always been an ugly word, mainly because of his parents' harping on him about this and that. They used the word a lot in a critical way. Later, he heard the same thing from women he was with, usually in combination with some kind of complaint about his actions. *Why was it*, Mike thought, *that women were always trying to "fix" him?* Then he had a horrible thought. Perhaps Violet appeared as a female in this house for the same purpose. *Another woman, sent from God to change him? What if God was a woman? What a sick joke that would be!* Suddenly, Mike smiled at the thought processes produced by his human maleness, knowing full well that this was not the truth. God was neither male nor female, but Mike was amused, nevertheless, by this imaginary scenario. What could the House of Responsibility be about?

Violet was leading them through a maze of smallish rooms on their way to Mike's dinner.

"What's in there?" Mike inquired as they came upon a set of large double doors.

"The theater," said Violet, never missing a step.

A theater? Mike's thoughts were racing as he continued to follow Violet. *What's a theater doing in an angelic place? Will there be a play?* He had another, stranger thought. *Maybe they were going to a movie!* Mike thought how funny it would be if tomorrow he and Violet went to a movie together—perhaps they could see one of the many angel movies that were popular? He almost laughed out loud. Violet, knowing exactly what Mike was thinking, was very amused also—but for other reasons.

Finally, they reached their destination. The dining room and lodging areas looked similar to those in the other houses. In the closet, there were slippers for Mike's feet and beautiful violet clothes that were obviously designed for him to wear during his stay. He smelled food. Again, he was led into a dining area that had a scrumptious selection. How did they know exactly when he was going to arrive? For that matter, Mike had never seen a single food preparer or a clean-up person. He remembered the mess that Green and he had left after their fun, and how the blueberries had stained his toes for days. Like gnomes, whoever prepared the food came and went undetected. What a place!

Mike expected to turn and find Violet gone, as the angels before had been. Instead, she was still there.

"Is everything to your satisfaction, Michael?" she asked. Violet was indeed a beautiful creature. Mike continued to be soothed by her motherly qualities.

"Yes, thank you." Mike felt like bowing in respect.

"In the morning, we shall begin. Good night, Michael Thomas of Pure Intent." With this, Violet exited.

This was different. Just as Green had changed the protocol by remaining on the porch when Mike left the House of Biology, Violet had done much the same thing here. Were the angels becoming more polite? Were they adopting human etiquette? Mike noted the difference but decided not to ask about it.

He ate, got ready for bed, and immediately fell fast asleep. He felt safe, warm, and loved. He would start still another adventure the next day, and he knew there would be discovery for him in Violet's lessons. He dreamed of his boyhood, his parents, and it felt good.

OUTSIDE THE HOUSE, the dark, elusive, vile shape that was IT took a position of watchfulness. IT was both contemplative and outraged. When Michael had appeared outside the green house on his way to this one, IT had been shocked by his changes. He had grown in power, and he had those blasted weapons! Michael's alertness was now suddenly warriorlike, and he had no fear! What had happened in the last house that would change him like that? IT seethed with anger that the chance to confront Michael had failed so miserably during the storm.

IT started to develop a better plan to trap the human. IT reasoned that if Michael Thomas had wanted to be an elusive warrior, he should have taken a less-known route instead of traveling on a known path as he did. Then, IT realized that Michael would always follow the path. He had to, since he didn't know where the next house would be. Therefore, IT decided, the answer was to go ahead of ITs prey and wait for him to step into a trap. If IT could be said to smile, IT did. IT didn't sleep but had visions of the imminent demise of Michael Thomas of Pure Intent.

✤ ✤ ✤

THE NEXT MORNING was typical of all of them. It was glorious! The meal was splendid, and Michael topped it off with a favorite blueberry muffin, shaking his head in disbelief at the freshness of it all and the wonderful flavor.

"It didn't taste this good between my toes." Mike laughed out loud as he again thought of himself and Green in their wild, humorous abandon in the dining area of the last house.

Just as he had finished dressing in his newly supplied clothes, a knock sounded at the door. *A knock? Since when did any angel knock?*

"Please enter," said a polite Mike. Violet seemed to float in, and Mike smiled at her. "Please thank whoever is responsible for such a fine human breakfast."

"You're welcome," said Violet.

"It's you?"

"It's all of us," she replied. "We are not separate."

"I've heard that before. Someday I'll understand it. Until then, thank all of you," Mike said.

"Are you ready?" Violet asked.

"I am."

Violet turned and led the way back to the area they had passed the day before. This time the double doors were open, and Mike followed her into the beautifully appointed violet-colored movie theater! Mike stopped in disbelief. He stood amazed, and Violet chuckled.

Before them was a giant wraparound movie screen. In the rear of the room, Michael saw a modern film projector, with reel after reel of film stacked in giant metal cans, ready for showing. It seemed as if there were hundreds!

"Guess what, Michael Thomas?" asked Violet. "We are going to watch movies together!"

"I don't believe it!" exclaimed Mike. "This has to be a joke."

With that comment, Violet dropped her smile and looked at Mike in a serious way.

"Far from that, Michael. Far from that. Please take a seat in the front row."

Violet went to the back of the room where she began warming up the machinery. Mike was still confused at the dichotomy he was observing. *Angels don't thread film projectors,* he thought. *They don't have movie theaters in sacred places. This is very strange indeed.* But he did as he was asked and took his place in the middle of the front row. Unlike movie houses where he had come from, the front row of this theater was at the midpoint of the room. He also noticed something else odd. The middle chair in the front row was plush and padded. All the rest of the seats in the room were not, almost as if they were only placed there for effect. Mike sat down in the plush violet chair and faced the giant white screen.

"What movie are we going to see, Violet?" Mike was a bit apprehensive about this.

"Home movies, Michael," she replied, continuing to prepare the first reel, not looking up. Mike didn't like the sound of that answer at all. He felt his stomach grip his ribs. There was that feeling again! His new intuition was working overtime, letting him know that what was coming might be unpleasant. He thought about trying humor—maybe a comment about some popcorn? He didn't get the chance. The lights dimmed in a very professional manner; Mike heard the clatter of the projector, and the screen came to life. Mike's eyes were glued to what he saw. His heart was in his throat from the first image.

The first film that played that day, just as all the others to follow, was of the finest reproduction quality Mike had ever seen. There was no flickering, and the image was somehow projected in 3-D, but without the dumb glasses! The sound was natural, coming from exactly where each sound should be on the wide screen in front of him, even as the characters moved from place to place. Mike instantly wished that the film was not so real. He was too close. The wraparound screen placed him right in each scene. He wanted to move back but couldn't.

Portrayed on the screen in front of Michael Thomas was Michael Thomas! If he had to title this home movie, it would be "All the Bad Things That Happened to Me in My Life." The film started with him as a child, and it was so real! His mother looked very young; and his father, so handsome. He was deeply moved by the remembrance of these dear ones. And the current presentation in this violet theater made them come alive to his tender heart. It was as though he were living it again! Each episode took an entire reel of film and was presented unedited in real time—just as it happened in his life, only jumping from one potent negative experience to the next.

The first few reels were actually funny. There was Mike as a cute, blond three-year-old, finding his mother's makeup. He made a mess of the bathroom, and his mom caught him. She was very upset, and it was the first time Mike received a spanking. The seated adult that was Mike was shocked at how he actually experienced the wounded feeling of that first spanking event again. He was being forced to actually relive the emotions of each event! Home movies, indeed! This had the potential of becoming a horror show as he aged in the films. Mike was beginning to feel like a freight train was approaching—and he was tied to the track.

More childhood events were presented, each one bringing Mike into a reality that he had not thought of in years. There he was, locked in the bathroom at six years old. He remembered how that felt—it wasn't his fault! Somehow the knob got turned, but his dad had to be called in from the field to remove the hinges. Then, there was his father's anger and another spanking. Mike again felt the violation of trust from the events of that long-ago day. He hadn't done anything wrong! Dad was angry and laid into him with the stinging leather of his biggest belt. It had cost his father a day's work in the field, and it had interrupted the harvest. The adult Mike was beginning to feel depressed.

Reel after reel played, and now Mike was ten. He was bused into the city to go to school. He remembered the face of Henry, the school bully, who came back each school term to torment him. All the kids seemed to hate this big kid, but they did nothing about him. They were all afraid. Because he was a farm kid from the funny-sounding town of Blue Earth, the other kids laughed at Mike. The bully, however, was merciless. The school contained children from many kinds of families, but in these modern days, farmers were a minority. His clothes gave him away, since Mom had made all of them. He didn't look the same as the others, and the bully never let him forget it. He and the other kids made fun of Mike's clothes, his smell, and even his parents' way of life.

As the projector clattered on, Mike saw the time a group of children called him over to play. He felt good about that. They actually wanted his company! Then, much to his dismay, it became a trick. Instead of including him in their fun, HE became their fun. They aligned him just right while another boy got on hands and knees behind him. Then, at just the right time, they pushed him over. He fell backwards, over the crouching boy behind him. They had a great laugh at his expense. Mike also laughed, trying to join them in the joke, but they discarded him, moving on without him when they were done.

This was painful. Mike didn't like seeing this at all. What good was all of it? He found himself getting angry at having his private life so exposed and presented in this manner—and of having to live it all again. Wasn't once enough?

More reels, and now he was 14—that fateful day in school when he was accused of cheating and he hadn't. Another student had taken some papers from the teacher's desk and put them back poorly so the teacher knew they had been disturbed. The boy who had done it pointed at Mike and said that he saw him do it. The teacher believed him; after all, Mike was just a poor farm boy, still wearing funny clothes, although his grades were very high. He was sent home with a reprimand and expelled for the day. On the way home, riding a special bus, he was thinking of how he was going to explain it all to his mom and dad. He relaxed a bit, knowing that they would believe him. They didn't, and again Mike felt alone in his life. He knew they loved him, but he wished they had given him the benefit of the doubt when he needed it most. He felt so alone.

Mike had been in the chair for hours, but the Mike in the movies wasn't even grown yet. He thought of how long he would have to endure this punishment. He didn't feel very spiritual anymore. He felt as though he were being beaten up! The films were compelling in their accuracy. Mike couldn't take his eyes or his mind away from them. Every detail was there; every voice and person was exactly as it had been. The process was astounding, but the subject matter was disastrous!

Now he was dating, and there was a lot to see! His clothing was still odd. Even though it was store-bought, his mother didn't understand fashion, and purchased weird combinations and materials. The girls at school and at church thought Mike was cute, but he overheard them making fun of his clothes. He was devastated! It wasn't long after that experience that Mike, then 16, began saving his allowance and started buying his own clothing. That's when his self-esteem started to grow, for Mike knew what looked good on him. He made a study of it and always brought along a girl acquaintance or two to help him shop. The girls loved that! Just think—a guy who liked to shop! It was the beginning of his big metamorphosis from teenage geek to handsome, desirable young man. His personality changed along with it, and Mike became more self-assured. His grades remained high, and he was involved in many school activities. Then, it happened—a smear campaign by someone jealous of Mike caused him to lose the school's presidential election in his senior year. They said he had been caught in the girls' lavatory doing obscene things. Everyone wanted to believe it. It was so sensational—and completely false. The election had been a shoo-in, since he had been president of his sophomore and junior classes, too, but the rumor mill won, and Mike lost—big. It also cost him the affections of Carol, his first real heartthrob. She wouldn't speak to him; he mourned the event for weeks and dropped out of all school functions. He had been victimized again! There it was in full "blow-by-blow" detail on the screen in front of him. The event dragged on in real time, showing every awful aspect of this part of his life. It changed Mike then, and it further weighed on him now, as he sat reliving his past.

The films played on and on. Lunch was not offered, since at some level the great angel in the back of the room knew that Mike would not be hungry. She was right. Each time a reel was finished, there would be a temporary flapping sound, and the room would go dark. There would follow an awkward silence, broken only by the sound of levers being engaged and switches being moved on the projection equipment. Neither Michael nor Violet said a word. Then, the screen would come to life again and carry on with the worst things that had ever happened to Mike. He knew, as the films played, that the "big event" was closing in. Then, it was there in front of him—the day his parents were killed.

Mike knew that he didn't have to stay in the chair if he really didn't want to. All the angels had told him that he had a choice. Right now, he wanted to run. In his mind, he begged "loudly" enough for all the angels to hear him. *Please God...I don't want to experience this again! Enough is enough!* It came anyway, and Mike felt like a truck had hit him.

Mike didn't break down and cry in his chair. He would wait until later that night. He sat stoically watching the play that was his life go forward in real time. He relived the phone call, the shock, the funeral, the grief, and the sorrow; the auction of the house, barn, and land; and the sale of his father's farm equipment, including the old tractor. He relived going through his mom and dad's things, the photos of better times, the pictures of their wedding, even some of their love letters to each other when they were falling in love. Mike sat very still and tried to escape his feelings. He disciplined his mind to make a wall for his emotions but felt victimized as he sat in the chair. He felt the involuntary convulsions of grief try to come in waves, sweeping through his body; he was aching to let out his sorrow in a burst of tears and anguish. The presentation was flawless, and its reality was a curse. This was the hardest thing he had ever been asked to do. Everything he had seen for hours and hours had made him the butt of a very bad joke. Now he was being punished and persecuted in this room! It wasn't fair. Where was the purpose in all this?

He breathed a sigh of relief when the death episode was over. Nothing could be worse than that. Mike felt very small. He was drenched in sweat and weary of the process. Still, the subject matter was commanding. He couldn't stop watching. It was so real!

When he saw "Cricket," his nickname for Shirley, he knew he was in trouble again. The next story to unfold was that of his final love affair in Los Angeles—and how it had gone sour so fast. He had thrown himself completely into it, and Cricket had treated it so lightly. It wasn't death, but it could have been, for it was the death of his heart. Again, he tried to harden his heart as he watched the images on the screen. She looked so good! Her voice was so memorable. The situation was still so recent. After all, it had been the reason for his recent depression, his lack of self-worth, and his crummy job. Mike watched all of it, reliving the details of the second most depressing incident in his life. The episodes moved forward to his workplace, highlighting his verbally abusive manager, and showing the claustrophobic cubicle he had so willingly worked in when he lived in Los Angeles.

The films ended at four o'clock; the last scenes were of the break-in and robbery of his apartment, ending with him being taken to the hospital. When the screen went blank, he heard the flapping noise that signaled the end of another reel. A piece of leader was being beaten ragged against the take-up reel. The flapping continued, but the lights did not come on. Mike stood up and, placing his hand over his forehead in salute style, shielded his eyes against the light of the raw projector bulb to see if Violet was still there in the back of the room. She was not. It marked the end of the lesson for that day—the end of the movie. As in the subject matter of the film, Mike was alone.

With the projector still flapping, Mike moved out of the room and into the hallway of the house, then to his quarters. He didn't need to eat dinner either. He was depressed. He had been beaten to a pulp emotionally, and he instantly fell into bed, fully clothed. Violet never appeared to say good night. Mike knew that it was a wise angel who left him alone that night. He was in no mood to talk.

Michael's dreams continued showing the film as he slept. They reran the part about the bully, his parents, and Cricket. They would not leave him alone, and he finally let go, sobbing uncontrollably into his pillow. Visions of his parents, so alive and vibrant, made his sorrow all the worse. It was the second time in this sacred, angelic, anointed land that Michael felt completely alone and black—a victim of life. And now he even had the movies to prove it!

IN THE MORNING, Mike felt a bit more rested, but pensive. He was hungry, too, and easily consumed a large breakfast. He still felt victimized from the day before, but somehow had convinced himself that the worst was over. He was tough, and although he didn't understand why all this was necessary, he had decided that it was not going to let him again slip into blackness and depression. Whatever awaited him today had to be better.

After breakfast Mike got dressed. New violet clothing had been magically provided, replacing the clothes he had slept in, and he was again ready. Violet appeared at the open doorway and was quiet. It was as if she were giving Mike space to react and say whatever he needed to say, or to chastise her for the painful experience of yesterday. Michael knew she was there. She watched him for a while then finally spoke.

"Michael Thomas of Pure Intent, is there anything you wish to say, or ask?"

"Yes." Michael was stoic. "Are there more films?"

"Yes," Violet replied softly.

"Then let's get to it." Michael stood and waited for her to move.

Violet was surprised. The angel's experience with humans in this house had never been like this. Green was right. This one was special. He might make it. He might be among the few to go all the way. She had never seen such resolve and vibrational shift so quickly. She felt special to be part of his training, and she loved him greatly. Violet turned and led Michael once again to the theater.

Mike knew the drill. He took his place in the big, violet, padded front seat of the theater, like a prisoner in the electric chair, waiting for the electricity to start flowing—or in this case, for the lights to go down and the movie to start. Mike was resolute with purpose and determination. Nothing would keep him from going home. NOTHING!

Again Mike's life unfolded before him on film, starting with his childhood. This time it was different. He quickly saw the subject matter had changed. This time he titled the film "All the Bad Things I Did in Life." The childhood episodes were funny, and Mike laughed heartily at many of them. It felt good to laugh, but his ribs were still sore from all the intense crying of the previous night.

As his age increased in the movies, some of the things he had done that were gloriously displayed began to embarrass him. Certainly, Violet knew of these things, but he didn't want to relive them. He found himself sliding down in the chair as they played out. He cringed and felt uncomfortable.

There he was in church at age ten, making fun of the preacher and passing notes that had silly, obscene drawings on them of crude body parts. He and his buddies in Sunday School had felt it very funny indeed to draw these things, and then place them in collection baskets, stuffed into the folders meant for dollar bills. They could just see the faces of the "blue hairs," the older women who opened the folders and counted the money. They laughed and laughed.

At age 12, Mike sneaked out and started his dad's tractor one Sunday morning when his parents were away at church. Mike had feigned illness and had been allowed to remain home. The tractor started okay, but Mike didn't understand how to make it move; he tried every lever and pedal in frustration. He didn't understand how a manual transmission worked, thinking it was like the family car with a pedal for GO and one for STOP. Lots of loud sounds ensued, and in the process of his tractor adventure, he ruined the transmission.

When his dad found the problem, he came in to face Mike. He asked his son for the absolute truth.

"Mike, did you try to start and drive the tractor?"

"No, sir." Mike lied to his dad.

Mike was ashamed of it then and now. His father somehow knew, and Mike could see it in his eyes. It was one of those times that had taught Mike what it felt like to violate the integrity of the family. It didn't feel good, and Mike remembered it all his life. The repair bill had been great, and Mike had his first realization of what his foolishness had cost his parents. They ate Spam and beans for weeks after that, trying to recover from the unexpected expense. Every time they sat down for dinner, Mike got to see the results of his folly and literally tasted his lie for some time. Now, he experienced it again—in living color and 3-D. He sank farther into his chair. Again, it seemed so real!

As Mike grew taller, he got stronger. In the school system of the day, most students transferred together from school to school as long as their parents lived in the same districts. Therefore, Henry, the "bully" of Mike's grade school days, came along with this package. While elementary school was one scenario, the bully wasn't so big when he got to high school. Most of the other boys' bodies had caught up with the bully's early growth, and the adolescent playing field was more level. Henry the bully didn't do well in school and just barely managed to graduate. Michael took every advantage he could to make Henry's school life miserable. He used his height and popularity as an intimidation tool, often taunting him personally or threatening him with harm.

As class president in his junior year, Mike used his power to exclude this former tough guy from everything good. He wielded his influence like a pro, and the ruffian of the past was denied many good things—from admittance to proms to elective subjects he was obviously good at. Mike never told anyone what he had done, but delighted in anything he could do to ruin the boy's high school years. Although Henry knew what was happening, he couldn't do anything about it. Later he was able to extract revenge, but Mike wasn't to know about it until now as he sat in his chair watching it all unfold. It had been Henry who had smeared him in his senior year! Henry had successfully started the damaging rumors that ruined his chances to become senior-class president.

Later in real life, Mike had learned that as a man, Henry had become a thug and was now in prison. Mike often wondered if things would have been different if Henry had been left alone during his high school years. Mike felt ashamed of what he had done, as he now watched it unfold again.

Mike was feeling stupid. This was a long movie about how bad he had been, how unethical his early years had become. He might have even hurt a man's chances at life! Mike felt very small, indeed. He continued to watch.

In his senior year, Mike had actually cheated on a test. He had a great grade point average, but was poor in U.S. history. He blamed a boring teacher for the problem, then proceeded to lift the test in advance using a key he had kept and made a copy of as class president the previous year. Mike felt it was poetic justice, and he vividly remembered how he had already been "punished" for this act when he hadn't actually done it in grade school. Therefore, it was somehow okay in his mind.

It got worse. As fate would have it, the teacher spotted Mike's instant improvement and accused him of exactly what he had done. Mike, using his charismatic personality, record of good grades in other classes, and previous reputation, blasted the teacher to the administration and got him reprimanded. It stayed in the teacher's file and might have kept him from advancing. Mike hadn't known that either until now as he sat in the big padded chair.

Damn! This is painful. Being victimized by life is bad enough; watching yourself lie and cheat is worse. Mike didn't want to see any more and wished it would all stop.

It did. There was very little, if anything, for Mike to see as a grown-up. His whole life had changed when his parents had died. Their deaths had made him grow up fast and awakened in him the steadfast integrity that he now claimed as an adult. It was almost as if he carried the family name on his sleeve, and all his parents' hard work with it. Mike breathed a great sigh of relief when he again heard the flapping of the last leader against the take-up reel. This time, the projector was stopped, and the lights came on gently. Violet approached him from the rear of the room.

"Michael, please come with me," she said gently.

Without speaking, Mike did as he was asked. He felt weary as he arose from the chair, having spent so many hours there! He hoped that he would never see it again, and he loathed this place where the films of his life were shown. He looked in the back where the projector was as he was led out of the room. He expected to see dozens of reels of film stacked everywhere from the last two days of viewing, but there were none. The area was clean and clear.

Violet was the kindest entity Mike had ever known. It's not that she was better than Blue; Orange; or even than his angel buddy, Green. She was different. Each angel had endearing qualities that Michael loved. This one emanated care and concern. Mike wanted to stay here and live under her umbrella of parental peace! It felt wonderful to sit across from her and listen to her speak. All was well as long as she was there. This feeling was not lost on Mike. He realized that this was the feeling of being a child and of having no responsibility. It was fitting, therefore, that her countenance was in the house of responsibility. Here was the parent, and Mike was the child again, feeling a release from life.

Violet took Mike into a large room. In any other circumstance, you could say it was a conference room, but in this case it only had two chairs. There was a display board of some kind on one wall and many symbols and charts on the others.

In the other houses, the angels hadn't spent so much time sitting. Since there was no fatigue for them and no need for sleep, they didn't need to sit down as humans did. Usually it was only to make the human comfortable, as in this case. Violet gracefully took a seat and faced Michael.

"Michael Thomas of Pure Intent, how do you feel?" She had opened the conversation with a question that would allow Mike to vent his feeling of the last day's theater viewing. He did and accompanied it with something that he had thought much about the evening before.

"Violet, oh precious one." Mike really loved this great caring angel. "I know that you cannot willingly hurt a human being. I know that it is not in your angelic consciousness to cause pain, suffering, doubt, or fear; but by showing these films, you have done all of these things, so I know there must be a fine reason for it all. How do I feel?"

Mike paused and thought for some time, trying to be totally honest about his emotions over these last few days.

"Violated," he paused again. "Horrible, victimized, saddened by my own failings, guilty about what I have done, angry at those who did things to me, devastated by the grief caused by circumstances beyond my control, beat up, introspective." Mike continued to pour out his heart to Violet. There was very little emotion, since it had been wrung from him during the previous night. Instead, Mike was trying his best to really tell Violet what his human side was feeling. The words kept coming, and then he started repeating himself. Violet didn't ask him to stop. His catharsis was beginning to run out of steam. He had expressed himself, complained about it all, then complained again. He never asked why he was shown the films. Intuitively, he knew that Violet would let him know this. He was right.

When he had finished, he needed water. Somehow, it had been provided for him. He took a drink and made a gesture to his silent companion, showing that he was finished with his discourse. Violet arose and began her gentle lecture.

"Michael," she looked deep within his soul with a caring intensity that he absolutely knew was from the mind of God. "As a human training for home, this is the last time you will ever feel any of these things." She let him think about that for a moment as she stood up and went over to a seemingly blank wall. She pulled down a chart that had been rolled up like a scroll and mounted at the top of the wall near the ceiling. It reminded Mike of how maps are displayed in classrooms, then rolled up to allow the chalkboard to be used. On the chart was writing. The writing was the same strange Arabic-looking script that he had seen on the labels in the House of Maps. He couldn't read any of it.

"I am here to explain that you, and all the others in your life, carefully planned the potential for everything you have just seen in the 'Theater of Life' for the two past days." Mike let that sink in. He didn't really understand how this could be.

"Planned it?"

"Yes."

"That couldn't be. There were accidents, coincidences, things that just happened, hundreds of factors that created chance." Mike paused.

"You planned it with the others, Mike."

"How?"

"Michael Thomas, you already know that you are an eternal entity. You are here seeking permission and training to go home—a place of sacredness—where you feel there will be answers, peace, and purpose, according to your own definition. What is hidden from you is that you have been on Earth many times before and have walked in the shoes of many human beings of different sizes and types. This time you are Michael Thomas."

Mike knew of the idea of past lives, but here it was being verified again by one he trusted. He accepted it, and marveled at the thought.

Violet continued, "When you are not on Earth, lessons for your next incarnation are planned for you by the only one who knows what you need—YOU! You and the others set up potentials for your learning. Some agreed to poke and prod you. Some agreed to be the sand in your oyster for years! Some agreed to partner with you, and yes, Michael, some agreed to die early within their contract, to help facilitate your needs as well as theirs."

Mike was overwhelmed by this information.

"Violet, my parents? —They knew?"

"Not only did you ALL know, Michael, but this was the greatest gift you ever received in your life." Violet's eyes were compassionate beyond anything Mike had ever known. She knew so much about him! She was ready to explain everything, expected much of the emotion, and was ready for all the questions. She was amazing.

"It's complex, Michael," Violet continued. "Each incarnation of a human being is connected and related to everyone else's. There are contracts you pen before you ever arrive that set up your potentials for learning and growth. You are someone else's thorn, as well as a pearl of great value. The situations you call accidents and coincidences are carefully planned."

"That sounds like predestination?"

"No. You have a choice in all of it. The road is created, but you can travel it or not—create a new one if you wish." She paused for effect. "That's exactly what you are doing now." She smiled at Mike, then continued. "When you gave intent to travel this road, you threw away the contract you made with the others. You went beyond the mundane that you planned could happen to facilitate ordinary lessons, and instead decided to go for the gold, Michael Thomas. Now you get to see this and understand the big picture."

"Why the films, Violet?" Mike had to ask this.

"To allow you to view every seemingly negative thing in your life, Michael, and understand that you helped create it. You helped plan it, and you executed it right on schedule. In other words, you were responsible for it."

Mike was astounded at the thought of it all. He still didn't understand the dynamics. "What if I had wanted to change it, Violet? How is it that I would have chosen such trouble and tragedy?" Violet was ready with the reply.

"When you are not here, Michael, you have the mind of God. This is hidden from you now, but it is so. Death and emotional circumstances are energy to God. You are eternal, and the comings and goings of humans are meant for a grander purpose than you know—one that you will understand again some day when you join me in my form. For now, you must understand that what you call tragedy, although horrible for you in your present mind-set, can be the catalyst for planetary change, vibrational increase, and a gift beyond measure. It's the overview that is important, not the actual event. I know this sounds confusing, but it is so." Violet paused again to let Mike think about it all. She continued.

"As for changing it? You always had that option and choice, but that fact is also hidden from most humans. It's all part of the test of life, Michael. Look at it this way: When you leave this place, you will have a tendency to stay on the road. The road is the most natural place to be. It's easy, and it requires little thought about where you are headed. It's already there, leading the way, so why not stay on it. The truth is that in this land of seven houses, the path always goes in the same direction, but it meanders a bit. Therefore, you could reach a house, perhaps, even sooner if you simply headed in that direction without taking the road. You might even discover wonderful new things along the way, off the road. In human life, it is the same. The road represents your potential plan with others. It meanders, but always leads you in the same direction—toward the future. Most humans stay on the road, never realizing that they have a choice to get off it if they wish. It's when humans leave the road that all manner of things change for them—especially their futures. They actually start writing a new future as soon as they give intent to leave the road. They find peace in being able to control their lives better; they experience purpose. Some of them even come through here, Michael." Violet smiled knowingly.

"And this House of Responsibility?" Mike asked.

"It's where you learn that YOU, Michael Thomas of Pure Intent, are directly responsible for everything in your life. The sadness, the grief, the seeming accidents, the loss, what others did to you, the pain, and yes, even death. You knew it coming in, you helped plan it with the others, and you played it out—until now."

"And the purpose of such a thing?"

"Is love, Michael. Love at the highest level. The grand plan is something you will know in time. For now, understand that it is all appropriate, and part of an overview of love that you already know of and are participating in right now. Things are not always as they seem."

The words rang in Michael's ears. *Things are not always as they seem*...were the words of the first angel, the one in the vision after the robbery. Then, he had heard it again from some of the others along the way. Mike's mind was reeling with these new concepts. Then, he remembered Blue's words in the House of Maps. *You are looking at the contracts of every human being on the planet.* In those small holes that Blue managed, millions of them, were the potential plans of all humanity, planned by each individual, and ready to be altered if humans wished it so.

The true message of all this suddenly slammed into Mike's mind like a hammer. If he had only known this when he was young! He would have understood so much more about life. He could have changed his future. He could have found peace with this kind of overview. The deaths, the lost love, the depression—what hope and wisdom this would have given him! The thought of choice changing his life was amazing. Violet was right. Mike had followed the path of life as a road, letting all the things unfold that he had—*planned*? That was a difficult word to think about. It meant that he was responsible for everything that had happened. That put an entirely new perspective on it all. Oh, could he have used this! His life would have been far different. No one in church had ever told him this. He loved God, and he had always felt the sacredness of that place, but he had always been told that he was a sheep following a shepherd. No spiritual teacher had ever told him that he had this power.

"Violet, if this is so, then why didn't I learn of it in church?"

"Church won't tell you everything about God, Michael. Sometimes it tells you a great deal about humans and what they think about God." Violet wasn't being critical or judgmental of any human, but simply factual and truthful.

"Was the church wrong?" Mike asked.

"Michael, the truth remains the truth, and there are pieces and parts of it throughout all your spiritual systems. You all are greatly honored for seeking the truth of God. Love, miracles, and the mechanics of the way things work are all represented to some degree in your places of worship. That's why you felt the Spirit of God when you went there, Michael. Spirit honors the quest, even if all the facts are not known. Remember that your true existence is veiled from you even now, as you hear the truth. Your church, and all the spiritual quests on your planet, are greatly honored, for they represent the search for God—and for spiritual truth. The only sadness is when humans control this quest and keep it from being enhanced by limiting it, sequestering those under their control with fear.

The honor is in the seeking, not in what you got right. Therefore, the sacredness of your planet lies within those who walk on it, not in the buildings with all the spires." Violet moved over to the chart she had pulled down earlier. "You think that your holy Scriptures are sacred? Take a look at this." She pointed to the cryptic writing on the chart. "This is the *akashic* record of humanity. It contains the records of your lives and of your potential contracts." She paused in reverence. "Michael, this is the most sacred writing in the Universe, and it was written and executed by those who decided to take the journey as HUMANS!"

She looked directly at Michael for the first time in many moments. The message was not lost on him. Suddenly, he realized that her posture showed her respect for him—spiritual respect! The role reversal was surprising and uncomfortable for Mike. He wanted to know more, and she gave it to him.

The next few days in the House of Responsibility were awesome in the profundity of the message of life and humanity. Mike not only learned more about who he was, but who he had *been*. It all came together like a puzzle of immense proportions. Violet showed him the records and contracts of his parents and of others in his life so far. There was nothing inappropriate given, and he didn't get to see anything that would change what was to come, but the larger picture of his existence was beginning to take shape.

The most amazing information? That humans were actually pieces of God, walking the planet with no concept of that fact in order to achieve a learning process that somehow changed the spiritual aspects and vibration of Earth itself! Violet continually referred to humans as "the exalted ones." Humans were somehow entities that would change the very fabric of reality; they would change what happened on a very large scale, and it was all centered in the lessons learned on Earth—lessons that they all planned together!

Finally, it was time to go. Mike felt as if he were a new creature. His knowledge had increased a hundredfold about how things actually worked. He had retained everything and felt as if he had been empowered with truth. As he put on his battle gear to begin the journey to the next house, the words of Orange rang in his ears. *The sword of truth...the shield of knowledge...the armor of wisdom.* Things were beginning to come together in a way that was making a great deal of spiritual sense. He recognized that the weapons were ceremonial and had intent. Much of the language was being repeated, explained, and was finally being understood.

Violet led Michael to the front door of the violet house.

"Michael Thomas of Pure Intent, I will miss you."

"Violet, I feel like I'm leaving home, not going to it!" Mike had felt cared for here, and Violet had become like a parental family member. So far he had met three fine brother angels and now a mother angel. *What is next?* he wondered.

"More family, Michael," Violet answered Mike's thoughts.

At the door, Mike noticed his shoes right where he had left them. He also remembered the unanswered question regarding them. He looked at the shoes and then back to Violet.

"There is unfinished business here, Violet," Mike said, wanting to know the answer to the question of why he'd been asked to remove his shoes.

"Yes, Michael. I remember. Now YOU can tell me why," she smiled at him and waited patiently for the answer. Mike knew, but he was embarrassed to verbalize it. It seemed so grandiose—so self-serving.

"Say it, Michael." Violet was the teacher again.

"Because the human is sacred." There, he had said it. He continued, "And because this house is where humans walk in a high vibration."

Violet sighed and was visibly moved. "I could not have wished for a finer answer, Michael Thomas of Pure intent," she said. "It is indeed the presence of the human, and not the angel, that makes this place sacred. Michael, you are indeed a special human being. I honor God within you! Now, I have a question for you." Mike knew the question, but allowed Violet to ask it anyway. "Michael, do you love God?"

"Yes, Violet. I do." Mike was beginning to tear up. He wasn't afraid to let Violet know of his emotional state. He was sorry to leave this place of violet color, where he had met an energy he thought he had lost so long ago when his parents died. Mike turned and walked a few steps, then turned around again. "I'll miss you, too, Violet, but you'll remain in my heart." Mike started down the path to the next house, then again turned back to say one more thing to the watching angel.

"Violet, watch me!"

With theatrical style and childlike motions, Michael Thomas left the path with great flare and struck out over the lush, grassy plain. He looked back and shouted at her.

"Look at me! I've decided to make my own path!" Mike laughed at the metaphor he was creating. He skipped and flailed along the uncharted topography until he could no longer see the violet house.

Violet stood and watched Michael until he was out of sight. Like a mother, she was proud indeed of this great entity called Michael Thomas. Then she went back inside and closed the door. She returned to her natural form, which was not humanlike, but magnificent, nonetheless. She spoke to the others.

"If this is an example of the new breed of human, we are in for a wild spiritual ride indeed!

A QUARTER MILE UP the path, a sickening creature had positioned itself in wait. IT had carefully prepared the trap, and IT felt there was no way that Michael Thomas could penetrate the deception. IT knew that Mike was out of the house now and traveling again. IT could feel it. IT was excited!

Not long now, IT thought. While Michael Thomas is looking behind him for me, I'll attack from the front. He won't know what hit him! The disgusting entity chuckled at how clever IT was becoming in this fairyland. Any moment now...

IT had a long wait. Michael Thomas had left the path.

CHAPTER NINE

The Fifth House

It didn't take Mike long to realize that being off the path had its challenges. He had to constantly check the position of the sun to align his direction. In addition, he continually checked his map so that he wouldn't accidentally miss the house by going past it. It was also a slower journey due to the uncertainties of footing.

Even with all these challenges, Mike realized that, at least this time, the journey was fun. He was fulfilling a wish to make Violet proud of him. He was also doing it for himself—to show that he could rebel against any form of the ordinary—even in a spiritual land. He was also beginning to feel that once was enough, and that as soon as he had found the next house, he would probably go back to using the path for the following ones. It was easier and didn't compromise any of his choices. In fact, now he felt more than ever that his choice to stay on the path in the future was validated by the fact that he knew what it was like not to! Now that he had done both, he felt that he could choose wisely which to do, instead of feeling forced by protocol to stay on the trail given to him.

Mike also realized that the feeling of being watched was gone. Had he broken the spell of his following nemesis? Had the dark and ominous thing that seemed to follow him on this journey simply gone away? No. Mike was wise. Rightly, he guessed that his change in habit regarding traveling on the path had simply confused the vile thing that had been dogging him from the beginning. No doubt IT would realize what had happened and go looking for Mike. This meant the Mike had to be wary and alert for surprises ahead of him as well as behind.

About four hours into his travels over the plain, the skies began to darken. Mike had no illusions about what this meant. Another of those weird, frightening, and violent weather anomalies was about to strike this place, and he'd better check for shelter immediately. He remembered that the last time this had happened, within ten minutes he was prone on the ground in a horrendous howling wind, praying for his very life.

Mike took out the map again and looked to see what was immediately around him. True to form, the map had the red dot showing only what was currently around Mike. The map showed that he had just passed an outcropping that contained a cavelike shelter. Mike remembered having passed it recently, but he hadn't passed on the side that would have revealed the cave. Mike stuffed the map in his pouch and retraced his steps until the indicated rocks again came into view.

Even in the few minutes it had taken to navigate back to the potential shelter, the storm had developed in an ominous way. The skies were blackening, and the gale-force winds were starting to howl. Rain was being added to the mix when Mike saw the opening and picked up his pace. Just as Mike passed into the mouth of the cavern, nature seemed to go wild again. Mike had to stand well back in the cave to avoid getting wet or being sucked into the uproar that raged outside. He again marveled at the ferocity of the event, and also whispered a thank you to Blue for the map that had removed him from harm, seemingly at the last possible moment. The "currentness" of the map had again aligned with his need.

Mike continued watching the spectacle from inside the cave, never taking his eyes off the constantly changing program of wailing mayhem. It was amazing! He was so glad that he wasn't out in it.

"Why are these storms allowed in such a sacred place as this?" he wondered aloud. Blue's voice sounded...in his head?

"Michael Thomas, there are no storms in this land unless a human is on the journey of lesson."

"You mean if I were not here, there would be no storm?"

"Yes," replied the voice of Blue.

"But I'm not in it. It's not affecting me."

"Exactly!" laughed Blue. *"You have learned to use the map! Believe it or not, there have been humans like you on this journey who discarded the map early, feeling that it was some kind of joke. You saw what it was, and the currentness of it has become your way of life. You have one foot in the spiritual 'now' time frame, but you are also learning to weigh linear time against it as you move through your trip here. Therefore, when the lesson of the storm comes into view, you escape it entirely and sit it out in peace. Michael, you are dearly loved!"*

Mike smiled at the thought. It was all for him! All this energy—all this planning! He looked outside and yelled at the wind.

"You can stop now. I'm safe!" Mike laughed and laughed.

The storm lasted about two hours, beginning to clear about dusk. He didn't know if there was time to reach the next house, and without the sun, he didn't know if he could even find it. Regardless, Mike also felt safe and able to defend himself if needed. He left the cave, observed for the last time the direction of the sunset, and again headed in a direction he knew to be north.

It was slow going as it got darker, and Mike began to realize that he had never been out at night in this land before. *Would there be stars or a moon?* He quickly found out. There was neither. When the last vestiges of twilight had bid farewell to the horizon, Mike was completely in the dark. And, oh, what a darkness! Without any light whatsoever, Mike couldn't even see his map. *He knew he should have stayed in the cave.* He was not prepared for this kind of blackness! He sat down, not wanting to stumble on something unseen in his pathway.

It took about an hour sitting in the dark for Mike to realize that his eyes were working in an odd manner—either that or something strange was occurring. Earlier, the sun had set firmly in the west where he had expected it to. Based on that, he had taken note of

where north was and had also aligned the tip of a hill with that perception so that he would have a marker to aim at even in the moonlight. When neither moonlight nor starlight materialized, the marker
was also lost—until now. Dimly, to the north, he saw the faint outline
of the marker. The same red glow from the setting sun was now
extending north, in a manner that illuminated the very marker that
Mike had observed. Something was over there giving off light!

Mike arose with great care and alertness. The faint red glow coming from the north was slowly letting his eyes become aware of the
immediate ground around him. He moved, slowly and quietly, toward
the glowing red light. He pushed his feet through the grass cautiously so as not to be surprised by a change in ground elevation or a boul-
der. Stooped over, eyes straining to see the faint outline of the ground
directly beneath his feet, he moved forward at a snail's pace.

In this crouching, step-by-step method of travel, Mike almost
stumbled and fell when he suddenly reached smooth ground. It was
the path! Mike chuckled to himself at the metaphor. Even though he
had chosen to forsake the path, it found him when he needed it most.
What a place!

Mike saw that the path ran at an oblique angle to his northern
marker, but he believed that it would indeed lead to the next house
and that he had not passed it. In addition, he noticed that the glow
was coming from an area where the path was heading. Mike moved
to what he perceived was the center of the path and picked up his
pace slightly. He was still traveling very slowly. He tried to stay in
the middle of the path but occasionally found himself at its edge. He
laughed.

This is worse than fog on the coast of Santa Monica in June! he
thought. He remembered riding his bike at night in the fog when he
all he could see was the white line in the center of the road. He
wished for that same white line now.

Mike noticed that as he approached the glowing area, he could
see more clearly. Gradually, the path became almost fully illuminated, or at least enough so that he could straighten up and walk in a
normal fashion. Still, he was cautious. He didn't know what the
light was, and he wanted to be ready for anything.

When Mike came around a curve, he realized where the light was coming from. He couldn't believe what he was seeing. There in the forest was the next house. It was brilliant red! Mike mused that while the other houses had *seemed* to be glowing from within—this one actually was.

Mike allowed himself to pick up the pace to almost normal as he approached the red house. The light from the house embraced him in its red glow. He turned up the pathway and caught sight of the posted red sign by the walkway: "House of Relationships." Mike stopped.

"Oh, dear," he said with a sigh. "Here is a subject that I have already failed in! Are we going to see more films?"

"Yes, we are!" The young red angel appeared out of nowhere on the steps leading to the door. "Greetings, Michael Thomas of Pure Intent. I thought we had lost you!"

"No such luck, my fine red friend," Mike answered. "I just took my time. I guess I wasn't in a hurry to see your new films. Are they like the ones Violet had?"

"No, Michael. They are not." The red angel was very handsome, indeed. He reminded Michael of a movie star—an action hero with a terrific build. The red angel was really big! His personality was outgoing and comfortable, however, so his size didn't cause any alarm—any more than the others had. His red robes seem to give him a look of sacredness. Mike remembered seeing this color in some of the robes of high church officials.

"Are you hungry, Michael?" the large red angel asked.

"Yes, sir."

Red led Mike into the house, but not before he motioned for him to remove his shoes. Red winked at Mike, as if to remind him why the ground was sacred. Mike felt timid at again being honored like this and said nothing. He removed his shoes quietly and placed them at the door.

As before, the outer appearance of the house was no indication of what it was like on the inside. This house was big. It had stairways and arches, and the windows opened on landscapes that could not be seen from outside. Mike would never get used to the seeming inconsistences between physics and reality. He was reminded of the *Alice in Wonderland* tale, and wondered if Lewis Carroll had ever been here in his dreams. What a funny thought! Should he start looking for a white rabbit?

"White is next, Michael," said Red smiling. "No rabbit, though."

Mike laughed. So the next house was white? The White House! thought an amused Mike. Red was also amused, and Mike had a good feeling about whatever lessons were to take place here. He felt Red was indeed family. Like Green, Red seemed to be a brother—perhaps a famous one. Blue and Orange were like uncles, and, of course, Violet was Mom. He could hardly wait to meet Dad!

"Are we feeling like family, Michael?" Red had stopped at what obviously were the quarters for food and lodging. Mike could smell dinner waiting.

"Yes, Red."

"How appropriate. That's what this house is all about." Red turned and escorted Mike into the dining room. As usual, an amazing meal was waiting.

"I'll see you in the morning, Michael Thomas. Sleep well and be peaceful with your lesson here." Red turned to leave, but said another good-bye just before he shut the door.

Mike laughed to himself at how polite the angels had become on his journey. Mike did indeed feel peaceful. He knew that Red was aware of the lessons in the violet house, and of the powerful emotions and upheaval it had created in Mike's very soul. He was kind to let Mike know that the next lessons were going to be different.

Mike ate like a horse! He had missed lunch while out on the plain, and traveling in the darkness had taken a great deal of energy—more than he had realized. He was also tired, and after dinner, he immediately fell asleep. He was peaceful, and he felt the comfort and safety of this fine red house envelop him. He slept deeply and calmly—almost as if he were already home.

♣ ♣ ♣

LATE THAT NIGHT while Michael Thomas was sleeping, a bedraggled, angry, stinking, greenish creature skulked up the road toward the Red House. IT took one look at the house and knew that Michael Thomas was in it. IT had waited and waited for Michael Thomas to appear on the path, but Mike had not obliged.

IT raged inside and burned with an anger that consumed IT with purpose. IT was confused! How had Michael Thomas known IT was there waiting? He must have gone around IT, leaving the path completely! Michael actually had made it to the Red House without the path! How? IT knew the angels were not allowed to interfere, so they had not told Michael where IT was. IT would have to rethink ITs plans now. When IT had gone ahead of Michael, IT had lost him. Should IT therefore go back to following him? That way, at least, IT would know where Mike was. What should be ITs course of action?

As before, IT found a place in the trees to take up a vigil while IT waited for Mike to leave the Red House. As long as IT knew where Mike was, IT was content. IT passed the time by anticipating the final confrontation with Michael. Over and over, IT reviewed plans, formulating and dismissing strategies. There would have to be a great deal of energy expended and some trickery, but IT knew Michael Thomas very well. IT knew what Michael Thomas reacted to and how he thought. IT began practicing the techniques that would be necessary for the plan to work. The confrontation would take place on the road to the final house. That's when Michael would be the most vulnerable. IT would again lie in wait. *Deception is the key,* IT thought. IT would have to pretend, and take another form—something that IT could only sustain for a few moments—but those few moments would be enough.

AS HE HAD IN the previous houses, Mike arose and put on clothing that was waiting for him in the closet. The clothes were fresh and clean—and red. Mike again remembered the words of Orange, who had told him that there would be no human waste associated with his meals. Mike also realized that he'd had no beard growth since he'd begun this journey. It was almost as if everything that was happening was somehow suspended in time, preventing his physical self from aging or functioning as it had before he got here. What a place!

Mike enjoyed the delicious breakfast laid out before him in the adjacent room and was sitting contemplating his journey, when he heard the knock at the door and Red entered.

"I see that you are well rested and ready, Michael Thomas."

"Yes, I am, Red." Michael was gracious and feeling good. Again he was amazed at how handsome Red was. "Thank you for your hospitality."

"You deserve all of it, Michael Thomas of Pure Intent." Red smiled and motioned for Mike to arise and join him in a walk to the learning portions of the House of Relationships. Red led Mike to areas that he had not seen the night before. The house was indeed different from the others. All the red made Mike feel alert and energetic. It was an amazing feeling. At length, they came to a large theater and entered. The wraparound screen was the same as in the previous theater, and the padded chair was there, too, except that now it was red. And, also, as before, the chair was just a little too close to the screen. Red knew that this place might cause Michael to be anxious after what he had experienced in the last house.

"It's not what you think, Michael," said a comforting Red.

"Thank you, my friend," said a grateful Mike. "Do you wish me to take my place?"

"Yes."

Red made his way to the back of the room as Violet had, and busied himself with the projection equipment. Mike took his place in the seat of honor in front—and the show began.

This time there was no sound accompanying the presentation. Instead, Red lectured and explained what Mike was seeing on the screen displayed before him. Red was right. It was invigorating, educational, enlightening, and amazing! There was no sadness or introspective, emotional feelings being elicited from Mike. This was more like a slide show with narration, instead of moving pictures.

"Mike, this is all about family," Red began, as the screen lit up with some still images. "You have already seen in the last house that you play many roles on your planet and that those with you do, also.

You have also learned that all humans agree and plan the potential directions of their lives before they ever arrive. Now it's time for you to understand the relationship between the players. Let's start with identifying the family."

Mike sat incredulous as Red introduced 27 beautiful faces on the screen. He gave names that were long and that Mike had never heard before. The names were angelic sounding, and, Mike thought, must be difficult to spell. Names like Angenon, Aleeilou, Beaurifee, Vereeifon, Kooigre, and on and on. Next, Red presented a chart of the lineage of each one. The chart started at the top with the Earth names and faces that Mike recognized, then branched off below with other names and faces that Mike did not know. Across the top were Mike's parents, friends from church or school, people from work, and many people he barely knew. There were also some strangers. Mike took a moment to identify each. He recognized teachers who had made an impression on him. He saw Henry the bully, and his real first love, Carol! He also recognized his friend John. And there was the thief who had almost done him in at the apartment! Then, he saw Shirley, the woman he had loved and lost in Los Angeles.

There were other images as well—people he did not know. One in particular caught his eye. A beautiful woman with a gorgeous smile. Her hair was red and her eyes green—an entrancing combination. He felt energy around this picture but didn't know why. The next picture made Mike's hair stand on end—it was the woman who had drunkenly steered her car into that of his parents' that fateful day! She had been killed, too, and Mike thought she had deserved it. Why was she here? Look—his own picture was there, too!

Below the top row of photos, connected with lines as in an organizational chart, were more images of people within more horizontal lines directly under the top ones Mike had recognized.

"Each horizontal line is a lifetime, Michael Thomas," Red said while Mike examined the entire scene. "They're the same players over and over. The names change, and the gender is different, but they are the same entities—and they are your real family. Like a group, you loosely travel through time, some coming and going, but all are family. Now it's time to hear their story."

What happened next was one of the most amazing and revolutionary things that Mike had ever experienced. He wasn't prepared for what took place in that red theater with the red seats and the wonderful red angel. He was transfixed and speechless as he sat in his big red chair wearing his red clothes.

The first picture on the top left of the chart suddenly zoomed to full size and became animated! Suddenly there was sound, too, and the one called Shirley, the love of Mike's life, came to life on the screen! Then she stepped from the screen into Mike's reality on the floor before him. She was real—no longer part of any movie or slide show! She called Mike by name and began her tale as she stood literally feet from him as a perfectly tangible object.

"Michael Thomas, I am Reenuei from Quadril Five. I am your family, and I love you dearly! I am Shirley, as you know me in this life. Before that I was Fred, your brother in the last century. Before I was Fred, I was Cynthia, your wife before that. Michael Thomas of Pure Intent, we have a contract, and the energy of it is called karma. We had planned together to meet again in this life, and we did. You and I have completed something we both started centuries ago, and we did it well. We agreed to generate feelings in you that would bring you to this crossroads in life. It is my gift to you, and yours to me. We did it together!"

Mike's mouth was agape. She wasn't an image on the screen. She was real! He was listening to a very familiar entity telling him that she was Shirley—and before that she was someone else he knew... and before that...it went on and on. What a loving presentation! Each word was dripping with truth and purpose. Each explanation felt authoritative and complete. What a story! What a place! Mike didn't know if Shirley could hear him as she stood there, but the undeniably solid form in front of him commanded that he speak.

"Thank you, dear Shirley!" Mike bowed in appreciation to this one he had known and loved. This gave an entirely new perspective to their relationship; she was more like a best friend than a female who had ruined his life. Shirley disappeared gradually from the space she had occupied in front of him.

The next image came forward and related a tale of love, intrigue, and complex relationships. It was Mike's favorite high school teacher, Mr. Burroughs. He explained that he had been in Mike's life many times, as many people. This time it was only to touch Mike during his education, which he had done. Mike's part was obvious, also. They actually helped each other in ways Mike was not aware of. They had a contract, too, and the energy of learning he called karma, even though it was subtle. Mike orally acknowledged him, and the image of Mr. Burroughs faded, as the last one had.

Suddenly, as big as life, he saw the image of his father. Mike was not sad—Dad was alive! His father's form descended from the screen and casually took its place as a living being before Mike. He began his narrative, and Mike listened with great joy.

"Michael Thomas, I am not who you think I am." The entity was gentle, and not exactly the countenance that was Mike's dad. It continued, "I am Anneehu from Quadril Five, and I am your real family. The face you see now is that of your father, and I played my role in human life exactly as I had planned it with your mother and you before we ever got to Earth. Everything that happened was appropriate, and we left early so that we could accomplish a great deal more in other spiritual areas. At the same time that we left for our own work, we facilitated your greatest gift, Michael. Our passing was the catalyst for your enlightenment. We came into your life with the heavy karmic lesson of death, Michael, and it played out perfectly. You are seated here because of it, and we love you dearly for your journey—and the fact that you now recognize the gift."

Mike felt keenly that this entity was alive and speaking to him personally. He memorized the name *Anneehu*. He wanted the sound to live in him from now on. How could there be sadness around his father's death when the truth was standing in front of him? The words *greatest gift* rang in Michael's ears as the being that had been his father continued. It told of the wars they had served in together, of the brothers they had been—and yes, even the sisters—a very long time ago on continents that no longer existed on Earth.

Finally, Mike's dad was finished. He smiled and faded away as had the others. Mike was moved, but not sad or pensive. It was exciting! He spoke to his father's image as it was fading.

"For the gift, Father, I am grateful." Mike knew this was absolutely true, and bowed his head in respect as he spoke.

Mom was next, and Mike was glued to his seat with his mouth open, listening to her tale of karmic lesson with him and the others in his life.

"I am Eleeuin, also from Quadril Five. I love you dearly and have been many faces in your past." She continued to explain the parts she had played in one life after another. She had even killed Mike once when they were both women—sisters! She told of the energy created from the actions of one life to another, and how it played out in building the lessons of interaction for the next. She did not pull on Mike's emotions or create any kind of melancholy in his soul. She was informative and beautiful in her presentation. She was real. She was alive! When Mom started to fade, Mike spoke to her as well.

"Thank you for your gift as well, Eleeuin." Mike felt it appropriate to remember at least the real names of his parents. Remembering all the names was beyond his ability, but he committed these two names to his memory forever.

One by one the faces took their place as real individuals before Mike. They introduced themselves and told of the great love they had for Michael Thomas. They spoke of the family often—all were from the strange place called Quadril Five—whatever that was.

There was only time for 9 of the 27 to bring their stories to Mike that day, and then the lights went on. Mike sat in silence, realizing that again lunchtime had gone by unnoticed. Red came from the rear of the room and faced Mike.

"Tired?"

"No—exhilarated!" was Mike's reply. "Do we have to stop?" Red laughed heartily and motioned for Mike to stand and join him on the way to dinner.

"There will be two more days of this, Michael Thomas. There is time for most of the family to speak." Mike had about a million questions as he was led back to the dining room.

"Red, will you stay for dinner? I mean—I know you don't eat, but I would like to ask some things."

"Yes, of course." Red was amused. Mike thought he probably had other things to do, not realizing that Red was there solely for Mike and others on the path at that moment.

They entered the dining area where two place settings were arranged. Mike looked at the table questioningly.

"Who is joining us?"

"I thought you invited me," replied Red with tongue in cheek.

"But you don't eat!"

"Says who?" Red was having fun, as he placed himself at the table opposite Mike and poured himself a refreshing fruit drink. Mike was still confused.

"I never—I mean—none of the other angels ate. I just thought—" Red interrupted Mike.

"Michael, angels don't have to eat, but I am joining you in this human necessity because it is enjoyable for you to have a companion who is also eating. Right?"

"Correct." Mike couldn't argue with that. It had been weeks since he had enjoyed a meal with anyone. The last time it had even come close to happening was when Green watched him. At least it had been company. Red was fun! He was perhaps the most human of them all.

"I feel honored that you would think so," replied Red, chewing his bread, reading Mike's thoughts completely. Mike ate his meal haltingly, stopping often to ask Red questions.

"Red, was what just happened real? I mean, when they were speaking to me—was that just some kind of new projection technique that I haven't seen yet?" Red again laughed, wiping his chin with a napkin.

"Why is it that humans want so desperately to assign reality to illusion? Even sometimes when truth is presented, humans deny it as a trick. I'll never understand that."

"Well?" inquired Mike.

"Absolutely real," replied Red. "More real than your own reality on Earth, Michael. They are here in person for you in this house."

Mike didn't understand that completely, but continued to ask questions.

"Red, all the strange-sounding names—I noticed that my image didn't have one—only that strange writing I have seen before."

"You do have one, Michael, but it is hidden for now. If appropriate, someday you can learn of it, or at least the part of it you can speak—but it has no bearing on your enlightenment. After all, you don't know my name, and it hasn't stopped you from enjoying your time here." Red took another bite.

Michael had never considered the fact that the angel names of those he had met in the various houses were unknown to him. He just called them by their colors. It was easier for everyone, and they encouraged it.

"Red, what is your real name?" Mike was really interested. He took another bite of salad as he waited for Red to answer.

"You make an assumption that a name is a sound, Michael."

Mike noticed that Red was an inept eater. You could tell that it was his first time. The food kept falling out of his mouth back onto the plate. He was on his fourth napkin and trying his best to emulate a human in the mannerisms and etiquette of consuming food. It was really quite funny, but Mike was so engrossed in his questions that he didn't react to it. Later, he would have a good laugh, but not at Red's expense. Red continued, after wiping his mouth again.

"All entity names in the Universe are energy, including yours and mine. They have color, vibration, sound—even intent! They cannot be given completely as a sound in the air as your Earth name can. Even the names written and spoken that you heard today are only a portion of the actual energy of an entity's complete name; they are given as best they can be just for you. When spiritual beings greet each other, they can 'see' the names. Each entity carries his entire lineage and accomplishments in the colors and vibrations within his Merkabah—the name for an angelic body. It's far more complex than you can understand at this moment, Michael, since it is interdimensional."

"Red," Mike began, wanting to know more, "today in the theater, why were some of the images in the top row skipped over when it was their turn to present their stories?" Mike was especially curious about the image of the red-haired woman whose energy had captivated him early on. She had appeared in the top row but had been skipped.

"These are humans you didn't meet, Michael." Red took a drink, and unsuccessfully tried to keep the fluid from running out of the corners of his mouth. Again the napkin was applied—the seventh one.

"So the ones I didn't meet—they don't count?"

"Unfulfilled contracts are not normally shown here, Michael. You wouldn't relate to any of them, since you didn't meet them in your life. The ones that will introduce themselves to you are only the family you have met so far."

Mike sat back for a moment and again reflected on a thought he had not had for some time. He wondered about the appropriateness of his journey in this land of seven houses. If he had stayed in Los Angeles, he would have obviously interacted with some people who had spiritual plans to meet him. Had he interrupted some kind of cosmic plan? What would be the consequences? Red was "listening" and addressed his unspoken question.

"Michael, listen to me. Not everything you contemplate is understood within the dimension of the three. Your mind isn't that of God here. You can't know what we know yet. You are still human, and you are greatly loved for being just that. There is more happening here than you know. You chose to leave the path, and it is an honor that you did. Nothing is inappropriate that you have chosen to do. We would not be helping you in this manner if it were not anointed that you were here at this time."

Mike had never thought of his choice to be on this path as an anointed one. He continued to think of it as an escape. He was in training to go home, and for some reason that was honored and blessed by these angelic beings. Red was right. He didn't see the big picture.

"Will I ever understand?"

"When you stand before the door to home and open it, you will."

Red stood up and graciously excused himself. After the door was shut, Mike arose and walked around the table to the chair where Red had sat eating with him. It looked like a three-year-old had been there! Crumbs, fruit juice, and pieces of food were everywhere. Mike burst out laughing.

"I love you, Red!" he exclaimed. Mike realized how thoughtful Red had been to offer to eat with him. He had tried. *I guess even angels have things they can't do,* Mike thought. Then he became introspective and wondered, *If there are things angels can't do, and angels are part of the whole, I wonder if there are things God can't do?* Mike heard an answer in his head immediately. It was the voice of Violet!

"*Yes. God can't lie. God can't hate. God can't make unbiased decisions out of the scope of love. This is the essence of why you have the lessons of Earth, so that God can have an unbiased test.*"

Wow! Mike knew that something profound had just been imparted, but he understood none of it. *Perhaps, in time, even this will make sense,* thought Mike. It was good to hear Violet's voice again. What a place!

Mike slept, but the two angelic names Anneehu and Eleeuin kept appearing before him, along with vivid colors and geometric patterns. It was all so wonderful! Despite the recurring light show, Mike slept well.

THE NEXT DAY, Mike could hardly wait to get started. He wolfed down his breakfast and followed Red to the theater. He literally scampered to the big padded chair and awaited more introductions and enlightened words from his new family. This time it was the turn of some of those who hadn't been so friendly. Still, it all seemed so correct.

The bully, Henry, came and stood before him, telling Mike of the contract between them and the heaviness of its origin. Mike and Henry had been shipmates in some distant past, and the interaction of their lives at that time had dictated lessons to be learned together this time. It was all so fascinating, and somehow it made sense. He and Mike were partners in a dance of energy that was ongoing. He faded, and Mike thanked him for playing his part so well.

Next, the woman who had killed his parents with her car spoke. She took pleasure in her explanation. She called herself the "walk-in catalyst for completion"—more spiritual talk that Mike didn't understand yet. It was as if she had an appointment with Mike's parents on that dark farm road that night, and she had been there right on schedule. She told of the planning session, and how all the entities had clapped their hands in glee when it was finished. Death didn't have the same energy behind it for those on the other side. It was almost like a play!

The woman never apologized for what she had done. She didn't have to, since it was in perfect order. There was no more judgment from Mike. In fact, Mike told her as much.

"Thank you for your gift, precious one." Mike meant it.

The procession of family origin for that day was completed, and Mike again arose and went to his meal. Nine more had given their stories and lineages. This time he did not ask Red to eat, but instead to remain while Mike ate. He had more questions and didn't want the distraction of flying food and spilling fluids.

"Red, many of these beings are still alive on Earth. How can they also stand before me in such a way and tell me their stories?"

"Again, Michael Thomas, you use your human experience to understand the reality of home. The 'real Michael Thomas' can be many places. The 'piece of God' that is the higher part of your soul is not fully present as you walk on Earth, but is elsewhere doing other things—such as making other plans for energy potentials with the family now that you have changed your path." Red smiled while he let Michael take in the full meaning of what he had just said.

"New plans?"

"Yes," replied Red.

Mike was astounded. It was starting to fit together. Planning sessions occurred not only in the beginning before he got here, but new ones due to his enlightened choices were ongoing even now, using a part of him that he was not even aware of!

"So does that make me some kind of split personality?"

"Michael, close your eyes." Red was giving Mike a lesson. "Concentrate. Remember the events of today. Imagine yourself back in the theater." Mike did so. Red continued, "Now, where are you?"

"In the theater," replied Mike.

"I thought you were eating here."

Mike opened his eyes and looked at Red in a disgusted manner. "Wait a minute, that's only my imagination. It doesn't count any more than my dreams. My real body is here. My thoughts are in the theater."

"Okay, which is real—your body or your thoughts?" Red asked.

"My body—I think," replied an uncertain Mike. Red didn't answer. Instead he leaned forward and gave Mike something to think about.

"Mike, last night..." Red paused for effect, "... you met your folks again, you know. This time they showed you their real energy, and you called them by their real names. You traveled places with them and had a great time." Mike stopped eating.

"You mean that was real?"

"Yes."

"But I was asleep—dreaming!"

"Your humanness won't let you understand the reality of Spirit, Michael. Your consciousness is the actual reality. The physical is only temporary. Your cellular structure, although a sacred vessel in itself, is only a place where the Spirit of your consciousness resides, and you can take that Spirit anywhere you want. Therefore, wherever your thoughts are, your reality is. Believe me, it is so." Red smiled.

"I can leave my body?" Mike was puzzled.

"You do it all the time, Michael!" Red was amused. "This puts you in two places at the same time, as you call it. Not so unusual as you think! As long as you remember to come back to the human vessel, it is appropriate. You are committed to carrying your consciousness in that vessel as long as you are on Earth, but you can still travel."

"You said there was part of me that is not here?"

"Yes." Red knew what the next question would be.

"Where is it?" Mike asked. Red arose from his seat and headed toward the door in order to let Mike retire for the night. He turned to honor the last question.

"It is in the most sacred place of places. It is with all the others. It is in the temple of physics. It is with God." Red left.

Mike was hearing all kinds of new information and couldn't decipher any of it. *The temple of physics? What could that be? It sounds like a church science project, or a movie with Harrison Ford. What could it mean?* It seemed like every answer to a question generated more questions.

Mike retired. Just before going to sleep, he remembered what Red had said about his dreams being his actual reality. Had he really traveled somewhere last night with his family? If so, why didn't he remember it clearly? It was all so new—all so amazing. Mike was still thinking about it when he dozed off into that state that left his human mind muddy about what was really happening. Then, he again traveled to his favorite spot—one he had been to so many times while asleep—where love meets reality, and family gathers to speak of things past, present, and future—where the laws of physics are seemingly violated, but are actually created. He would remember none of it later.

IT WAS THE FINAL day in the Red House. In the theater, only a few astral presenters came forward, since at least five had been skipped over as ones that were not current to Mike's experience so far. He met the school teacher he had reported to the faculty, and the thief who had seemingly started all this by his actions in Mike's apartment. It all seemed so long ago.

Mike listened to them all. He honored the fact that they were family and were connected in so many ways to his current and past lives. When finished, Mike had an overview that almost no human had ever possessed. He had a far more enlightened idea of what life was all about. Again, he lamented the fact that he could carry none of this back to Los Angeles, or that he hadn't known it originally.

If he had understood contract and karmic energy, he would have had such a peaceful understanding of even the most emotional experiences! It would have helped make Mike the finest human who had ever walked the planet. Perhaps these things were never to be known by humans on Earth. Perhaps that was the lesson that was spoken about so often. It was almost like being in the dark and seeing if you could discover the light anyway. It was a giant puzzle, but Mike was grateful for this educational and enlightening journey.

That night, Mike spent some time in ceremony with his body, as Green had taught him. He felt another shift coming and treated it exactly as Green had shown him. It passed within a few hours, and Mike knew absolutely that he had graduated to another level where the biology had melded with his spirit in some way. It seemed as if Mike's acceptance of what he had learned from the different houses had caused a physiological reaction within his cells. Then, he remembered again what Green had told him about how his actual spirit was carried in each cell. It made sense.

He slept well again, oblivious to his astral travels and his family meetings, and awoke refreshed. After breakfast, he put on his full complement of sword, shield, and armor and left to meet Red. Red was there, ready to accompany Michael to the door of the house. On seeing Mike approach, Red was obviously affected.

"Michael Thomas of Pure Intent. You've changed."

"I know." Mike was timid about the ceremony and shift that he'd experienced the night before. "How can you tell, Red? How can an angel tell if a human has shifted vibration?" Red was still looking at Mike with an awed expression.

"Your colors give you away," said Red softly. "Never has a human shifted so far, so fast, Michael. You are one-of-a-kind in this place. You have embraced everything and understood quickly what was put before you. You are indeed a special human!" Red turned and led Mike back out of the maze of hallways to the small door of the red house. Mike walked into the sunlight and began to put on his shoes, which he found undisturbed where he had left them. He hadn't understood about the colors, but it didn't matter.

"I shall never forget this place, my red friend," Mike said. "Here I met my family for the first time."

Red smiled. He knew the truth. Michael had met his real family for the first time as Michael Thomas, the human. Michael actually knew the family well.

"Michael Thomas, you are still in for many surprises in the two houses to come. Your new vibration will make these all the more intense. Are you prepared for these?" Mike thought this sounded ominous.

"Is there a problem ahead, Red?" Mike was concerned.

"There will be some challenges, physically, spiritually, and for the human heart, before you get to the door marked home," Red answered seriously. "These will be perhaps the greatest ones you have faced so far in this land. Some may call into question this very path and the reality of it. Some will astound you in their scope. Some may even frighten you."

Mike straightened up when he heard that. He knew that some kind of test was ahead. As before, Mike was resolute. He hadn't come this far to back out now.

"I understand," said Mike. "I'm ready."

"Indeed you are, my human friend." Red continued to look at Mike as though he had never seen him before. "I have a question," Red asked. "You will hear it this morning, and only two more times. The last time will be the most important one."

Finally! thought Mike, glad that an angel was giving him some information about why this last question was being asked at every house. It must have to do with the seventh house and what Mike would find there.

"I'm ready for the question, Red." Mike knew the question but wanted to give Red the honor of asking it. Red could tell that Mike was letting him have his moment, and he appreciated it.

"Michael Thomas of Pure Intent, do you love God?"

"As I do you, and all the others—yes, I love God." Mike stepped forward and did something he had not done before. He hugged Red! The large red angel was a tough package to get his arms around, but Mike did his best. Red quickly accepted the physical good-bye and stooped down to allow Mike to hug him at eye level. Red encircled Mike completely, swallowing him up in the gossamer red robes.

"There is significance in this, Michael," Red said as he let go of Mike. "As Green and Violet have told me, you are the first to have the vibration that would allow touch with an angel." Red was emotional. "We never got to hug humans physically in the past. I will always remember this time."

Mike took the compliment well and then walked down the trail from the house to the main path. Mike had a choice—path or not. Yes, this time he would use the path to the next house, which he already knew was white. Mike turned one more time and waved a farewell to Red. Red stood there on the porch and watched Mike stroll out of sight. He marveled at Mike's progress. He was proud that Mike's gifts and weaponry were so attuned to this human. Never had this happened so completely.

It was only a matter of moments before the looming menace of the repugnant creature with the stench of death itself appeared out of the tree and began to follow the human to the next house. IT left no footprints as it moved along the margins of the path. IT passed very close to Red and glared at him with two fiery eyes. Red, for the first time, spoke to the apparition.

"Phantom, you haven't got a chance." With that, Red spun around and disappeared into the house of his color.

CHAPTER TEN

The Sixth House

T he trek to the next house went almost without incident. Mike was more aware than ever that he was being followed. Instead of fear, however, he felt only caution. He could actually feel the dark energy of IT following not too far behind. He hadn't been able to sense the creature's energy before. It was almost as though Michael Thomas had been given a new gift of second sight—perhaps a sixth sense? He absolutely could tell that this energy existed! What did this all mean? What or who was this—thing? What did it want? Why didn't it just show itself? Why just follow him all the time?

Mike remembered the storm and how the dark greenish figure had come out of hiding and attacked him while he was vulnerable—seemingly only to disappear when lightning struck. Perhaps it was afraid of Michael? In that case, Mike had nothing to worry about, and he would simply keep the phantom at bay throughout the remainder of his journey to the last two houses.

Mike intuitively knew, however, that there would probably be a time of reckoning with the sinister thing that shadowed him from house to house. Red had intimated as much, and Mike's new intuitive sense was telling him the same thing. *Be careful, Mike!* were the words he heard over and over regarding the subject. It was his mind talking—or was it? He was beginning to realize that the voices of the angels were somehow melding into his own, giving him advice about his journey. It was all so new!

As he continued, twice he caught a glimpse of the thing when he looked back. At least it was behind him. Mike considered the fact that if it was smart, it could get ahead of him in his journey from the sixth to the seventh house. *Better be watchful for that*, an intuitive voice spoke clearly in his mind. Mike took out his map to see if the shadowy phantom had any kind of energy that would appear. The map was normal, however, showing all things around the red "you are here" dot for a couple of hundred yards. Mike looked back to where he had seen movement and realized that the thing was lurking just out of range of the map. He wondered if it knew that it might show up on the map and therefore kept itself far enough away. He would have to keep that firmly in mind. Somehow, he felt, it was valuable information.

Mike found the white house fairly soon in the afternoon. It was small and unassuming; a cottage just like the others. He approached it and looked for the sign so that he could have a preview of the lessons to be learned there. His curiosity didn't disappoint him, for indeed, the sign was there. It read "House of Love." Mike was instantly curious. What could this be about? He had felt loved in each house. He had been through the House of Relationships, yet here was an entire house dedicated to love.

Mike turned from the path and walked up to the door. There was no angel to greet him. He looked for the place to put his shoes, and it was there, waiting for him. Mike wondered if he should wait for the white angel but decided not to. He removed his shoes, placed them in the appropriate area, opened the door, and went inside.

He was overcome by the smell of flowers! He remembered this feeling. He was standing in a hallway that led to a vast area of indistinct whiteness. He slowly made his way down the hall until he was standing in a great, open void of white. He remembered this place. This was where he'd experienced his original vision! Suddenly, the great white angel who had been in the vision stood before him.

"Greetings, Michael Thomas of Pure Intent! We meet again." The angel smiled a phenomenal smile—and what a voice!

Mike was extremely pleased to see this wonderful entity. The gossamer quality of his garments again astonished Mike. The angel seemed to blend into the house. He intuitively recognized that White, as he would call this angel, was different from the rest. He floated! The others walked. White had a countenance about him that somehow gave him a greater badge of divinity—if such a thing was possible. The other angels on this journey had become his friends, his family. This one was like a priest. He glowed! Mike felt that White shouldn't be touched and that he carried a great energy with him. Mike's new intuitive powers were serving him well.

"You have a face this time." Michael winked at White. He remembered that everything about the angel had been indistinct the last time they had met.

"Indeed, I do, and it is because you have made it this far that you are able to see it. You have done very well, Michael. Your vibration is higher than that of any human who has traveled this land. Already there are colors in your name that announce this—colors that will remain forever regardless of your success here, whether you go forward to the next house or not."

There it was again. Was it a warning that he wasn't going to make it? Was it doubt? Red had given him the same feeling—that perhaps he might fail in the last moments of this sacred journey. *What was coming that would be so tough?*

"It is this house that will test your resolve to continue," said White, again reading Mike's energy. "Not everything is as it seems. Use this comment as your guide, and you will fare well in what is to come."

Mike remembered that he was standing before the angel who had originally spoken those words, and how true they had been! It was an admonishment not to make assumptions. It was a warning to heed, and it would somehow help him. Mike wanted to know more about White.

"White, you are different?"

"Yes, Michael. I AM. This is the house of love. It is next to the purest house you will ever enter. It isn't a house of lessons as the ones before. It is the source house. It's the center."

"But it's number six of seven—in a row of houses!" Mike exclaimed.

"Again, not everything is as it seems." The angel smiled. "Believe me, it's the center. The order of the houses is only for your lesson, Michael. The layout you see only represents a human attribute."

Mike was immediately curious to know more about the house.

"What will take place here?"

"Revelation…"

The angel floated closer to Mike. What a face he had! If love had a face, this was it. Beautiful, astounding, and peaceful. White continued with his answers.

"A journey into choice. A re-examination of all that is. Another vibrational shift, if you want it."

"Who are you, really?" Michael inquired of White. You're not just the white angel in the sixth house. I know that.

"I AM known by all, Michael Thomas, and THAT I AM known by all, therefore I exist." This was the identical answer that White had given the first time Mike had asked the question. It made no sense to him.

"I don't fully understand your answer, White, but undoubtedly someday I will. Of all the angels I have met so far, you are indeed the grandest." Mike was speaking truthfully, for he was beginning to understand that what stood before him now was an entity of great spiritual importance and potent energy.

"That may be so, Michael Thomas, but there is one coming who is grander than us all." White was patient while Mike pondered the statement. Then White turned and floated ahead, beckoning for Mike to follow. White led Mike through a nondescript and almost indistinguishable maze of pseudo hallways. Mike couldn't see details in this place! They rooms and halls, if that's what they were, could have been any shape.

"What is wrong with my vision, White? Everything blends in with everything else."

"Much of what you perceive is in higher dimensions, Michael Thomas, and your mind is not able to make sense of it at the moment. That is why I did not meet you at the door. I cannot easily go outside of this place, for the physics there would not accept my dimension." Mike knew he was in an area of knowledge he didn't begin to comprehend, and he did not pursue it. White led Mike to a familiar-looking door, one Mike could actually see distinctly, and then he spoke.

"Your quarters and dining area are in your dimension. You must enter alone. I will be here to greet you in the morning after your first meal." White was very gracious. He smiled broadly at Mike and made him feel very good, indeed. There was something about his voice that made Mike wish to hear him speak over and over. White's voice was beautiful! Mike remembered how he had reacted to White's laughter the first time he had heard it. He wanted to be in White's company.

"Must you go?"

"Yes, but only for now. I will be here in the morning."

"I'll miss you." Mike felt as if he were saying good-bye to a long-lost relative. He actually didn't want White to go. The energy between them was addictive to him! Mike recognized that this was unusual. He verbalized it in only a few words and formed a question. White knew it was coming.

"White, what is it I am feeling? Are you able to explain it so that I can understand?"

"No." White was honest and smiled at Mike. "But I will tell you anyway." This magnificent angel was very willing to talk about everything, even if it was over Mike's head spiritually. He continued.

"I represent the source for all matter. I exist that I exist and am the reason for the Universe to exist. I live in the highest scientific paradoxes imaginable, but I am responsible for the emotions of a single human heart. I am the smallest part of physics and the largest part of the Universe. I represent all light. I am the space between the nucleus of the atom and the electron haze. I am the most abundant force in the Universe and the most powerful source of energy. I am from the most distant, yet most powerful force in the Universe. I am the sands in the hourglass of time, yet I am the center, where there is no time. I am the creative force that allows physics to respond to consciousness; therefore, I am a miracle. I AM love."

Mike understood none of this, but he was awed by the message anyway. White had sanctity and holiness. Mike was standing before a part of God that was sacred and anointed. He was faced not with a teacher this time, but a personality—a celebrity—with a voice like none that Mike had ever heard. Mike had felt this same thing the first time he had met White.

"Thank you, White," Mike said gratefully. "Thank you."

White looked at Michael Thomas for a very long time before he spoke again. His silken voice slid into Mike's ears like the morning dew on a moist flower petal.

"You will not spend much time here, Michael Thomas. Tomorrow I will explain the four attributes of love, then I have someone for you to meet." Mike could tell that there was something potent coming just by the way White looked at him. Mike felt the angel's love and compassion for him.

White exited, leaving Mike wishing for more of everything: more of that wonderful voice, more information, more peace! That was it! White carried peace when he was around, yet White was gone, and the peace remained. What a feeling!

Mike had forgotten how hungry he was until he smelled food in the other room. He knew the routine and quickly placed his belongings in the closet, washed himself, and prepared for his evening meal and an early retirement.

After dinner, Mike slept better than he had ever slept in his life. Whatever he had experienced in the other houses, this topped it. The sense of peace was so thick he could taste and smell it. The serenity was awesome, and the result was complete and ultimate rest.

✤ ✤ ✤

WHEN THE DISGUSTING and vile entity with the red eyes came upon the white house on the path, IT did not stop to take refuge in a tree or wait behind a rock. Michael had already entered the cottage, and IT knew that all was safe, and IT could pass without notice. IT continued with a dark purpose that compelled IT forward. For about an hour, IT moved quickly up the road in the direction of the next house and found a place perfect for the ambush. IT scouted the land and thought of all the escape contingencies that Michael Thomas might try. Then, IT settled in and began the waiting process, practicing what IT was going to do. The deception was perfect, IT thought. Michael didn't stand a chance. His guard would be down.

If you had been a traveler on that path in the dusk of that closing day where IT had set the trap, you would have seen a solitary man standing under a tree, repeating the same words over and over—as if practicing a speech. If you had come closer to this seemingly gentle soul, you would have observed the features of an honest farmer and heard the voice of a loving father—Michael Thomas's father.

MIKE AWOKE EARLY and prepared himself. His quarters were similar to that of the other houses except that they were completely white. He had often considered the "white-on-white" look as feminine decor, but this experience changed his mind. In this place, all the whiteness conveyed a sense of peace, of serenity. Mike found some white clothes to wear, complete with white slippers if he had wanted them.

He ate—and what a meal! Not only did it taste good, but the food looked wonderful. He was seated at a table with a white tablecloth and white china; there were white cups and glasses and even white utensils. The color of the food contrasted dramatically with the whiteness and gave the appearance of a gallery painting. Mike ate slowly, taking in all the elegance in his new surroundings. All the white made him feel as if he were in a palace—as if he were among royalty.

When he was finished eating, Mike took a deep breath. He absolutely knew that the grand, white angel was just on the other side of the door, waiting. *What was going to happen here?* If love was the greatest power of the Universe, and Mike was increasing his vibration toward it, then what could be waiting that would tempt him to leave this path?

Mike opened his door and stepped into the wispy hallway of the white house. He was right. The white angel was waiting for him right where Mike had taken leave of him the evening before.

"Good morning, Michael Thomas," said the cheerful entity. Mike immediately felt the grandness of the energy around White.

"Good morning, White."

"Are you ready to move forward?"

"Yes." Mike loved the feeling here but was a bit apprehensive. White led him into a room where he could sit. He was invited to seat himself and did so. There were no teaching aids, screens, or charts here, only a white room with a chair in which Mike was now seated. The angel took a place in front of him and began the information exchange.

"Michael Thomas of Pure Intent, I am here to present to you the four attributes of love. When the pure love of God permeates your being, your very cells will vibrate with its integrity. You will see things differently. You will treat others differently. You will have powerful discernment. It is the essence of all creation, but oddly enough, your language has only one word for this astounding property." The angel smiled. "I wish to show you how it works. Please, come with me."

Mike was surprised by what followed. He thought he had been through a great deal in the first six houses and had seen everything, but suddenly the angel was taking him on a journey! Seated, he was being whisked into an interdimensional reality. He and White seemed real, but everything else became dreamlike. He had the feeling of motion but was not dizzy in any way. The white, indistinct room became a maze of colors and sounds, changing greatly before his eyes. Still in his chair, Mike was being taken somewhere else, and although surprised, he was not afraid. It was all so wondrous!

After some time, he and White finally "arrived" at whatever destination the angel had in mind. The indistinctness of the dimensional shift started to fade, and Mike found himself and White in a hospital setting. This surprised Mike. He thought White was taking him to some heavenly place to look at divine love. Instead, he was observing an average hospital room where a patient was lying in a bed. Multiple tubes were attached to the individual, and Mike recognized the area as one hospitals called *intensive care.*

It was so real! He could hear everything as it was happening, and he could smell the antiseptic the hospital used on the floors and walls. After being on a sacred path in a spiritual land for so long, the sounds and smells assaulted Mike's nostrils and made him wince. It was so different, yet still familiar. The two travelers took up a place where they could observe everything that happened in the room. They seemed to float in a stationary way in one corner. There was stillness, and Mike was quiet. Only the beeping, hissing, and clicking sounds of the medical apparatus were apparent. Mike looked around. The man in the bed was obviously of advanced years. He looked ashen, very old, and very sick. His eyes were closed.

"What's wrong with him?" Mike quietly spoke to White, as if the patient might hear him.

"He's dying," replied the white one. Mike started to ask another question when a woman in her early forties entered the room alone. She stood there for some moments just inside the room, looking at the man in the bed. Mike realized that somehow she was special. His intuition remained alert, even within this seeming vision.

"Who is she?" Mike inquired.

"She is the daughter of the dying man," stated White. "The story you are seeing is really about her." Mike took it all in as White continued to speak. "Her name is Mary, and she has every reason to despise the man in the bed."

"Why should she hate her father?"

"Because he abused her greatly when she was just a child," replied White. "It scarred her emotionally and physically. It ruined her life." White paused, and they both watched Mary approach the bed. The angel continued, "Her mother never knew about it, since Mary was too frightened to tell her. It affected their relationship as mother and daughter, and Mary moved out of her home early to get away from her lusting father. Her mother thought that Mary didn't want her, and they never were able to enjoy any adult friendship. Mary never told her anything, and she died thinking that Mary didn't love her."

"That's terrible!" Mike was genuinely distressed. He could feel the unfairness of the situation and felt very sorry for Mary. The angel looked at Mike quizzically.

"They are family, Michael. Certainly you didn't already forget your lessons in the Red House?" Mike felt ashamed. No, he hadn't forgotten, but this was the first time he had tried to relate what he learned about his own spiritual family to another human. He realized that White was alluding to the fact that the father and daughter had a karmic contract together, just like those he had with his own spiritual family.

"It gets worse." White was still speaking. "When she tried to have a normal relationship and find a husband, the early experiences with her father always somehow spoiled it for her. She never was able to successfully marry and have children of her own."

Mike sighed, and then spoke. "That's quite an agreement they had." He was overwhelmed by the heaviness of what Mary must have gone through. The angel looked at Mike in an admiring way. He didn't have to say anything. It was White's way of giving Mike a compliment from what he had learned so far along the path.

"Do you understand, Michael Thomas, that what happened with Mary and her father was a contract of incredible love?"

"I do, White. But as a human, I still find it a very hard concept to understand and accept."

"That's your duality working, Michael," stated White. "You may never completely accept some of these things while you are in human form, and that is totally appropriate." Mike continued to look upon the situation in the hospital room. Mary was quietly staring at her father, perhaps waiting for him to awaken. She placed some of her things on the bedside table.

"She must hate him very much," Mike said sadly and softly to White.

"No, Mike. She loves him greatly." Mike was shocked by this statement.

"After all he did?" Mike questioned. White turned and faced him.

"Mary has something in common with you, Michael Thomas—and something not in common." The angel stopped and looked hard at Mike for his reaction. Mike was listening. "Unlike you, she is on Earth now, but like you she has a full realization of the information you have received in the first six houses." Mike was stunned! He had believed that his spiritual training was something a human only received by going through the journey he was now on. He didn't know what to say. *How could this be?* The angel saw Mike's anguish and confusion and continued.

"Mary made her vibrational shifts on her own, Michael, and it took almost nine years of her life. You have done yours in only a few weeks! You are indeed special. The information you have gleaned in the first five houses, plus the information found in the last two, how-ever, has been on Earth for eons. For a human to obtain it, he just has to realize his duality and give intent to find the truth of his existence. There has been much written about the way things work, and there are many human teachers who can help attain understanding."

Mike was very quiet. This was very new information, and he had to take it in slowly and understand what it meant. He was begin-ning to feel uneasy. Had he made a mistake in the original vision, asking White to allow him to leave Earth and go Home? Now, he realized, everything he was learning would also have been available had he stayed.

"White, why did it take her nine years?"

"She went at her own pace, Michael, and was honored for it. She did not have the benefit you did of angels who explained and tutored. She did not have the honor you had of meeting your family face to face. She doesn't know their angel names as you do. It took far longer for her since she is still in the vibration of the three and lives within an energy that is lower. Her duality is stronger, therefore, and her awareness and enlightenment took longer because of it."

Mike sat and looked at Mary. Here she was, vibrating at a very high level, but she looked so small and frail.

"Don't let appearances fool you, Michael. Everything is not as it seems." The white angel had again read Mike's energy. "She is a warrior of the light. She has slain the giant and is powerful!"

Mike was really starting to feel uneasy now. *What exactly did that mean?* He started to ask about it when White spoke again.

"Michael Thomas of Pure Intent, we are here to watch this seemingly insignificant woman teach you the four attributes of love." Mike was very still. He knew intuitively that there was a great deal yet to learn. Just when he thought he was approaching Home, things were becoming more complicated. The angel continued, "Pay attention, for she carries with her the same power I do. She understands love, Michael, and part of me resides in her because of it. There is no greater power than this. She has also accepted the golden one."

Mike knew this was no time to ask any more questions. He watched while White continued the explanation of what was taking place.

"Michael Thomas, the first attribute of Love is this: LOVE IS QUIET. Notice that she did not enter the room with a fanfare. Her abusive father is very ill. He cannot defend himself and is weak. It would have been a grand opportunity for revenge. She could have entered in a noisy fashion, announcing herself and making him fear her. He knows what he did, Michael, and he is ashamed and guilty. It has affected his life as well, and he has dealt with it poorly for years. He does not know what she knows spiritually. He does not have her new power. Watch her quietness, Michael Thomas."

Mike and White watched in silence as Mary straightened her father's sheets. She seated herself beside the frail man and lay her head gently on his chest. Mike could feel what she was feeling! Somehow White was allowing for this. There was peace and serenity in her attitude and her mind. There was no thought whatsoever of retribution in her heart. She had forgiven her father so completely that her mind and heart had no feelings of victimization or anger. What a woman! Mike felt her compassion for this man who had fulfilled his contract so completely and had made such a compelling and serious mark on her life.

It was a long time coming, but finally the father opened his eyes and discovered her presence. She stood up when he awakened. His eyes got very wide, and you could see his instant feelings of fear and surprise. Here she was! What was she doing here? He hadn't seen her in years and years! Was she going to yell at him—or worse? He was beginning to react. The instruments measuring his bodily diagnostics began to increase in their activity. The beeping, hissing, and clicking got faster.

"Watch, Michael," White spoke in his wonderful mellifluous voice. "Here is the second attribute of pure love. LOVE HAS NO AGENDA. She could ask anything she wants of her father right now, for he is weak and guilty. He is a wealthy man. She could demand abundance, legal reparation for what he did, or perhaps just demand that he recant his past performance aloud for her to hear. She could threaten him with harm or estate ruin—or both. Watch her, Michael."

Mary placed her hand on her father's head and whispered in his ear. Immediately, the activity of the instruments quieted. He sighed, and Mike could see the beginning of tears in his eyes.

"What did she say, White?" Mike didn't hear Mary's whisper.

"She said, *I love you father, and I forgive you completely,*" the angel replied. Mike was amazed at this drama playing out before his eyes. He wondered if he would have had the power and wisdom to do the same had he been in her situation. He admired Mary greatly.

"She didn't ask for anything?"

"No, Michael. She is content to simply BE."

Again, Mike felt what Mary felt. Everything was finalized and gone regarding the karma between them. She was clear and was somehow giving him the same clearance and closure on a potent feature of their lives together. She had just disarmed something that had consumed him with grief and guilt for more than 35 years! You could see it in his face. Instead of demanding something in retribution, she had given him a gift. Now, the tears were large, and flowing silently down his cheeks. Mary again sat and wrapped her arms around this precious man who was her father, and again lay her head on his chest. There was no dialogue at all. It wasn't necessary.

"Michael Thomas, the third attribute of love is this: LOVE DOES NOT PUFF ITSELF UP. Now that she has established the fact that her maturity is glorious, indeed, she says nothing. He owes her a great deal right now due to her divine reconciliation, yet she remains quiet. She could have gloated in her power and stood tall with pride that she had been able to forgive him, yet she remains quiet. She has every right to stand up and beat her chest about the nine years that it took to get to this place—yet she remains quiet."

Mike was in awe of this woman. Indeed she was a warrior of the light, and understood things that Mike was just learning. Imagine such a thing! She was still on Earth with all this knowledge! What a peaceful and rich life she must have. Mike was introspective, but he was absolutely enthralled by the scene unfolding before him.

There was nothing the father could say. All had been forgiven, and a wonderful peace and release were being felt by his very fiber. Mary hadn't done anything spiritual for her father; in fact, she had only improved herself—yet it was affecting him. Here was something else to look at clearly. Mike knew that what he was seeing had great significance.

The father took a long look at his wonderful daughter and gently closed his eyes. The smile on his face was pure peace. She had given him the gift of a lifetime—just in time. The instruments plugged into the man began to howl different tones and volumes. The hissing stopped, and Mike knew that the father had just passed on. Attendants rushed in, but there was nothing to be done. After much activity and some final preparations, they covered his head and left him alone with Mary. White spoke again.

"Michael Thomas, the fourth attribute of pure love is this: LOVE HAS THE WISDOM TO USE THE OTHER THREE PERFECTLY! She timed everything appropriately and arrived correctly. She used her intuitive map, Michael Thomas, to know exactly when to come. Now watch what she does."

Mike's attention turned from White back to what was taking place in the room. Mary was not sobbing uncontrollably at the loss of her father. She was not filled with grief, even though her love for this man was great. She had asked the attendants to allow her to remain. Mike watched as Mary placed her hand on the chest of the covered figure that had been her father—the seed of her existence. She lifted up her head and faced White and Mike! She seemed to speak right to them! It was Mary's strong voice that they both now heard for the first time.

"Let the Earth remember this man, whom I love dearly." Mary's voice had authority as she continued. "He came and discharged his agreement perfectly. I accept his gift! Celebrate his return home."

Mary quietly lowered her eyes, gathered her things, and left the room. Michael's mouth was agape at what he had just seen. He felt the emotion of the moment and was overwhelmed by it. He had just watched the completion and closure of a life-long contract, and what a finish!

"It was the wisdom of love that allowed Mary to celebrate his death and not mourn it," said a very wise White. White looked at Michael Thomas and immediately asked for his reaction.

"What do you feel, Michael Thomas of Pure Intent?" White was not impatient and waited for Mike to recover some composure.

"I feel," Mike had to clear his throat. "I feel...that I have been taught as much in these few moments by this small woman, as I have by all the angels in my journey so far." Mike realized what he was saying, and he instantly felt sheepish. "Not that I don't appreciate—" White held up his indistinct hand and stopped Mike from continuing.

"Your answer was perfect, Michael Thomas. Perfect. It is the human who has been able to make the difference. That is as it should be and as it will be also in the next test."

Instantly the scene blurred, and again Mike had the feeling of motion as he was transported. Before long they were back in the white room of the white house where they had started. Mike was very quiet.

"Do you have any questions, Michael Thomas?" White inquired. Mike thought about what he really wanted. He knew that he was not as powerful as Mary. He knew that although he had learned a great deal and had understood much of the workings of things, he still did not have Mary's quiet power. He had tools, a magic map, and much knowledge. He had a high vibration and had experienced much, but he did not have the love that Mary had. He asked the magic question.

"Can I have this powerful Love, White?"

"Is it your intent that it be so, Michael Thomas?"

"Yes, it is."

"Michael Thomas of Pure Intent, do you love God?"

Mike straightened, thinking that this must be the reason all the angels had asked this question—for this very moment—so that he could stand here and answer.

"Yes, I do, White." Michael was formal.

"Then let your pure intent create the power!"

Mike didn't remember what happened next. He lost consciousness as a human. He had dreams...he was somehow carried somewhere...there was a ceremony...there was celebration...something was given to him...a gift that he would carry in his cellular biological structure. There were his parents again! It was all so indistinct. All so wonderful.

When he awoke, Mike found himself on his white bed, in his white quarters. It was evening, and he was exhausted. He felt that he had been through some kind of gymnastic ceremonial ordeal. His mind was bleary, and he couldn't concentrate. *What had happened?* He would sort it all out later. Now, he had to sleep. Mike crawled under the covers and instantly slept. As before, he slept very well.

WHEN HE AWOKE the next morning, Mike knew that again a shift had taken place within his very biology. He sat on the edge of his bed for a very long time, thinking about it all. He felt rested and peaceful. He felt renewed! Although he couldn't assign a particular feeling to it, he also felt somehow wiser within the scope of his being. Mike knew so much —and that's where the trouble was brewing.

He couldn't get the picture of Mary and her father out of his mind. Mary was on Earth, yet she was such a wonderful spiritual being. She had accomplished great changes in her vibration and was powerful in her life. She had stayed. She hadn't ask to go "home." She had endured life on Earth and had gone the whole route. Mike had bailed!

Where was the integrity in this? Mike was just beginning to see where his new wisdom was actually creating a kind of introspection and integrity check of the kind he had never known before. Oh, Mike was honest—perhaps one of the most honest men around. All that farm living and being trained by wonderfully honest parents had paid off, but it never gave him feelings like this. Earth honesty wasn't the same as spiritual honesty. Spiritual honesty seemed to include the wisdom of several more dimensions before the integrity check was complete.

Mike was beginning to understand what Red and White might have meant regarding his choice to continue. With his newfound wisdom, his thinking had begun to change. Was all that he was doing correct? Was there a greater spiritual quest for Mike than what he had asked for?

Mike continued to contemplate it all as he arose, dressed, and ate his morning meal. He was going to ask White some very pointed questions when he saw him. White could be his counselor in these things, and he knew that White would help him.

White was waiting, as usual, on the other side of the door. Mike stepped into his presence but said nothing. White stood there while Mike gaped at his new surroundings. All the indistinctness of the walls and floors and hallways was now crystal clear. He saw intricacies of design he was never aware of before. It was beautiful! But that wasn't all.

The feeling of stepping into the angel's light was overwhelming! He shared something with this grand white entity that spoke somehow of partnership. Mike felt he was somehow a part of what White was. Mike loved White. He felt his breath quicken in response to it all.

"It is your new sight, Michael Thomas." The angel spoke without Mike having to ask. "It is the beginning of a dimensional shift as well as a biological one. It is the same as Mary's, and it is yours because you have intended it with a purity we have seldom seen."

"I have to ask you some important questions, White." Mike had tried to be very quiet and respectful in his phrasing of this statement, but he was shocked by how his own voice sounded! It was larger than it should have been—or was it louder? No. It was different in an odd way, and Mike was uncomfortable with the change. It was almost a violation of his person. He felt anxious.

"Michael, be still for a moment," the angel said in a comforting and compassionate voice. "What is it that you hear when my voice speaks to you? There is a complement of love and peace that has affected you from the beginning of our partnership. You even asked about it, remember? Your intent to move forward may seemingly rob you of precious personal things. This is a staple of your journey. Remember when Blue told you this? He told you that your old vibration was comfortable, and the new one would take some getting used to. Outside the house of Orange you also learned of this when your precious belongings were discarded. You lamented and mourned their loss, but it was necessary for you to move forward. After a while you did not think of them again. Yesterday you gave intent for the largest personal change so far, and in response to your request, you have changed greatly. It gets more personal as you go along, Michael. Your sight, your voice, and your very thoughts will take on more purpose. You are turning into a warrior of the light—just like Mary."

Mike felt a rush of understanding and wisdom from White's words, but the information also heightened his need to ask White about his spiritual quest. As well as he could, he ignored the odd-sounding voice that was now his.

"Thank you, White. I understand. I am grateful for the gift and will get used to it as I did the other things. Please, White. We need to speak. I need counsel."

White knew what was coming and spoke.

"There is much I can tell you, Michael, and I will answer whatever I can. There is also an area that is reserved for your wisdom only. Your intent has given you the power of ultimate choice and wise discernment. These choices are anointed and filled with your own essence. They mold your future and create your reality. They affect others around you and must be, therefore, of your own making."

Mike expected this. He knew from being in this place that the angels were not going to walk his path for him. He knew that the lessons were his own, and that what he did had to come from within his own mind. Still, he was going to try to extract some knowledge that might help him to better understand what was really going on, and what he should do next.

"You are a fine teacher, White." His new voice was driving him crazy. He remembered the first time he had heard his own voice on a tape recorder as a boy. "I sound like that?" he had wondered. "No way!" This was similar.

White quickly turned before Mike could ask anything more and moved down the corridor. Mike followed the large floating entity. It was like being given a tour of an entirely new house. Things were so different. The beauty was astounding and spectacular. It was like a wonderful gallery of architecture and sculpture all at the same time. Everywhere there were breathtaking things to see! He had missed all of this with his old vision, and it made him wonder what it was that he was currently missing, and what he might see in even higher dimensions.

"The colors, Michael," White answered Mike without even turning around.

"Sir?" Mike didn't understand the statement. He followed along.

"What you are missing are the colors."

"But this is the white house," Mike stated as they moved forward. The angel laughed a great laugh. It filled the corridors and made Mike smile.

"Only to your human eyes, Michael. The actual color of Love is far beyond the vibration you perceive. It is not white as you see it. You see white because none of the other vibrations are available. It is actually devoid of color for you. In reality, the color shimmers with an overlay of all Universal vibrations together. It is pure, and is at the top of the spectrum. It is the color of an interdimensional light so great that it has substance and thickness. It is a billion, billion times as bright as your Earth sun. It is the color of truth. There is much you cannot see as a human."

"I love this place!" exclaimed Mike.

"We shall see if that feeling remains," said White.

Mike again reacted with curiosity to the angel's suggestion that he might change in some way. He had to ask more questions. They continued down the dazzling hallways until White led Mike into a room that had windows and one chair.

"Another journey?" Mike inquired.

"Not exactly," stated White. "But it will take you somewhere."

White again took up a place before Mike and announced his readiness to continue with business.

"Michael Thomas of Pure Intent, what is it you wish to know?" Mike had his questions all ready for White.

"White, from the depth of your wisdom, and in a way that I might be able to understand, can you tell me if my quest in this great land is appropriate spiritually." Mike needed to know from the source if what he was doing was correct.

"Yes, I can." White remained quiet for a moment, as though he were going to answer literally *yes* or *no* to the question. Then, he continued before Mike could press him further on the issue.

"I told you from the beginning that what you are doing is appropriate for your life. In addition, there is no way that we would all be in support of something that was not correct for you."

"But Mary?" Mike blurted out in his new uncontrollable voice. "She had all the gifts and tools, but was still on Earth. Isn't that a better thing? Doesn't it represent a higher spiritual purpose?"

"For her," replied a wise White.

"But I'm in training to serve myself, White! I'm going 'home' to where love is. I've asked for something selfish. How does it serve Earth? I'm on a path that *seems* to provide nothing but what I want!"

"Seems?" White interrupted.

"Yes. It *seems* that way." Mike was exasperated. He fell silent.

"Since when did you care about serving Earth, Michael?" White was having fun. Mike was taken with the question. He didn't answer right away.

"I don't know." Mike was pensive. "I guess it's all part of the new me."

"What did I tell you when we first met about the way things seem?" White was testing Mike.

"That things are not always as they seem," said Mike. That had been the recurring theme of his journey, and both Blue and Violet had actually stated those very words. With the addition of White, three angels had said this.

"Very good!" replied White. "What else?" Mike fell silent. He didn't remember. The angel continued. "Your wish for home is not selfish but natural, and it is not in conflict with the desire to honor your purpose for being human." White paused. "Now that you have made it this far, I will tell you one other thing." The grand angel moved to one side, as though preparing for something. "There is a new energy on your planet. It vibrates with potential change and a wonderful purpose. Your request for home is honored because of this new energy. Your journey, therefore, is one taken by few humans, since it has not been available until recently. You, Michael Thomas, are a forerunner of this process. That is why we celebrate you so with your success and wisdom."

Mike was silent for a long time. Finally, he spoke.

"Okay, so it's sanctioned." Mike was being logical, yet weighing the facts as he knew them. "But for me, would it have been better to return to Earth? To do what Mary did?"

"For you?" White tilted his head. "Are we being selfish?"

"I didn't mean it that way." Mike realized that a logical argument wasn't going to work with the master of Love. "I mean, where should I really be? What should be my action that fulfills the greatest good for all? This is my real question."

This statement caused White to swell up with great pride. He smiled broadly at Mike and spoke intently.

"When this question is asked, Michael Thomas, it shows that you truly are beginning to understand the way things work. Your wisdom is starting to show, Michael."

"Thank you, White, but what is the answer?" Mike ignored the compliment and winced a bit as he pressed the angel for more. It was uncomfortable to be so aggressive with such an entity of gentleness.

"The greatest good?" White began to move away. "It's your own reality, Michael. And you, as a human vibrating with a new intensity, will create it for yourself. There isn't one entity in the Universe that can do it for you." White had moved to the door.

Mike understood that he had shifted into a discussion that would go no further. These were the questions that the angels would not— or could not—answer. He tried one more tactic.

"White, will I be able to discern what is the highest good for all?"

"The next event will be the test of that." White opened the door and was about to leave. Mike wondered where the angel was going. White continued speaking.

"You don't have all the information yet, Michael. This is the house of love. There is still more for you to see here." White moved out into the corridor.

"And Michael," the angel said as he was closing the door, "it gets harder now." White left and silently shut the door to the room. Mike heard the click of the latch, and all was still.

Mike knew that something was coming, something potent. What else could there be? What could be shown to him that would cause an even greater disquietude in his soul about the appropriateness of his journey? Mike turned in his chair and faced the area where White had stood. He was patient. The fact wasn't lost on him that whatever was going to happen was going to happen without White. Whatever it was, he was required to go through it alone, and obviously White wanted it that way.

The entire room seemed to change slowly, and the light became different around him. The white of the walls dimmed, and a concentrated space about 15 feet in front of Mike's chair was turning into a glowing haze. Slowly, the haze turned into an indistinct figure of some kind. Mike was very attentive. He was about to meet someone. He remembered that White had mentioned earlier that this would be so. The figure continued to emerge. Like a stage being flooded with light, the area around the emanating silhouette grew gradually brighter so that Mike could watch the developing persona that was coming into view. Mike was actually becoming used to this magical way of presenting things, and he sat on the edge of his chair peering into the changing space before him.

It was a female! The shape took form slowly as Mike watched. He took some long breaths as his apprehension mounted. His intuition was set on high. The very cells of his body vibrated with excitement, telling him that what was before him was extraordinary. His new gifts of discernment were shouting that what was coming was unique and powerful. The image finally became solid. His visitor was here!

The woman before him took his breath away. There was far more here than simple loveliness. He had an instant feeling of family, of connection, and it agitated Mike's inner being. She was spectacular! What was it he was feeling? Why were the alarms of his heart going off?

Her flowing red hair set off a perfect face of compassion and incredible beauty. She smiled at Mike, and his heart just about leaped out of his chest. Her green eyes sparkled like emeralds set in the perfect ivory of her skin. Mike swore that he again smelled violets. All kinds of things went through Mike's mind. Perhaps this was the goddess of love—like the sirens of old legends. Mike was having trouble with his breathing, until he realized that he was holding his breath! What was this about? He looked at her in amazement. What could make him swoon in this manner? What was his heart doing? His brain felt like mush, and he could only sigh with longing at the sight of this glorious creature.

Mike had seen many angels along the way, but this one had to be the grandest. Perhaps this is what White meant when he had told him that there was one even grander. Mike could not speak. The heart connection of this woman to him was astounding. He felt as though he was at a reunion and was about to greet a long-lost love. The haze was now gone completely, and she stood in his dimension in all her grandeur.

Mike was in a stupor. In all his experience, he had never felt himself vibrate in this fashion. He could not concentrate on the words that he wanted to say. He didn't know what to ask. He knew her—or did he? How could her presence affect him like this? What was the feeling he had of remembrance? Then he realized that he did recognize her! It was one of the faces in the Red House within the chart of family. She was one of those who had not come forward to meet him as the others had. It had been the image of the red-haired woman whose energy had captivated his interest right away. Why hadn't he met her then? What was it that Red had told him about the faces he didn't meet? They were unfulfilled contracts? What did that mean?

The revelation was slowly unfolding in Mike's mind as the two of them continued looking at each other in a charged silence. *If she is on the chart in the Red House*, Mike thought, *then she is not an angel! She is part of his human karmic family!* Mike was beginning to have a bad feeling about this encounter, although his soul continued to sing a song that was brand new to him. It was a song that spoke of joy, purpose, and love. What a feeling, and what a dichotomy! Part of his brain was telling him that he was about to be in trouble, and another part was rejoicing. The rejoicing part was like the child who sees Disneyland for the first time and has been counting the days, enduring the agonizing wait for the grand payoff. The troubled part, however, was his heart. It felt like it was in a wringer!

Mike felt stupid. He again realized that he was not breathing properly. The figure before him was affecting his physiology. The very sight of her magnificence was causing a reaction in his body. *Why were his hands sweating?* She wasn't an angel, yet the woman before him was affecting every cell in his body. He didn't know if he had the physical power to speak. He felt teary-eyed and emotional, like seeing a long-lost friend who he thought had died. This was indeed an experience to remember. Luckily, she spoke first.

"Mike, it's me."

The familiarity and kindness of her voice practically knocked him over. Mike was glad he was seated, for his knees were weak, and his legs were vibrating like so much jelly. His entire body reacted to a voice that he absolutely knew! But who was she? Her gleaming eyes and expression pleaded for him to recognize her. He did, but not the way she wanted. Mike had to speak. His adrenaline was pumping like that of a school boy reacting to the beautiful girl across the room who finally had spoken to him. Her physical body was glorious, and her clothes were a perfect fit. He could just imagine what it would be like to hold her. Oh my God! Mike realized with some embarrassment and disgust that he was in the first stages of physical desire! What had Green said about that? That intimate physical relationships within pure love represented the catalyst for enlightenment? Mike's humanness made his thoughts somehow seem out of place here, but it was happening, and these feelings seemed to be appropriate and spiritually perfect. Suddenly, he could hear Green laughing. He ignored the sound and mustered up his courage. He spoke in a shaky voice.

"Your outfit is nice."

Good God, what had he said? What kind of ignorant, unimportant, inappropriate, inane, insipid thing had he done? This gorgeous creature comes into his space in the House of Love, he is filled with awe, and that's the only thing he has to say? Mike was mortified at his stupidity. She smiled. He melted.

"Thank you, Michael." She winked. "I am Anolee, your love contract, Mike." Somehow Mike had known that. His heart was pounding at the sound of her voice. He wiped his wet hands on his pants, then realized she had seen him do it. She stepped forward and came closer. The light she was bathed in followed her. Mike felt himself try to disappear into the chair as he forced himself backward in reaction. The sound of the cushion wheezed in response. He wanted to stand, but knew he would probably fall over—something that he did not dare risk her seeing. He had been foolish enough already. She was amused at his shyness but did not comment on it. He felt overwhelmed by her presence. When she had come forward, he had watched her walk, and he recognized the motion. Indeed, there was part of him that knew her intimately. Her new proximity to him only heightened his awareness of who she was. She continued.

"Had you stayed on Earth, Mike, there was the energy potential for our meeting. We planned it together, remember?" Mike didn't, and he didn't want to hear this. She saw the beginning of his pained expression and his sinking heart.

"It's okay," she said. "I'm here to tell you that what you are doing is honored. The family is proud, and we are all celebrating. Especially me."

Mike couldn't get past the obvious. It didn't matter that it was okay. He didn't care that the family was celebrating. All he wanted was her! All his life he had looked for true love. All his life he had searched for this very thing. He had known that perfect love was possible, that he could enter into a partnership that was ordained and correct before God. He had prayed for it as a boy, observing how much in love his parents had been and how they had treated each other. He had expected it as a man, and that was why he had been so depressed after his relationship had fallen apart. This had been the crux of his search for completion back on Earth. It had been his contract! Now, it was manifesting itself before him, and he was allowed to greet it—and learn that it had been there all along. The realization hit him like a sledgehammer in the heart. HE HAD LEFT TOO SOON!

Then, he was struck by another thought and was compelled to ask, "Anolee, did we have a contract for children?"

"There were to be three," she replied.

Mike was emotionally devastated by this answer. He could not speak. He let her continue to tell him the spiritual names of the children, but he agonized as he heard every word. Even though she was there to honor him in love, he felt tortured. His heart was being torn apart piece by piece with every word, as he realized what he had missed. The unborn children! The experiences! What had he done? Mike began to lose control, his emotions welling up. He wanted to hold her and tell her how sorry he was that he had not stayed. That's not why she was there, but that's what he wanted to do anyway. Tears began to stream down his cheeks, and he began to shake. She had finished her story and had given him the information she had come to give.

She stood before Michael Thomas in silence. The potential energy between them was so thick you could cut it. Before him stood a splendid female entity who was beautiful beyond belief, and he could only sit in a chair and sob. It was pathetic. All Mike's senses were filled with the essence of failure.

There was electricity in the air that crackled with the energy of spiritual purpose and love, though seemingly unfulfilled and lost forever. The smell of irony was pungent. The only rose in his life was never to be admired and loved for its beauty. Its fragrance would go unappreciated, and the precious rose would wilt by itself—never to be held or adored for its perfect beauty and natural elegance.

The contract between them had been powerful, and this realization was breaking the spirit and heart of Michael Thomas as he sat in the white chair in the house of Love. Her reality began to fade, and he reacted instantly. He felt himself shouting.

"NO! Please don't go! Please!" Mike felt he would never see her again. He just wanted a few more moments. The words she spoke in farewell sounded like more angelic gibberish.

"Michael, things are not necessarily what they seem." The resplendent and magnificent woman who represented the potential love of Michael Thomas's life faded before his eyes, speaking seemingly trite words that he had heard before. With her fading away went the hopes of a human lifetime. He had watched and listened to his dreams of joy being dashed on the rocks of so-called spiritual purpose.

Mike was petrified with grief. He couldn't move. Like a statue, he stared straight ahead for hours in the faint hope that this precious entity would return to the very spot she had occupied—a spot made sacred by her very presence. He pleaded with God to allow just a few more moments with his lost partner.

The light in the room grew dim and changed color with the close of the day. Finally, it turned into a blackness that echoed the moonless night outside and reflected the hopelessness of Mike's heart inside. He sat in the dark silence of one who has been firmly and decisively defeated. There was no joy in his heart. The peace of his spiritual journey had been replaced by the agony of hurt and the sick, dark, tormenting feeling of loss. His energy sapped by the intensity of an injured heart and a revelation of profundity, Mike eventually fell into a deep slumber. Still he did not move, as his dreams replayed the anguish of the potent and tragic meeting over and over.

Mike's heart was broken.

✤ ✤ ✤

THE NEW DAY DAWNED and filled the room with light. Mike found himself in the chair where he had been all night. He felt as if he had run a marathon, and his joints ached—not from activity, but from being in the same position for so many hours. He needed to eat, but did not feel hungry. Still, Mike forced himself slowly out of his seat and made his way to his quarters.

As usual, the food was prepared, and he fed himself automatically without appreciating the fine beauty around him or the incredible taste of the meal. When finished, he went into the sleeping area where the bed was still freshly made, not having been slept in. He opened the closet. There, where he had left them, were the gifts from the angels, given to him with love while visiting and learning in their houses.

A feeling of sad wisdom spread over Michael Thomas. He remembered his question to White: *Will I be able to discern the action for the highest good of all?* Now he understood the test. The very essence of his existence cried out to return to Earth right now. All he had to do was close the closet, proceed out of the house, and turn left instead of right on the path. He knew it. That would indicate his intent to stop this journey and go back. White had told him that there would be no judgment in it, no guilt, and, of course, no enlightenment.

Mike absolutely knew what the right thing was. Even Anolee had told him that they were all proud of him, and he realized that her heart probably hurt as well. Yet, she had encouraged him to go on. He knew what the greatest good for all was. To turn left would be to serve only himself and his human desires for love. White had told him that his discernment of truth would be keen, and so it was. He felt no doubt as to the correct path, only the incredible pull not to take it. His heart cried out for him to acquiesce to the situation and go back. Nothing would be harmed, and he could continue with his life and find Anolee. Life on Earth would be good then.

He picked up his map and held it close to him, closing his eyes and replaying his time in the Blue House. He slowly put on his armor and felt the power it bestowed on him. He blessed it and thanked God for the precious symbol it represented. He took up the shield and held it with both hands against his chest, savoring what it meant to him. Then he placed it in its carry position, hooked onto his back so it would be instantly available if needed. Like a warrior preparing for battle, he grasped his sword and brandished it with a flourish. He heard the whistling of the wind as the blade sliced the air. He remembered the ceremony with Orange and what the sword represented. Then, he blessed the sword, also, and deftly slid it into the scabbard, sheathed but ready. Mike stood tall in his handsome traveling clothes, and then purposefully left the room.

White was there when Mike came out of the room. He saw the armor, shield, and sword and instantly knew what Mike's intent was. White smiled and gave Mike a bow, with his hands in a position of prayer—an honor that was completely lost on Mike. Then, he spoke.

"Michael Thomas of Pure Intent, how do you feel?"

"This is difficult, White. You were right. I didn't know how hard it would be. It is the most difficult thing I have ever had to do. I still don't feel good about it…but I know what is appropriate and correct. Please, I wish to leave this place. It does not have fond memories."

"As it shall be." White turned and led Mike toward the entrance. The angel spoke to Mike over his shoulder as he led the way.

"It's not over, my human friend." White was now floating down the grand hallway that led to the front door.

"I know." Mike didn't know any details, but his intuition was telling him that there was still much to see and do within his journey, even though he had but one house to visit. His intuition was again correct.

White stood just inside the door while Mike put on his shoes. In retrospect, Mike hadn't liked the white house very much. White had been correct in his prediction about what Mike might feel, and Mike was glad to be leaving this place. White knew it, but he did not judge Mike's feelings. Instead, White was actually in awe of this human. The others had been right. Mike was different. He would make it if he could get through the final portion of his journey. His discernment was great, and his resolve was even greater.

Mike had finished with his shoes and took a few steps into the front yard. He stopped and faced the door. White spoke from within his position just inside the doorway, since he could not venture outside.

"Michael Thomas of Pure Intent, there is no greater love than this...that a man would sacrifice his heart for the benefit of the whole." White smiled at Mike and slowly shut the door to the house. His last words were barely audible as the door swung shut.

"Not all is at it seems. You will see. You will see. You are dearly loved..."

Mike slowly and wearily sauntered down the walkway of the white house and approached the path. This had not been his favorite house, and he was beginning to tire of that particular phrase uttered so often. It now felt as though everyone had said it—several times. He felt that this white place had extracted much from him, while the reality was that he had extracted much from it. He stood for a long time at the white gate to the house, looking left and then right. Finally, he opened the gate and took his place in the middle of the path itself and stayed very still. He faced left and closed his eyes, being careful not to take a step. He held a small ceremony of his own, and started it by silently asking that the angels he had met be present to hear his pronouncement. Then, he spoke aloud.

"There is no sacrifice here, for I shall meet you face to face, Anolee, and I shall know my unborn children, all in time, when I reach the door to home." Mike was taking to heart the teachings of the angels about the temporary nature of Earth and the absolute reality of Spirit. His statement carried with it the promise of a different kind of love in a very different place, but a reunion, nevertheless. He had resolutely hung his heart on the reality of a sacred meeting in the future, where he would again see the love of his life—his glorious partner. That is where he would spend time loving her—and she, him.

Mike sighed and did an about-face. With long, purposeful strides, Michael Thomas resumed his journey to the final house. His armor softly clanked around him as he walked in the sunshine. He was aware that he was leaving behind one of the greatest promises of happiness that he had ever known. He had turned his back on all of it, and although he was aching inside from the decision, he had the promise of the incredible love of God as his solace, as well as the absolute knowledge that he would indeed see Anolee again. He was pensive, resolute, and serious. Michael Thomas had learned a great deal about love. This house had taught him the most about himself—and God— and it had been the one that had wrung his very soul until the drops of truth and discernment came weeping out for him to recognize and use.

He didn't look behind him this time. There was no timidness in his deliberate stride. Although somewhat weary, Mike felt empowered and safe. This was now his land. He felt he owned it. He had paid for it. He deserved it. He would soon find out if this was so, for an hour up the road another great test awaited Michael Thomas. IT would provide the battle for his very soul.

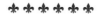

CHAPTER ELEVEN

The Seventh House

It wasn't that the weather had turned sour, but it certainly wasn't what it could have been. Mike was used to either wonderful sunshine with accompanying mild temperatures, or an assault of the elements that would arise almost instantly and pummel a watermelon into a raisin within ten minutes. Today, however, the skies were overcast and had slowly turned a gunmetal gray, giving everything an appearance of sameness. The temperature was becoming a bit chilly, and there was a slight breeze that somehow felt ominous. It pulsed instead of remaining steady, like some kind of forbidding, rhythmic messenger. The clouds didn't develop into anything worse, but they didn't seem about to clear, either. Mike had been on the road slightly less than an hour. He wasn't concerned about the weather, but he was aware of the change.

Mike had pretty much been on "automatic" during this journey to the next house. He remained vigilant, watching behind him for trouble, but his mind was filled with thoughts of the decision he had made. When he had started toward the last house, there was an intense feeling that he had somehow passed an invisible spiritual marker—a seeming demarcation point in his journey. He hadn't yet let go of the vision of being back on Earth with Anolee and the children at his side, everyone smiling. When his thoughts went there, his heart soared, and he felt relaxed. When he looked ahead of him and saw the winding path leading to an unknown challenge, he felt alone, and his heart grew heavy with a deep sense of permanent loss. No one had died, yet there was a spot in his heart that grieved. Still, he walked forward in deep thought, not noticing that the terrain was changing slowly but dramatically.

Mike rounded the corner of an especially sharp curve. He noticed that he had passed into a canyon of some kind with steep sides sloping up sharply on each side of the path. He observed for the first time that instead of slow rolling hills and lush grass, he now was standing in an almost desertlike landscape with outcroppings of large boulders and cliffs, and an occasional large tree accenting the barrenness of it all. He recognized that he had completely missed the change of topography due to his preoccupation with his thoughts. The path was leading into a gorge with very steep sides. This, plus the gray clouds, diminished the light level even more, so that it might have been dusk rather than early morning. Mike was being "poked" by his intuition. Objects in the distance were not clear. Were they rocks, or...?

Be more alert! Watch for danger!

Mike suddenly became aware that he had been in a mental daze for the last hour. He stopped and took a number of deep breaths, clearing his mind. There was a tingling feeling. What did it mean? Mike obeyed his instincts and looked around him for trouble. He searched the path behind him, looking for the dark entity that had been dogging him each time he ventured out, but he saw nothing. There was no motion. The gray sameness of the past hour had also added to his complacency and his lethargy of thought. Apart from the odd weather and new-looking surroundings, he could see nothing that was unusual or threatening, but his instincts told him that he was being somehow prepared for something. Mike softly thanked his new vibratory power for doing its job. He took out his map. Perhaps it would tell him something.

Mike examined the map. Something was odd. It showed the narrow chasm he was in and the area immediately around him, but there was something different. He looked closer. There! About a hundred yards up the path on the map, just out of sight from where Mike actually stood, was a blank spot. This was unusual. Ordinarily, the odd but very useful map was filled in around the red "you are here" dot. The chart didn't show much of the future or the past, but what it did show was generally accurate, portrayed in elegant detail. Now, there appeared to be a blank spot up ahead, as if it had been erased. What could a blank spot mean?

"Blue, what does a blank spot on the map indicate?" Mike asked out loud.

Blue didn't answer, but Mike's own intuition did. Almost immediately the answer came to him. He remembered that the "thing" that had been following him had kept out of range of the map. Perhaps this was why, because it showed up as a blank spot! Blue had told him that the map was compatible with the "now." It was the "current" kind of energy around a sacred journey and reflected a certain vibration. Something was ahead that did not belong in the now. Something was just around the corner that was invisible to the map's high vibratory rate. The absence of information on the map was due to something that was not vibrating at the same level as the sacred land around it.

Mike felt that his analysis was accurate. The thing was lying in wait for him. He should have been more alert! What would he have done had his new intuitive powers not awakened him? He softly cursed his seemingly helpless romantic mind and concentrated instead on the mind of the new warrior inside. It didn't take long. He felt a peace and power that reflected his intent. He was waking up each cell with the message that something was coming—something important.

"Wake up, everyone!" Mike smiled at the thought of speaking to his biology, and again thought he could hear Green laughing. He missed Green. Humor was a wonderful medicine in this time of preparation. Preparation? For what? A battle?

Suddenly, Mike had a revelation. Like an enormous tidal wave of understanding, thoughts and visualizations came crashing down on him with a horrendous weight of realization. He was motionless. He verbalized his new fear to whatever was listening.

"MY GOD! WHAT IF I AM ACTUALLY SUPPOSED TO USE THESE WEAPONS?"

Mike was shaken. He felt anxiety run through his body. No. This couldn't be.

"These are New Age symbols of being a warrior of the light! SYMBOLS!" he yelled as he looked skyward and spun around, as if expecting to see some of his angel friends lurking against the walls of the dimly lit gorge. His voice echoed back at him.

"Orange, you never taught me how to fight! So I assumed there would be no real use—" he stopped in mid-sentence. Mike realized that he was shouting. He heard his voice echoing back from the canyon walls. More thoughts ran through his mind. Words spoken by those he had met along the way started coming back to him. He recalled that Red had told him that some tests would frighten him, but he had assumed Red was referring to the storm he had encountered. Now he realized Red had been speaking of things to come, not things past. What was coming? He remembered the recent words of White as he described Mary in the hospital room.

"Don't let appearances fool you, Michael. She is a warrior of the light. She has slain the giant and is powerful!"

Slain the giant? Then, he remembered the words White had spoken as Mike was leaving the white cottage.

"It's not over, my human friend."

All these warnings and nuances. *Is there is a battle coming? A real one? One where I'll have to actually USE the sword?* Mike sat down on the path. His knees were weak with fear and panic. He wasn't a warrior—not a real one!

"Angels, you didn't prepare me for this!" he said to the gray sky and the menacing canyon walls. "I don't fight! Why would such a thing be? Real battles and real weapons represent an old vibration. They represent an old way of thinking. They are not appropriate here!" There was an odd stillness. The wind died. It was deathly quiet, and then the voices began.

"Unless you are about to fight an old energy." He heard the clear voice of Orange. Mike instantly stood up and twirled around as if to find out where the voice was coming from.

"And unless you are about to fight a biology that doesn't vibrate as high as yours." He recognized the voice of Green! The angels' voices were coming from inside him.

"And unless who you are about to meet really isn't part of your family, Michael." It was the voice of Red!

"And unless there is no love there, Michael." He heard the soothing and wonderful voice of White!

"I DIDN'T KNOW!" cried an anxious Michael Thomas. "I'm not a real warrior, White!"

"Neither was Mary, Michael." White's voice was comforting.

"The old energy responds to the old paradigm, Michael. That's what it understands." It was the lovely feminine voice of Violet!

"Orange, tell me how to fight!" Mike was distressed.

"I did." He heard the encouraging voice of Orange again. *"You are ready, Michael Thomas of Pure Intent. You are ready."*

"What should I do?" cried Mike to the walls of the canyon.

Silence. Then, he distinguished the voice of Blue.

"Remember, Michael Thomas, things may not be as they seem!"

The words rang out like they never had before. They carried admonishment, warning, and advice that might be needed right now! The entire entourage of angels were there with him. *With power like that,* thought Mike, *there must be something really scary ahead.*

Mike was nervous. He knew that he didn't actually have battle skills, and yet the angels were telling him that he did. He had to trust them, and after all, what choice did he have now? He was there, at the front line. He looked around him again and nodded sarcastically. *No way of escape,* he thought. Whatever or whoever was waiting for him had chosen a good place to attack. The walls were too high to climb, and retreat would only be possible within a narrow channel—an easy chase. Everything had been thought of. At least he knew where IT was, and there would be no surprise.

The more he thought about it all, the more confident he became about the ordeal ahead. His new vibration was helping out, and he knew it. He began to feel a peace that he knew wasn't logical, but spiritual. He was beginning to feel enabled, even though he didn't exactly know in advance what he would be facing, or how he would deal with it. *That was appropriate,* Mike thought. *After all, this is the way of this place.* He analyzed it. *The future is not available to me, but somehow it has already happened in the mind of God. Therefore, the solution to this situation has already been revealed. I'm just not privy to it yet. Like before, I'll know when I get there. I have the knowledge and the power, and this is my land. I have the home advantage!*

"Okay," Mike spoke out loud. "I've been beaten up by a storm; stomped on by an angel; lost all my precious belongings; my emotions have been subjected to wringer after wringer; my biology has been lifted and altered; and I've had my heart wrenched out, examined, and put back wet. What else is there? I have the tools. I am ready." Mike thought for a moment, then added, "I just wish I knew how to fight!" He sighed and looked in the direction of the upcoming challenge.

Mike decided to do something that a few weeks ago would have seemed silly and ridiculous. He knelt and held a small ceremony over what was about to happen. He touched each piece of battle equipment and named its purpose. He drilled himself with the things Orange had taught him about balance. He spent almost 20 minutes in gratitude that he had been chosen to battle whatever it was around the corner. He honored the land and his very existence. He acknowledged his place in the family of Spirit; then Michael Thomas arose, ready for battle—as ready as he could be, anyway.

Mike started forward again. He rounded the pathway that exposed the long distance ahead. The sharp walls of the canyon made the path look like a dark, fateful tunnel of doom. He knew IT was ahead. The map had clearly shown him so. Ordinarily this entire episode would be calling for Michael's body to go into shock. All his fear alarms would have been sounding, and he would have been a shaking mass. After all, he was just a salesman, not a warrior preparing to meet some huge dark ghoul! Instead, though, his senses were alert, and he was filled with commitment, not fear. All his vibratory powers and new gifts were starting to "kick in." His intuition was king, and with each step, he "listened" to it, knowing that it would not fail him.

Nothing.

Then, motion to the left!

Michael spun quickly and saw a large tree to the side of the path about 30 yards away. Where had the motion been? Drat this darkness in the middle of the day! Is this all part of the test? Why hasn't Spirit provided more light?

The motion was there again! Mike saw that it came from just under the branches of the tree.

"WHO IS IT? COME OUT!" Mike's voice was empowered and commanding. "IF YOU DON'T, I'M COMING IN!" He stood waiting, his every cell alert.

Slowly, a normal-looking man emerged and stopped just under the outer branches. He was dressed like a farmer, except that his feet were bare. He held up his hands in a pushing motion with his palms turned toward Mike. He spoke.

"Mike, please don't hurt me! I'll come out." The man slowly materialized from under the tree and walked toward Mike. As he came into clearer view, Mike thought he recognized the walk. No! It couldn't be! Now the man's face was clearly recognizable.

"DAD?" Michael's father gradually walked up to the path and stood not six feet from Mike. Mike swore in his mind that he could smell the familiar odor of the farm coming from the man.

"Yes, son. It's me. Please don't hurt me." Mike wasn't a fool. He knew that this could all be deception. After all, *things are not always as they seem.* The man who appeared to be his father could actually be something else; in fact, the odds were highly in favor of it. He continued his watchfulness and was alert to a trick as he spoke.

"Sir, you are standing right where I was told an enemy is supposed to be. Don't come any closer."

"I know, Mike. It's just up ahead, son. You are being duped! The thing waiting for you is going to capture your very soul. All this is wrong. Please, you must believe me!" Mike still didn't buy it.

"What are you doing here?"

"By the grace of God, I am here to stop you before it is too late. I was allowed to return to this place to warn you! I have been waiting here for days, knowing that eventually you would come to this spot. All who venture forward will be defeated by the beast! Many have come this way, and all have died. This is an evil land. You are being tricked!"

Mike still didn't believe that this was his father. After all, it was just a bit too convenient.

"Please forgive me, Father, but I necd proof. Tell me what my childhood nickname was."

The man spoke instantly. "Mykee-Wykee."

Mike winced at the truth. "What happened in Mr. Connell's barn in 1964?"

"A giant party celebrating the birth of twins, whom he named Sarah and Helen."

Mike was examining everything this man told him with a fine-tooth comb. The voice and body were perfect. He continued by asking the man to tell the story of Michael's childhood—schools, friends, clothing, and events. As both men stood facing each other, his father droned on for half an hour, relating every part of Mike's past perfectly and accurately. Slowly, Michael begin to relax. This man knew everything. He really was there. No evil entity could have memorized things known only to Mike. Mike's intuition was still on "alarm," but this really was his dad! His father was starting to sweat.

"Father, what's going on? I still don't understand."

"Michael, I love you so! Right now you are lying in a hospital bed with grave injuries to your neck. Remember? Surely you have to remember what happened in your apartment? You have been floating ever since—in a coma, susceptible to the workings of the devil himself. All this..." Michael's father swept his hand around indicating the surrounding mountains. "... is a fairyland. It's fake! Nothing here is real. Everything you have been shown and all the cute-colored fairy houses are nothing but a trick to take away your soul!" The man's breathing was becoming labored.

Mike knew that what he father was telling him couldn't be so. It was so confusing! He knew who he was and what he had experienced, yet his father's words seemed to ring with authority. And this man knew so much! Why was his father suffering health problems as he stood there? Wasn't he a spirit himself? After all, he was dead and had come from the other side. He shouldn't be having physical problems.

"Father, are you okay?"

"Yes, son, but I can't stay much longer. This place is evil, and I am from a heavenly place. The two don't mix, you know."

"So I've been told," Mike said.

"Mike, come with me. There's a heavenly portal under the tree. I can take you back. You can regain consciousness back on Earth and come out of the coma. It will save your life and your soul. Please come with me!" The man was growing weaker by the moment, and Mike thought he saw a blurring of the image in front of him.

Mike was torn with indecision. He knew better. Everything in his body told him better, yet here was his trusted father with a very believable story. What if this land was a fake? NO. It wasn't. Mike's inner being knew it. He wanted to try one more thing. What was the name? He had memorized it. He remembered and instantly spoke it.

"Anneehu!" Mike stared at his father, and the man stared back.

"What, son?"

"Anneehu!" Mike said again, slowly backing away.

"Is that some fairy word you learned here, boy?" The man was obviously nervous. His clothing was becoming wet with sweat.

Mike stood very still. Chills crept up the back of his spine. His father had never called him "boy." Mike stood prepared. This was it. He felt the armor on his body begin to vibrate. The shield on his back was beginning to oscillate on its hook, as if it wanted off. He gave the appropriate answer.

"No, sir. Anneehu is your heavenly name, and you didn't know it."

The two figures stared at each other in a standoff that seemed to last an eternity, but which, in actuality, was only a few seconds. The game was up. The deception hadn't been good enough, and IT was unable to hold the energy to preserve it. IT was ready to fight.

"**ENOUGH!**" With a shout that had the volume of ten men, the figure that had been Mike's father began to change its form completely. Gradually, the sweating farmer transformed into a huge, menacing, ghoulish shape. Mike traveled backward as IT grew, alert and ready. IT was at least 15 feet tall, with fearsome red eyes. ITs mottled wart-covered skin was an ugly green; the creature looked as though IT hadn't washed in eons. IT had enormous hands with large, dirty fingernails and arms that were far too long for ITs symmetry—and IT smelled! Short, stubby legs added to the oddness of ITs appearance, but Mike knew just how swift IT could be. He had seen IT many times as a blur behind him. The distance between Mike and the hideous creature had grown to about 20 feet, and he was going to keep it that way for a while, perhaps allow even a bit more space between them.

Mike was repulsed by the thing unfolding before him. IT was neither human nor beast. IT was unnatural and didn't belong in any dimension that Mike had ever been in. The stench was unbelievable! The face on the enormous bald head was constantly changing from one horror to another. When IT opened ITs mouth, Mike could see ITs large, razor-sharp teeth. When IT closed ITs mouth, the fearsome cavity disappeared into the ugly mass of warts and skin. ITs bulbous nose obviously didn't work, or IT couldn't have lived with itself. Everything disgusting and repulsive that a human could imagine was embodied by this creature. Was it real, or was it illusion? Mike didn't know. Whatever else it might be, IT was a shocking revelation of the energy of old things and ways. IT represented the antithesis of peace and love, and IT stank of death. The hatred and viciousness of ITs consciousness was overwhelming. IT looked at Mike with contempt, as if he were an ant about to be smashed without thought or remorse. The creature was driven by loathing for Mike's world. IT projected that energy directly at Mike, who had become the focus of ITs wrath.

Mike could barely stand to look at IT. He was repulsed and revolted. He felt the creature's projected hatred. But when he realized that he was reacting to the creature in a way that IT wanted him to react, he stifled the waves of nausea. *Not everything is as it seems,* Mike repeated to himself. He suddenly realized that IT was showing off—creating the illusion of a fiend, a trollish ogre just for effect.

Mike's body responded to the situation instinctively. The vibratory level of his new being was on full alert. Like a seasoned warrior, a veteran of numerous battles, Mike felt ready for any move from the green-skinned horror in front of him. Although his body hummed with strength and vitality, Mike remained motionless. His sword began to vibrate. He could hear it! The subtle hum of the *F* note was starting to sing. Still, Mike did nothing. His curiosity was too great. He had to know more. Now, it was Mike's turn for deception.

"You're so big!" Mike feigned fear. He cowered and raised his arms defensively to cover his face. He made his voice shake convincingly. "You're the real beast—here to take my soul?"

Folds of green skin and warts parted as the creature opened ITs mouth cavity to speak. Mike heard ITs real voice for the first time.

"**So weak!**" the thing gloated. "**I knew it.**" ITs voice was deep and menacing. IT reminded Mike of something out of a bad horror movie.

"Please! I'll do whatever you want," Mike squeaked. "Do you want me to go to the tree? To the portal?" Mike felt his sword beginning to jump up and down in its sheath. He hoped the creature wouldn't notice the metallic noise.

"**Don't be ridiculous. I'm here to kill you.**" If it were possible, the thing seemed to be getting even bigger! Mike realized that IT probably had the ability to be any size IT wanted.

"Who are you?" Mike shrieked. He hoped his acting wasn't too clumsy, but the thing seemed to believe him completely. What an ego IT had!

"**I'm the part of you, Mykee-Wykee, that's the real Mike Thomas!**" the creature boasted. "**I'm the strong part! Take a look at your power! I'm the essence of your intellect and the basis of your logic. Taking on the appearance of your father may have been just a disguise, but the words were true, boy. You are indeed lying in a hospital bed in a coma, and I'm here to get you out of this pretend land of nonsense entities and good witches and bring you back to real life. To get you out of there, I have to destroy the ridiculous pixie spirit you have become!**"

Mike realized that at one level what the ghoulish thing was telling him was accurate. IT really was part of Mike; it was a part he wanted put away forever—an old, ugly part that he recognized and hoped no one would ever see. He shuddered and crouched a bit more. *Don't overdo it*, said a voice inside.

"And you have to kill me?" His sword was violently rattling against the scabbard now, but Mike realized that the noise added to the deception that he was shaking with fear.

"Figuratively, yes. Your demise in this fairyland of idiocy will end your self-deception and bring you squarely back to the real world. I have been aware of your silliness from the moment you entered the gate, and thankfully was able to slip in after you. I have been trying to bring you back to reality ever since." The thing was starting to move toward him.

"Am I that bad?" *Keep IT talking*, Mike thought. *Keep shaking, sword!* He sent his thoughts to his weapon. *It's good for the deception.*

"In your physical weakness, you have embraced their clap-trap, their silly drivel. Nothing here is real, boy. You have been so tricked by the illusions here that I will have to completely destroy this part of you to save your mind and your soul. I detest everything you have become!"

Mike had to act fast. "Before you kill me, can you prove what you are saying is real? If you are logic and intellect, then help me see the logic of it!" Mike knew that this ugly thing wasn't going to wait much longer, but by appealing to its monstrous ego, he thought he could buy a little more time. Mike cowered some more and shook convincingly. His vibrating sword helped the image.

"Of course I can." IT knew IT was in control, and IT was about to squash this New Age fairyland forever. IT hated this land of make-believe. IT represented the real world, where there were no pathetic weaklings like Michael Thomas. IT embraced logic and pragmatism, a system of beliefs based on previous experience and substantiated by reputable men of history and science.

The creature rose to full height and announced:

"THE ONE WHO IS CORRECT HERE HAS ABSOLUTE POWER. LOGIC AND REASON REPRESENT THE TRUTH! THAT'S WHY I CAN EXIST IN THIS INSUB-STANTIAL WORLD—BECAUSE I AM TRUTH. NOTHING HERE HAS POWER OVER ME!" IT let out a roar that hurt Mike's ears, and actually seem to bend the grass around Mike's feet, instantly turning it greenish brown—so that it matched the horrible creature's skin.

"Really?" Mike asked, smirking at the beast. He dropped his act and stood up to full height.

"Then let the proof begin!" shouted Mike.

Mike never realized that he could move so fast. With expert balance and a swiftness practiced in the house of Orange, he found himself on a 6-foot-high rock, not 15 feet from the beast. He had actually advanced on the monster! His sword literally leaped from its scabbard and began to sing the fundamental F note with accompanying harmonics as it found itself firmly in Mike's grasp. It was an eerie sound, but full of strength and promise. Michael held the sword, not pointing toward the creature, but pointing skyward. Mike also found that he held the shield in his left hand. Somehow, as he made his lightning move to the rock, the shield had found his hand. He now held it aloft, its ornate silver inlay facing the beast. Michael Thomas, the warrior, stood ready.

To say that the creature was taken by surprise would have been an understatement. IT looked at the situation. Suddenly, the frivolous-minded, easily frightened prey had become a threat, and it was doing unexpected things. Was the boy going to attack? How foolish, IT thought. IT would swat this upstart like an irritating gnat; this would be almost too easy now.

Mike's proximity made it necessary for the creature to back up in order to use ITs long, monstrous arms. IT drew back, clenching ITs powerful fingers into huge fists, and prepared to attack.

As the creature positioned itself for the onslaught, Mike's voice rang out: "BEHOLD THE SWORD OF TRUTH. LET IT DETERMINE WHO HAS THE POWER."

Mike had no sooner finished speaking when the beast attacked.

Mike felt as if he were watching an ocean liner approach at top speed. It was all he could do not to close his eyes! At that moment, a light of unbelievable intensity seemed to leap from the blade of Mike's weapon and strike the beast with incredible force. The blow did not stop ITs forward motion, but served to deflect ITs attack off to one side. Even though the creature was thrown off-balance, IT was still able to send a blow in Mike's direction. Mike automatically thrust his shield up protectively, although he was sure the mighty fist was going to smash him and the shield with a single blow.

But the shield and armor again did what they had done during the earlier storm, even though Michael Thomas hadn't realized it. The armor instantly surrounded Michael Thomas with a bubble of protective light. The shield shot a series of intense dartlike pulses into the approaching arm. Light seemed to blaze up around Michael, to fly in all directions! The smell of ozone from the ionized air and the interaction of matter meeting antimatter was pungent. Instead of the crashing blow Mike expected from the creature's arm, the monstrous extremity was instantly repelled by the protective light. So powerful was this force that it had the effect of actually lifting the creature off the ground and knocking IT backward for some distance. Mike was unscathed and continued to stand where he had been.

The light was beautiful. Michael Thomas was astounded by the gifts he held in his hands! They had worked perfectly in tandem and had repulsed the attack of the giant. Mike noticed that while the battle-created light was pleasing to him, the massive beast had to shield ITs eyes from the intensity. The light continued to work in Mike's favor. Used to the dimness of the gray day, the creature was finding it difficult to adjust to light. Mike smiled in recognition at the gift of weather. He indeed was on home ground! He spoke confidently to the beast—something he remembered Orange had said.

"Does the shield of knowledge irritate you, my ugly green nemesis? Darkness cannot exist where there is knowledge. No secrets can survive in the light, and light will be created when truth is revealed!"

At these words, the creature was up on ITs feet and charging Mike again, this time with menacing resolve. Mike didn't think he could stop the freight-train attack this time. An arm was one thing, but the whole package? Mike waited until the last possible moment, then he darted forward off the rock just as the creature reached him. Again, Mike advanced instead of retreating, and again he created an unexpected situation where he was too close to be captured or dealt with easily. The size and weight of the beast was working against it.

Mike actually found himself running between the giant's enormous stubby legs. As he passed beneath the creature, he extended his arm, thrusting his sword so that the blade tore into the beast's crotch with a glorious light display. Additionally, Mike swung the shield so that it struck one of the legs, and the green-skinned extremity was again powerfully repelled—like a magnet slamming against a larger one of the opposite polarity. A sudden burst of light from the shield upended the creature. IT instantly recoiled and was airborne. IT clutched itself and writhed in the air, like a high-diving champion performing a "double twist." IT landed on the ground hard in unceremonious and undignified agony. IT rolled and roared ITs protest, ending up in a smoking, wounded heap. Sparks were still erupting between ITs legs where Mike's sword had done ITs damage.

"No little green-skinned uglies in your future!" Mike's repartee was delivered calmly and smugly. He advanced on the huge, loathsome troll. Mike held his sword aloft as he slowly and cautiously walked toward the repulsive beast lying on the ground. He stopped just out of ITs colossal arm's reach.

"Will you capitulate? Who has the truth here? Exactly where is the power?"

"**I WILL DIE FIRST!**" croaked the wretched creature. The voice was a raw groan, barely comprehensible.

"So it shall be," announced a fearless Michael Thomas, ignoring the increasing stench of the wounded beast.

The smelly creature was not through yet. IT was not a spiritual being. IT was, like Mike, a biological entity in this strange land of colored angels and lightning swords. IT hurt and IT bled. Mike could see the grievous wound that had been inflicted by his magic sword in the last foray, and he winced at the sight. A black, sticky substance gushed from the nasty wound, staining the already ugly and diseased-looking skin, turning the giant's legs black. Mike thought that the creature must be in incredible pain, but it was getting up again! When IT stood upright, it swayed slightly. ITs eyes appeared as narrow slits now, the light that surrounded IT almost too bright to bear. Mike knew that he had won.

Killing wasn't in Mike's repertoire. He had never killed anyone or anything on purpose—even on the farm he had refused to kill the chickens. But he knew that any killing here was symbolic, and the detestable thing before him was not actually going to die. It would just be ultimately and painfully defeated.

The scene of the two battling entities was classic. The light from the previous pyrotechnic blows still seemed to linger from the glowing sword, shield, and armor. Sparks continued to snap and pop from different parts of ITs smoking body as IT righted itself in preparation for a final attack. Now, Mike's armor was also starting to sing a victorious song. The highly outlined hard shadows created from the light of truth, knowledge, and wisdom revealed the dismal, stark sight of a huge, wounded, swaying, vile creature about to desperately sacrifice itself to the power of Mike's small weapon. It was David and Goliath, and the vision was surreal against the walls of the narrow canyon of no escape. The two unequally matched warriors stood barely 30 feet apart, each stubbornly standing his ground. It was again Mike who moved first.

Mike was far too swift for the wounded behemoth. He focused on ITs most vulnerable areas, and before the immense beast could react, was again allowing the searing light from his sword and the reverse polarity of the marvelous shield to do their work. In a desperate, mindless attempt to stave off ITs attacker, the creature began to flail ITs arms wildly. In so doing, the creature did even more damage to itself against the invincible spiritual weapons of light, truth, and knowledge. The spectacle was something to behold. Not only was there a light show of incredible proportions, but the sounds were thrilling! The spiritual battle weapons lifted their combined voices in a loud, harmonious song of victory. Orange had never mentioned that the weapons all sang!

The final skirmish was over in less than a minute. The energy discharged from the sword and shield quickly defeated the leviathan. ITs entire nauseating length was stretched out before Mike like some kind of quivering, rotting mound of putrid flesh. The stench of ITs blood gushing from numerous wounds assaulted Mike's nostrils. Suddenly, Mike's battle weapons ceased their singing, and the smoldering, green-skinned thing on the ground began to lose substance.

"I'm not gone, Michael Thomas. There will be another day," it groaned as it began to fade away.

"I know," Mike said, as he looked into the red eyes of the revolting titan. He knew the death of the evil creature was symbolic. But he also knew that the battle was extremely real. He shuddered to think that the outcome might have been reversed. Michael could have been the injured, dying one. He might have been the one fading into obscurity were it not for his spiritual weapons.

He was glad it was over. Mike slowly sheathed his wonderful sword of truth, but not before thanking it out loud. He did the same for his shield, as he returned it to the hook on the back of his armor. He hugged his armor and celebrated how well it had worked. Then, it happened!

Mike felt the three gifts start to leave. They were vanishing as the beast had done.

"NO!" he cried. "I need you! Please!"

But Michael Thomas's weapons were being absorbed into his biology. A meld was taking place that was only possible due to the intent of his own ceremony and because of the victory the weapons had just facilitated. Mike was startled. He cried out for an explanation.

"What now? Why are they leaving?"

"Michael Thomas of Pure Intent, your marvelous gifts are still there, but now you carry them inside!" It was the soothing voice of Orange. It was Orange who had bestowed the gifts in the first place. The angel continued, *"You have earned the right to assimilate them. They are now part of you, Michael Thomas, and will reside within your very cells."*

Mike sat down on a nearby rock. "And the next battle...?" Mike inquired of Orange.

"...will be won the same way, Michael, but without the tangible appearance of the weapons. Truth lives within you now, as well as the power of knowledge and wisdom. There is no beast that can ever take them away."

Mike considered Orange's words, then he invoked another angel. "Green, have I shifted again?"

"*Yes, Michael. Absorbing the gifts has made you complete. There is only one more of us for you to meet.*" It was comforting to hear Green's voice again.

"Who will it be?" Michael didn't want to wait until the next house.

"*The grandest angel of them all, Michael. You shall see,*" Green replied.

Michael stood up. He felt strange. Everything had happened so quickly—meeting the creature disguised as his father, realizing that he would have to fight an actual battle, defeating the monster, and now the seeming removal of the gifts he had grown so used to. He sat back down and began to go over the events of the past 20 minutes.

"White, who was the beast, really?" Mike asked White, since he intuitively felt that White's answer would be the most enlightening. He was not disappointed.

"*It was the part of you without love, Michael. It was the human part that is always present and that must always be dealt with. If left unchecked, humanity without love actually creates darkness.*" White's voice was amazing, and it instantly put Mike at ease.

"Will it come again, White?"

"*As long as you are human, it is in the background, ready to pounce,*" replied White. "*But love will keep it weak!*"

Mike was introspective. *I have but one more lesson here,* he thought, *and then I can shed my human form.* Mike was anxious to open the door to home. That magic door was his ultimate goal. He thought about what it would mean: a peaceful, loving existence—an existence with spiritual purpose. Mike was suddenly aware that the weather had cleared completely. In the warm sunlight, he looked around the battle scene. He could see the scorch marks where his powerful weapons had defeated the enemy. He touched his waist where his sword belt had been and touched his chest where he had worn the armor. He missed it, but he knew that what the angels had said was true. He didn't feel any different, or any lighter. He now carried the power inside, and it made Michael a mighty warrior of love indeed—just as Mary had been in the hospital. He smiled when he thought of her strength and thanked her mentally for the vision. Then Mike felt his chest again and realized the map was gone, too!

"The map!" Mike spoke out loud. He was disappointed.

"*It's inside you, also, Michael.*" It was Blue again. "*Your intuition will be every bit as valuable.*"

Mike felt naked. *But it's okay,* he thought. *I won't be human long. I won't need these gifts when I pass into heaven and go home. Only one more house!*

It didn't take long to walk out of the canyon, but there was a grand vision awaiting Michael Thomas as he drew close to the end of its craggy outline. As the end of the narrow ravine came into view, he could see a more serene landscape awaiting him in the distance. Mike also beheld a glorious rainbow arching over the ravine. It glowed brightly against the increasingly clear blue sky of the magic land; it marked the end of the canyon and symbolized the end of his journey. He moved forward, transfixed by the rainbow's majesty, only occasionally glancing down to see where he was walking.

Then, Mike realized what had created the rainbow. Six enormous friends ablaze with color were there in the sky before him. They were so grand—so proud!—all holding hands and forming a rainbow of celebration for the human they called Michael Thomas of Pure Intent. He passed beneath them, emotionally calling their color names and thanking each one. There was Blue who had given him his map and the direction of his journey; Orange, giver of the wonderful gifts that had slain the giant; Green, his comedic friend, who had explained biology, stomped on his toe, and had given him the experience of his first vibratory shift; Violet, the maternal one, who had exposed the lessons of his life, and revealed the responsibility he had for it all; Red, the horrible eater, and marvelous introducer of his spirit family; and the loving White, the essence of purity, from whom Mike had learned of real love by watching a pure woman of incredible strength, and where he had also felt the heartbreak of his own missed opportunity. Mike knew it was their way of celebrating his victory, for the next house was the last one, and he would no longer need them in this land. His training was almost over. He had learned well and had passed a great test, conquering the beast on his own. He knew that they were saying good-bye.

"I honor you, my friends!" Mike called to them. And he watched the glorious colors slowly fade, revealing a totally blue sky once again.

MIKE DID NOT have to travel very far before the next cottage came into view, but this one was different. It was no cottage. It was an enormous mansion! As he approached it, Mike not only saw its size was unusual, but he realized that what he first thought might be a brown house, slowly revealed itself as the House of Gold!

As Mike got closer and closer to the house, his perception of its size continued to change. What had appeared to be a single-story large structure slowly became a multistory gargantuan edifice of enormous proportions. And it wasn't just gold in color, but it actually seemed to be made of gold!

A huge, well-kept green lawn set off the building in a grand style, and many rich-looking fountains and streams surrounded it, all gurgling and splashing in a splendid manner. Everything was offset with gorgeous flowers of almost every kind conceivable, arranged in groups of colors that were breathtaking! Mike saw something else that momentarily took away his breath. The path ended at the entrance to the house. The final goal must indeed be inside! This wasn't just a house, it was also a portal—an entrance into heaven itself. It was the door to home!

Mike realized that he was anxious, breathing rather hard, as he cautiously turned from the main path and traveled up the long, winding footpath to the door of the great golden palace. Finally, he approached the large ornate door made entirely of gold. He wondered how he would ever open it, since it must be heavy indeed! He stooped down and removed his shoes, placing them in the obvious area made for them and waited. He knew he would never see them again.

No angel came.

He wondered about the appropriateness of trying to open the massive door and stepping inside, then remembered that this had happened before in the sixth house, where White could not venture out of the house into the yard. Mike made his decision. He pulled on the great golden door. It was far too large and tall for any practical use, but Mike felt it easily swing open!

He stepped inside and stood in absolute amazement. Everything was gold! The walls, pillars, and floors. Grand décor everywhere! It was breathtaking! There was the smell again—flowers! The fragrance of a thousand lilacs burst on his nostrils, filling him with a wonderful feeling of love. It was truly an amazing, sacred place.

Then, Mike understood the joke immediately. While the other houses in this great land had appeared small on the outside and huge on the inside, this one was huge on the outside, but the inside, although grand indeed, was restricted. There was no labyrinth of room after room as in the others houses. Instead, all doors and hallways led to one place. There were no choices as to where to turn, and there was only one direction to go. The path through the house was simple. Elegant, grand, glorious, and exquisite—but simple. There were no ancillary rooms, no living quarters for Mike. Nothing looked as it had in the other houses. There was also another feeling here. Mike was trying to locate in his mind what the feeling was as he slowly made his way through the few hallways to wherever they were leading him. Yes. He remembered. It was the feeling he had when he entered a great worship hall. He felt a reverence for it. It had majesty, as if he were in a sacred sanctuary.

Mike didn't know what to expect. There still was no angel. This was a first—the only time he had ever entered a house without being greeted. After his great battle and all the excitement, Mike should have been hungry, but he wasn't. He was too excited.

He continued forward until he reached a door that looked somehow different. It had a name etched on it. The writing was that same strange Arabic-looking script that he had seen on the labels in the House of Maps, then he had seen it again in Violet's charts. He knew it must be the name of the golden angel, wherever it was. Mike opened the door and went in.

What greeted Michael Thomas was never to be forgotten. He stood in a grand chamber of majestic beauty. It was a great hall of worship, or so it seemed. It was cathedral-like, with finely crafted, multicolored glass windows lining the walls. At each glorious window, the outside light was converted into rainbows that spilled onto the immense golden floor in pools of undulating color. As he cast his gaze upward, he could see into a golden area that had no end. The walls of the room were circular, and Mike could see that the door he had come through was the only entrance to the chamber. There was a golden fog that gently swirled around the room, giving the scene a feeling of being a pond in the early morning, when everything is fresh. The fog interacted with the light in an astoundingly gorgeous way. Each time the fog swirled into the rainbow pools of light, a burst of brilliant color would be absorbed into the fog, turning the moist air into a gossamer rainbow, painting the area with the hues of the entire color spectrum. Mike realized that he was holding his breath and forced himself to breathe.

Slowly, he realized that all the light, the décor, and the focus of the architecture was dedicated to honoring the center of the oval sanctuary. There were grand staircases at the edges of the great oval, but they only led to balconies that overlooked and focused on the center of the room. Mike concentrated on the room. The center of the grand chamber was heavy with the golden fog, but there WAS something else there as well. Mike started forward, realizing that he was certainly approaching the end of his journey.

As he moved toward the center of the area of golden fog, he realized that the shrine was far larger then he had originally thought. All the gold and the deceptive design lent itself to tricking the space perception of the human eye. He walked toward the center and found that it was taking him far longer than it should have. Finally, he was only a few feet from the focal point. He stopped. What was there? Something solid was inside the cloak of fog. Another structure?

He was almost at the center when an astounding burst of energy hit him. Mike was suddenly on his knees! A sense of incredible sacredness and sanctity had descended upon him with a power that demanded he kneel. He was breathless, and his eyes were cast down so as not to violate some unspoken, sacred protocol. His body was starting to shake with a feeling of amazing vibration that could only have come from the presence of God. This was it! He was approaching the final door to heaven—and home? Perhaps, there would be no angel. And yet all the other angels had told him that he was about to meet the grandest entity of them all. Mike felt that there was an awesome presence here, the anointed and miraculous presence of God itself! He was having a hard time breathing.

Mike lifted his eyes and saw the fog clearing. He remained on his knees but sat up straighter to watch what was taking place. The clearing fog revealed a large, golden blocklike structure. Further clearing showed that the block had steps cut into it. A stairway led upward. Was the door to home at the top of the stairs? The energy was growing very intense, and Mike didn't feel worthy of being there. There are times when a human knows his place, and no matter what Mike had been through, he didn't measure up to the sanctity and grandeur of what was before him. He was at the portal to heaven itself and felt like a rubber doll. He felt immobilized by the power of Spirit and the resplendence of God. He knew that just a few steps away was something far more powerful than anything he had ever imagined—something so potently loving and spectacular in its beauty that it represented creation itself!

Mike felt himself laboring for oxygen, but he kept his head up. He had to see it. Now, he knew that indeed there was an entity yet to meet—the grandest one of all, they had said. Indeed, it must be so. What stupendous angelic creature could bring this energy? He hoped he could survive the intensity of the vibration long enough to meet it. Even if the next moments vaporized him in some burst of heavenly multidimensional light, he had to see it! He remembered the stories of what had happened to those who had touched the Ark of the Covenant in Jewish history. They had vanished in a burst of vapor due to the fact that they had touched God. He felt that this could happen to him, too, if the energy of the moment increased much more. His cells felt as if they were going to burst. All of them were trying to celebrate at the same time! He had a feeling of expansion from within. Mike was beginning to be afraid—not for his life, but afraid that he would not get to see the entity that belonged in this last unbelievable house. The fog continued to lift.

The ornamented, golden block with stairs cut into it became clearer. It wasn't just a block; it was a throne! Ornate, radiant beyond words, superbly built, and as gold as anything could be, it seemed to glow with its own sacredness. The angel must be sitting on it. *Who could it be?*

Now, Mike suddenly found himself sobbing! His biology was bursting apart inside with the grandness of this holy energy, and he felt waves of gratitude and love pour from his heart. He simply could not control his emotions. The energy upon him was thick, and he knew that the golden entity he was expecting was indeed coming down the steps. The greatest angel of them all was about to emerge from the golden fog that hid the top of the throne. It was actually coming—he knew it! Perhaps he was about to meet the guardian to the doorway to home, the one he had wanted to meet all along—the one that knew everything!

Mike was a basket case. He didn't want to be seen like this. He wanted to be strong, but he couldn't even stand up. He wanted the golden one to know that he had passed the tests and had slain the giant, but he couldn't even speak. He felt childlike and unable to control his emotions. His chest heaved with gratitude and honor—and lack of oxygen. Mike's head was starting to hurt. *Who was this approaching that carried such power? What entity in the Universe represented the God force in such a dramatic manner?*

"Fear not, Michael Thomas of Pure Intent. You have been expected," said the great angel whose torso had dimly come into view as it descended the stairs. The voice—it was familiar! Who was it?

The voice, although carrying with it a sacredness of the highest order, was quiet and peaceful. The entity who was approaching was perhaps the highest of them all, yet the meeting began in a quiet manner—unassuming, with a message of reassuring safety. Despite the message, Mike could not adequately use his voice at the moment. He was still too moved to speak, and the seeming assault on his emotional state wasn't getting any better. He continued to watch as he grasped his chest with his hand, covering his heart so that it would not burst out of his body in anticipation of the golden master of love, who was now speaking to him. He didn't want to miss this and hoped he wouldn't pass out. His sight was beginning to blur.

The magnificent, heavenly angel came floating down the carved glistening-gold steps, slowly approaching the kneeling and shaking Michael Thomas. Even in his rapturous state, Michael wondered about the seeming dichotomy of stairs for an entity that didn't need them.

Michael saw the great, glowing body first; the head of the golden one remained above him enveloped in the golden fog. The angel paused, its face still out of sight. Mike saw that it was huge, bigger than all the others he had met. The golden hue of its garments was so brilliant that the folds seemed to be electric. He could see the bottom of the wings now. He knew there would be wings! They vibrated like 10,000 butterflies, but without sound. Mike was certain that when the head came into view, there would be a magnificent halo—such was the consecrated feeling of this great creature.

It wasn't that Mike was becoming used to this energy, but he realized that something was happening to him as the angel paused. He was being given a gift, and he knew it. A bubble of soft, white light was forming around him, caressing him and creating feelings of peacefulness within him. Mike breathed a sigh of relief. He knew that he couldn't have taken much more of that divine energy! Slowly, he started breathing normally as he now sat on the floor. The emotional wash of overwhelming love became a wash of peace, and he slowly recovered his normal human balance. Ten minutes passed, and the angel remained stationary. Mike was growing stronger and knew that the angel had created a place for him, protected by this bubble of light, where his vibration could exist next to the Godly vibration of a stupendous creature from heaven itself. Finally, he spoke, but did not get up.

"Thank you, great golden angel." Mike took a deep breath. "I am not afraid."

"I know exactly what you are feeling, Michael, and indeed you are not afraid." The angel still didn't move. Michael was trying to place the voice. It had the same kind of peaceful energy that White's had, and it tended to soothe Mike's very soul when he heard it. The voice was big, filling the entire space around him, yet quiet at the same time. He knew he had heard it before, but where? In what other area in this great spiritual place had he heard it? When he knew he could speak again, he did.

"Do I know you, great sacred one?" Mike inquired softly and reverently.

"Oh, yes," replied the partially exposed giant angel. "We know each other well." The majesty of the voice was powerful, filled with glory and splendor. Mike didn't understand, but he also didn't push the subject. The situation was thick with protocol and ceremony. It was better to sit and be spoken to in this energy, and Mike honored the difference in vibration between them. Now the angel spoke again.

"Our entire time in this house, Michael Thomas, will last not more than a few moments. It will be filled with revelation and great purpose. The vibrational difference between us is so great that we cannot sustain the meeting for long—but long enough."

Long enough for what? Mike thought. The angel continued, and the glorious strains of its voice again softened the very molecules in Mike's body as they fell on his ears and were absorbed by his internal biology.

"Michael Thomas of Pure Intent, do you love God?"

Mike's cells buzzed with action. That question again! Chills of realization raced up his spine. He had felt that White was the last one required to ask this, but he had been wrong. Here it was being asked again. *This was it!* His cells were all trying to speak again at the same time. *Tell him YES!* they pleaded. Perhaps the answer he would give to the golden one would be his passport through the door home. This was the last time the question would be asked, and the most important time. He wanted this moment to be profound. Mike paused but couldn't think of an eloquent answer. His mind was empty of anything but honor to be in such a place, before such a Godly entity.

"Yes, I do." His voice was honest and pure. It didn't shake.

"And Michael Thomas of Pure Intent," the wonderful voice continued from the invisible face in the dancing fog, "Do you wish to view the face of God? The one you profess to love?" Michael was frozen by the possibilities suggested by these holy words. *What did this mean? What was the revelation? Where was this going?* Again his cells demanded that Mike say yes. He answered automatically and simply.

"Yes, I do." His voice shook this time, and he knew the angel had heard it.

"Then, Michael Thomas of Pure Intent," said the angel as he was starting to move down the stairs, "behold the face of God, the one you have told us that you loved—eight times."

The shimmering magnificence of the most sacred of all entities closed in on Michael Thomas. Even with the protection bubble he had been given, Mike felt the energy level increase as the entity once again began to emerge from the thick golden fog and move down the steps of the golden stairway to the level that Mike was on. The entity was so large that part of the fog clung to him as he descended. When he finally stood before Mike, the fog was still gradually clearing around his face, as he again spoke.

"Get up, Michael. You need to stand for this."

Michael knew something profound was coming. He slowly arose on shaky legs and searched the clearing fog with his eyes and his mind at full alert, staring at the place where the face would emerge. Finally it did, and Michael Thomas of Pure Intent—the human who had seen just about everything on his path, who had faced the beast and slain it, who had made his transition better than any other human had in this great spiritual place—became as jelly in the revelation that ensued. Astonishment filled his teary eyes. Understanding teetered within his logical and spiritual mind as he tried to sort out what he was viewing and what it could mean. His emotions were suspended, unable to process the information that his eyes were suddenly revealing to him. His legs became weak, and he went down involuntarily on his knees for the second time in this sacred chamber of ornate gold.

The face of the great spiritual entity that had descended the chiseled stairs in the great golden throne was the face of Michael Thomas! There was no illusion here. It belonged to the angel. It WAS the angel. The angel was Michael!

"Therefore, as you love God, so it is that you love me." The gold one knew Mike wasn't really listening. His mind was still confounded. Overwhelming shock had filled every cell, and Mike was still trying to sort it out. *What did this mean? Was it real?* The angel continued. Mike sat motionless on the floor, still unable to take it all in. "Time for another gift, Michael." The angel's voice continued to be calming and reassuring, sending peace and understanding into Mike's very being. "I give you the gift of discernment, Michael, as you listen to my explanation."

Mike's mind started to clear. He again realized that the angel was giving him direct conscious help with his own understanding. This time it would be to clear his mind of human predisposition and bias. The angel again spoke.

"There is something within each human that dramatically fights to the last logical synapse of brain matter to keep from believing that it is anything other than human, Michael." The angel smiled, and Mike again seemingly saw himself in the mirror, smiling to himself. The voice was his own, but he had not recognized it. The only time humans hear their own voice accurately is on tape—which he had, but only a few times. He needed to hear what the angel was saying, and now his mind was clearing to allow for it. The angel continued.

"I AM your higher self, Michael Thomas, the part of God that resides in you as you walk the planet Earth. This is your last revelation and lesson before you continue to your goal. This is the last hurdle of information for you to absorb. It is the highest and most potent truth for all humanity—the one that is the best hidden and hardest to accept."

The angel was fascinating to hear, but Mike found him very distracting to watch now, because he had Mike's face! Still, Mike was absorbed by the information and desired to learn what it meant. He had to go forward. He had to know more. The angel moved slightly and floated to one side, revealing more of the upper portion of where it had previously stood on the carved-out staircase. It continued.

"This is the golden "House of Self-Worth," Michael. Nothing will stop you in your enlightened journey faster than a feeling that you don't deserve it. Therefore, we chose to reveal to you who you really are. You are part of me, Michael. We are an angel of the highest order, like all humans are. We are the ones who have chosen to visit planet Earth, go through the trials of human life, and raise the planet's vibration by our journey's lessons and experience. We are the ones who can make a difference for all humanity as well as the Universe. Believe me, Michael Thomas, what you did on Earth made great changes in other areas."

"But I didn't stay!" Mike blurted out what was on his mind, hearing this information and again feeling that he had surrendered early. "And I didn't learn anything!"

"It doesn't matter, Michael," stated the angel. "It's the intent to make the journey, and the original agreement to participate in the sacrifice that is honored so greatly. Just your presence on the planet is honorable and correct. Didn't you realize this? Did you ever hear the story of the prodigal son? It's told in every culture, you know."

Mike knew the story, but he hadn't applied it to this situation. He remembered that the son in the story was loved and welcomed by the father, even though he hadn't honored the family's ways. The angel moved again as it continued the explanation.

"Michael, the other angels loved you so much! Didn't you wonder what you had done to deserve such a thing? Now, you know. We—you and I—are an elite group. We are among those highly loved and honored who have elected to come to Earth, live in a lower biology, and have that fact hidden from us. YOU are actually a piece of God, walking the planet in lesson for the sake of a grander purpose, and you get to view that piece before you now."

Michael was awed by it all. He thought back over the past few weeks. The family and contracts he had learned about in the House of Violet he found amazing. The family revealed to him in the House of Red was astounding! But now, the revelation that he, the human Michael Thomas, was actually among the highest angels of all? And the other humans, also? *Could he really be so grand?*

"Yes, you are, Michael. Yes, WE are! It is now time for you to understand and realize that you deserved to come to earth. You planned to come and actually stood in line! You are honored among entities for what you have done, and you are worthy now to move into the next phase. As you have professed to love God so many times through your journey, SO IT IS, THEREFORE, THAT YOU MUST ALSO LOVE YOURSELF! Think about this, Michael Thomas, for its truth must change your perspective and the very essence of your human purpose."

Mike was now far more alert to the information, since the angel had given the gift of calming and discernment to him. He was clear. This was indeed hard information to digest. The angel continued to speak.

"The final step now—and would have been had you continued on Earth—will be to absorb this partnership. Know that it is real! Feel the worthiness and divinity of your humanness. Know that you are actually a sacred entity of heaven itself. Feel the fact that you belong here and are eternal! Own the badge of gold that it gives to you, Michael Thomas."

Mike had a flashback from his time in the white house, when White had shown him the vision of Mary in the hospital. He now remembered something that had remained hidden from his mind. White had uttered words that were meaningless until now. The angel had said that Mary had *accepted the golden one*!

"Did Mary know about you?" Mike had to ask.

"Mary knew about her own higher self, Michael, if that's what you mean. She was partnering with her higher self the whole time you observed her. That is what you felt. She knew who she was. She knew about the golden room and the golden throne. She knew she was sacred and that she deserved to be on Earth. She *owned* her sacredness."

Again, Michael was in awe of Mary, this small woman who had shown him so much, and he had never even known her.

"Oh, she knows you, Mike," said the golden one.

"She does? How?"

"Just as all of us know each other," the angel replied. "She was very aware that her gift to her father that day was having profound effects on others. Her intuition told her so. She even knew she was being watched. She, like you now, had all the gifts and tools and maps within her, and also the golden gift of divine discernment that I am passing to you. Such is the power of an enlightened human on Earth."

"Wow." Michael was learning so much, and his respect for Mary was soaring even beyond what it had been. She knew! Her intuition told her that her actions were being watched and used to help me.

"The test is at hand, Michael Thomas." The angel was getting down to business. Michael knew there would have to be some kind of test. *What would it be? How could this entity with his face and his soul know if the human Michael Thomas had accepted the reality of his self-worth or not?*

"There is only one way." The angel floated off to one side. "Do not be alarmed, Michael, but I must now remove your gift of vibrational protection for the rest of our time together. You have either absorbed the truth or not. This test may not seem difficult, but it is impossible to pass unless you are pure and have accepted the truth of the partnership."

"I have," said Mike, feeling anxious. *What was the golden one going to do?* The white bubble was beginning to fade around him, and he was once again seemingly assaulted by the vibration of the sanctity of the God force around him. There it was again. All that love. All that energy of purpose and focus of millions of entities. This time, however, Michael also felt something new. He felt a slight tingle of being part of it all. *Could this be the test?*

"I feel it!" called out Michael. He was hoping that this was it. Would the test, whatever it was, be over now? No such luck. Instead, the great golden angel with the face of Michael Thomas approached him.

"Michael Thomas of Pure Intent, sit down on the third step." Mike was starting to breathe with difficulty again. His cells simply didn't understand being in a vibration that was so high. Mike spoke out loud to his body, not thinking about the fact that the golden angel was even there. He had to get control over his biology—and right now!

"WE are okay," Mike said to his cells. "Don't react in fear! WE deserve this. WE are worthy of this!" Mike was shouting and he knew it. He was automatically doing what Green had taught him, and he was getting instant results. He sat down on the third stair of the great golden throne and began to grow calm. Mike suddenly realized that the golden one was watching him intently. He saw the biggest smile on that golden face!

"You really do know what to do, my human counterpart. These are things that I could not impart to you, but you have learned them well from the others. Now, let's see if you have fully absorbed what I had to give you in the same way."

The next thing that happened shocked Michael Thomas even more than the revelation of the angel's face a few moments before. The great golden one, who moments before had represented the epitome of the God force itself, was beginning to kneel before Michael Thomas. The magnificent golden wings spread and unfurled in a royal manner, like a cape of gold unfolding and expanding with the angel's movements toward the floor. The two magnificent appendages fanned out just enough to allow the great body to move gracefully down without his wings touching the ground.

Mike's body did indeed have a strong reaction, but it didn't disable him this time. Instead, it overwhelmed him in a loving way as he continued to watch what the angel was going to do.

As he knelt, the grand angel produced a golden bowl from somewhere and held it gently before him ceremoniously. He looked directly at Mike and spoke loving words to him.

"In this bowl are figuratively the tears of my joy for YOU, Michael Thomas. With this, I wish to anoint and wash your feet, for you are worthy of the honor."

Oh no! This Godly entity is going to actually touch me! Now Mike understood the test. A touch from this golden one would determine if Mike's cells had really understood the worthiness issue, and if his body was truly aware of its lineage of sacredness. No wonder the test couldn't be faked. This was it! The angel paused before he touched the left foot of Michael Thomas, and answered the questions in Mike's mind.

"It isn't a test of vibrational shift, Michael. For you and I will never be the same vibration until we meld together again at the end. This is a test of your human belief. WE must *own* the fact that WE, as God, deserve to be human. This will test if you truly understand that you are worthy of having your feet washed by Spirit itself, and if the love you have for God is reflected in the love you have for yourself."

Mike relaxed. He knew his own mind and knew he had accepted this thought and lesson from the grand one. He suddenly realized that the test would reveal it to the angel as well. He was ready. There he sat, before the grandest of the grand. The angel, even with its largeness, had positioned itself below Mike's eye level. The protocol was not lost on Mike, and he felt his emotions well up inside at what was taking place.

The noble one gently took his foot, and an unbelievable tingling feeling crept up Michael's body—right up into his very heart and mind. He was starting to overflow with compassion, and tears began streaming down his face. He said nothing as the angel gently washed his foot. Michael felt he was loved beyond measure. He didn't disappear. He didn't vanish in a flash of energy. Although he was feeling the pressure of the vibrational energy between them, and was barely coping with it, he was aware that he was worthy to receive it. Still he remained silent, for he knew that love is quiet. He knew that pure love has no agenda, so the glorious gold one wasn't going to ask him for anything in return. He knew that love didn't puff itself up, and that the angel wasn't going to suddenly be joined by a legion from the heavenly hosts. This was personal, and the angel was silently asking Michael to accept the honor and just BE. The feeling in Michael Thomas was indescribable. Tears of great joy and gratitude continued to flow, but he was not ashamed. He knew that the angel understood that this was a human's way of saying thank you—odd as it might seem. Finally, the angel spoke again. His voice was full of pride for Michael.

"Michael Thomas of Pure Intent, you have indeed passed this great test—one of the greatest of all. But now I will show you something even greater. Even though you have passed all tests, and even though you stand ready to move to the door of home itself, I will now wash your other foot. It is my honor to do so and exemplifies the love that God has for you. There is no more test here. There is nothing I gain from this. I do it because I love you. Never forget this moment."

If there could have been a more sacred moment in Mike's life, he couldn't fathom it. The tears continued to flow, and the love continued to be shared by the two entities of the same soul force, as the great golden angel gently washed Mike's other foot, which looked small in the angel's large hands. Finally, it was over. The bowl magically vanished, and the angel straightened to full height, his wings again folded appropriately and perfectly against his body.

"You may now arise, Michael Thomas. Your intent has been shown to be pure indeed, and you are ready to go home!"

Michael got up, looked around the chamber, and then back at the angel. As if reading his mind, the angel took his hand and motioned to something behind Mike.

"Up the stairs, Michael," the angel again smiled.

Mike turned and looked up into the swirling golden fog. The steps on the golden throne beckoned him into yet another unknown place of great purpose. He looked back at the angel as if to confirm that he was to climb the stairs for himself.

"The door you seek is there, Michael. Oh yes, and remember this: *Things are not always as they seem.*"

Mike didn't stop to ask about that statement at this point. It was slowly becoming the mantra of this place. He was aware that he could not stay here for long. The angel knew it, too, and gently moved next to Michael, touching him again, this time with a great encircling arm around Mike's shoulder. In a soft, reassuring voice, the angel spoke his last words.

"I just came from there myself, Michael. It's okay. You must go now. The goal is at hand. I will join you there shortly. We never say good-bye, since we are one."

Mike knew he had to remove himself from this potent energy. He turned and quickly started up the steps. Now, he understood why there were stairs. It was for the human, not the angel, and the steps were spaced apart perfectly for Mike's foot size. It was all starting to make sense, but Mike didn't want to analyze anymore. It was time to graduate! It was his time to move into that place called home. He moved forward up the steps of the great ornate golden throne. He stopped to look one more time at the golden one, the piece of God that was he, now standing regally with its hands clasped together, smiling at Michael Thomas from the foot of the steps. The angel was right. There was no feeling here of any farewell. It really was part of him! Mike began to realize that within the last day he had met two parts of himself. The one without love, and the one with it. Somewhere in between was the human consciousness, and it was for him to choose where it would settle. *What a concept!*

Mike turned and began to climb the steps. The thick fog hid what was immediately above him, and he could only see about ten golden stairs at a time. He was careful to watch his footing. The last thing he wanted was to fall off this tower at the pinnacle of his sacred journey. He laughed to himself at the thought of ingloriously tumbling back to the bottom and apologizing to his grand higher self for being a klutz. The mild humor immediately made him feel more relaxed.

He was aware that he had climbed at least two stories of steps, and a landing of some sort was just ahead. *What a magnificent throne,* he thought. It's really huge! And it's his! Finally, he had reached the top of the steps. Michael was not disappointed. There, next to an enormous ornate and regally carved golden chair, was the door he had planned on viewing for these many weeks. His vision of so long ago now loomed before him, within easy reach. It was well lit and the main feature next to the chair. It seemed to be suspended, without walls around it, and it was not apparent where its reality met the reality of the golden throne. Mike realized that it was not part of the House of Self-Worth, or the structure he was in. It was a portal, and therefore had a different dimensional attribute. The door had a great deal of writing on it, some of which he could not interpret, but in plain English he also saw the word *HOME.*

Mike had waited a long time for this. He had been through a great deal, learned much, and had altered his very cellular structure in preparation for what was on the other side of this portal. Now it almost seemed anticlimactic. He stood there thinking of all that had happened, and of the breathtakingly beautiful golden angel at the foot of the stairs. He thought again of what had happened there on the third step a few moments before. Indeed, that last experience had made the final difference in how he felt. Mike faced the door in a ceremonious way.

"I deserve this!" said a confident Michael Thomas. "And I honor the Universe for allowing me to do what I am about to do. With complete love, I enter the place I have asked to be."

The ceremony completed, Michael Thomas breathed one more giant breath of human air, and bravely opened the door marked *HOME*.

Mike vomited.

CHAPTER TWELVE

Through the Door to Home

"Hold his head to the left, next to the tray!" cried the nurse to the orderly. "He's vomiting." The emergency ward was crowded that night, as often takes place on a Friday. This time the full moon also complicated things.

"Is he awake?" asked the neighbor who had accompanied Mike to the ward. The orderly bent down to closely examine Mike's eyes.

"Yeah. He's coming out of it," the white-coated orderly replied. "When you can speak to him, don't let him up. He's got a nasty head bump with a few stitches. Don't want them pulled out of place."

The orderly moved out of the cubicle, an area separated by a curtain on a semicircular rod, offering some privacy from many others just like it.

Mike opened his eyes. He knew immediately where he was. He was back on Earth in the hospital where this had all begun. The fluorescent fixtures that bathed the emergency area in a bright sterile light made Mike wince and close his eyes. The temperature in the room was cold, and Mike instantly felt the need for a blanket. The orderly returned with one, as though he had heard Mike's silent request. Then he left again.

"You've been out for a while, buddy," said the neighbor, feeling a bit embarrassed that he didn't even know Mike's name. "They sewed up your head. Don't try to talk." The neighbor patted Mike's chest nervously and exited the curtained area to the waiting room.

Mike was alone. His head was swimming with the reality of what had happened. This all had been a dream! The ugly, vile thing that he had defeated in the vision had been right all along! Mike had been on Earth the whole time, lying in a hospital in a daze—a coma—and none of the wonderful things he had experienced had been real.

Mike felt like he was going to vomit again, this time from the reality of the situation. He was back. Home was just a pipe dream, and the land of angels was exactly what the monster had said—so much fairy talk. None of it had happened, and Mike was still in the hospital! Nothing he had seen or had been taught had any substance or validity. He closed his eyes and wished for death.

The head night nurse came into the cubicle and bent over Mike. He could smell her slight perfume over the other smells of the disinfectant around him. She examined the bandage on his forehead and touched him slightly.

"Mr. Thomas, are you awake?"

"Yes," said a weary and depressed Mike.

"You can go now. We sutured and dressed your cut and you're fine. It's okay to leave now." Mike knew something was different.

"My jaw—my throat?"

"Nothing's wrong with them, Mr. Thomas. Was there a problem we missed?" Mike exercised his jaw and felt his neck as the concerned nurse watched. All seemed to be in good order.

"No. I guess I just dreamed it." Mike was back to reality. He thought briefly about business. "Nurse, how long have I been here?"

"About three hours, Mr. Thomas." The nurse smiled and was attentive.

"And what about the bill?" Mike needed to know.

"It's covered under some kind of policy your apartment has, sir. There are some papers to sign, but nothing to pay."

"Thank you, Miss." The nurse left the cubicle, and Mike was again alone. Something didn't add up. Although it seemed like a couple of months ago, Mike vividly remembered that the thief had indeed crushed his throat in the struggle. All these injuries had happened before his vision, or dream, or whatever it had been. So nothing he dreamed could have changed that. Now, however, not only was there no damage to his throat, but none to his jaw either. *Was this still another dream?* No. Mike was overwhelmed with the pressure on his bladder. He had to go the bathroom! This was back-to-basic Earth reality, the kind he was used to as a real human.

Mike arose and ignored the ache in his head. He was still in his street clothes, he realized, as he went in search of the bathroom. He found it immediately. It was a small, one-person, generic hospital bathroom, reeking of disinfectant and extremely clean. He relieved himself. It seemed foreign—like something he had not done for months, and it seemed to go on and on and on.

Mike was washing up when he caught a glimpse of himself in the mirror. Something was different about his face. He drew closer to the mirror, looked into his own eyes for a long time, and questioned what he was seeing. He was standing up straight and felt good! Perhaps the three-hour rest in the hospital was exactly what he had needed.

Mike slowly walked out of the treatment area and was greeted by his neighbor who was there waiting for him. Mike saw him and shook his hand.

"Thanks Mr.—uh—" Mike was at a loss for a name.

"Please call me Hal, Mr. Thomas." The neighbor was grateful to see Mike up and better.

"Hal, have you been waiting all this time?" Mike was curious.

"It was nothin', Mr.—" Mike interrupted him.

"Please, call me Mike."

"Okay, Mike. My car is just outside. Let's go home." Mike suddenly reacted to the word *home,* and felt a stab in the pit of his stomach that reminded him how his dream had disappointed him so miserably.

"Sounds good, Hal." Mike was genuinely appreciative. While Hal went for the car, Mike signed the necessary papers and went outside.

On the way home, Mike questioned his neighbor about the incident. All seemed to be as he remembered, except the injuries. *Did I imagine that?* Mike wondered to himself.

Mike thanked Hal again for his gracious hospitality and went into his apartment. He opened the door in the usual manner, snapped on the meager light, stepped inside, and closed the door.

He was overcome with smells and sights that should have been very familiar to him but were not. Although there was a mess to clean up and a stereo to put back, the fish tank had not been broken as he had remembered. Something was very wrong here. He felt as though he were visiting some poor person and helping to clean the guy's place! Mike stopped and looked around at everything.

This place didn't belong to him! Why would he have ever thought so? Why was it so dark and dingy? Three hours ago it was his, and now it seemed to belong to a guy from an entirely different world. *What was happening?*

Mike realized that his consciousness did not match that of the man who used to live here. It somehow seemed odd and inappropriate for him to even think about sleeping here. Mike went to his top drawer and searched through his things. There, where he had left it, was a current credit card that he had never felt he would use. *It's too much money to pay for credit,* he used to say. *I don't need nice things,* he would say. Mike flipped it into his wallet, checked to see that he had at least a few dollars, and began gathering some belongings and toiletries. Finally, he snapped off the light and left the apartment. He knew he would have to come back to get his personal things and his fish, but he made a mental note to himself to give notice immediately. He then went to Hal's apartment and briefly told him what he was intending to do in case a police report would be needed later.

The cab Mike hired took him to a better part of town, where he immediately checked into a fine hotel. He breathed a sigh of relief as he looked at the lush furnishings and the brightly lit and ornately decorated lobby area. This was more like it! He would look for another apartment in the morning—after he obtained the kind of new employment he deserved. Even as Mike crossed the lobby to find the elevators, heads turned in his direction. There was a positive presence about Mike, and he commanded attention. Was he someone special— a star, perhaps?

Mike was lying on the bed of his hotel room when he began to wonder what had happened to him. He felt wonderful! He felt peaceful. He absolutely knew that he could find a great job tomorrow, in one day—even in Los Angeles—because he was very good at what he did. He could hardly wait to meet people and give of himself, perhaps even start a great career.

Then it happened. He thought of Shirley, his lost love, and there was no pain. There was no stab of remorse over losing a precious relationship, or of feeling pathetic and needing to hide because of it. Mike actually made a face when he thought about the kind of person he had recently been. *UGH! What was I thinking that would cause me to behave in such a manner? She was only fulfilling her contract. I was as responsible as she was for the event.*

Good grief, what was he saying? But it was true! Mike did something that would have mortified him a few hours ago. He went to the phone and dialed the number he had known so well. It rang once, twice, then a delightful feminine voice came on the line.

"Hello?"

"Shirley!" Mike was elated to hear her voice.

"Mike?" Shirley didn't seemed pleased to hear his.

"Listen, I just wanted to make sure that you were okay, and tell you that I really feel good about everything that happened."

"Mike? Is this really you? You sound different."

"I just wanted closure on our time together, and to tell you that I hope your life is really good. You deserve it, and I think you are really a great gal."

"Mike? This can't be you."

"It's me."

"You've got another girlfriend?"

"No, Shirley. I really am serious. I just called to tell you that I'm okay and that I wish you well in whatever you do in the future. We had a good time, and I hope you remember me in a good light."

"Mike? What's happened?"

"Can't talk now, but maybe some other day. Good-bye!"

"Mike? This is a joke, right?"

Mike hung up the phone with a feeling of wonderful serenity. He had closed that part of his life and was extremely glad to have put it away. The sound of her voice hadn't stirred up any negative feelings at all, only the peacefulness of completion and a sense of moving forward.

Mike felt odd. Something was very different. He was doing things that were not like the old Mike. He felt the energy of the moment and was not worried about being in a hotel, spending a hundred dollars a night. He absolutely knew that his abundance would be able to cover the hotel charges from the income of his new employment—a job he didn't even have yet! This was not the old Mike. This was a "current" Mike who understood self-worth and the universal workings of things. Mike was beginning to feel like he had been reborn, and all the healthy feelings that accompany a man who is happy with himself were solidly in place. He felt chills going up his back, and somehow he knew what they meant. He went directly to the door of his room and opened it. There, with fist poised to knock, was his friend John!

"Hi, John!" Mike hugged his friend.

"How did you know I was out here?" John was perplexed.

"Intuition, I guess. Come on in."

"You're a hard guy to track! I heard about the break-in at your place and came right over after the night shift. Your neighbor told me you were here. Are you okay? Your head okay? And what's wrong with your apartment? What's the deal with a hotel and all?" Mike held up his hands as if to stop the machine-gun approach to the questioning, and smiled at John.

"John, my head's fine, and I don't belong in that dump. I also don't belong in the job I have. You and I both know that." John was dumbfounded. He had been hoping that Mike would snap out of it eventually, but he wasn't expecting Superman overnight.

"Michael, what has happened? You are really different!"

"I know. I can't tell you why, but I just know so much! And I feel good about everything, peaceful and energetic about life." John was absorbing it all and said very little. "I would get you something refreshing to drink, but I just got here myself. Want to go to dinner downstairs?"

"You mean in the restaurant?"

"Yes. It's on me."

"Sure!" John looked hard at Mike. "Boy, have you changed!"

Both men exited the small hotel room together and ended up in the fine restaurant within the lobby of the hotel. There, John listened to Mike talk about everything except his dream. He spoke of closure with Shirley, his plans for a new job, and his outlook on life. Mike spoke eloquently about how truth always wins, and how forgiveness and integrity create peace in any life. The things that he had criticized before, he now spoke gently of, and allowed for differences in opinion. He spoke about the fact that a human didn't have to accept what was just handed to him, and that a person could create his own reality.

John didn't say anything. He was transfixed! He let Mike go on and on, through a nice large dinner, then dessert, and then coffee. He felt like he was attending some kind of "feel good" lecture, but it was affecting him. It all made perfect sense. Finally, he spoke while Mike's mouth was full.

"Mike, did you have a near-death experience or something like that?" John was serious. The day before, Mike had been his old worthless self, ready to be homeless, mope around, and suffer willingly.

"No, John, I guess I had a NEAR-LIFE experience." Both men laughed with the release of tension. Although the situation was comical, Mike was also contemplating exactly what had happened. He wasn't ready yet to claim that his vision had been real, but he felt so good about life!

John didn't want to say goodnight. He was benefitting by the energy around Mike and knew it. He was even convinced to search for a new job himself. Mike had convinced him that he was worth more, and John had agreed. He was invigorated by Mike's enthusiasm and the newfound positive personality. It was addictive, this positive attitude, and as for the high-minded thoughts? Well, he didn't know about those, but it certainly didn't hurt to listen. It made him feel like he was worth something.

The two men said goodnight, and again Mike gave John a warm hug. John realized that Mike had never done that before, and now in one evening, he had done it twice. What was with this man? What a good friend to have! It seemed as though Mike were in a different world, or somehow still here, but full of peace and love for humanity in general. He was nonjudgmental and happy. What a guy—what a difference!

Mike went back to the hotel room and sat alone on the bed. Dare he believe for even a moment that his dream journey was real? If it had been real, then why was he back on Earth? Nothing seemed correct. Nothing seemed to be what it was supposed to be. *What? Things are not what they seem?* Mike was starting to feel a strange but familiar presence. His intuition was prodding him forward, and his body was speaking to him.

Mike got up and went to a chair across the room. There, he did something that felt absolutely normal to him. He closed his eyes, held out his hands, and spoke out loud ceremoniously.

"In the name of Spirit, I ask that I should be shown what I need to know about this situation. I celebrate it, even though I do not understand it." Mike was silent, his eyes closed. Then, everything exploded in a burst of brilliant light.

Mike was whisked through the portal of dimensionality into a place that had been prepared for him and him only. It was the inner sanctum of Michael Thomas's communication with Spirit, a place he would return to often in his meditations. He floated there in space, totally aware that he was again in his "dream" state, only this state really wasn't a dream, was it?

"No, it isn't, Michael Thomas." The voice of White! Did Mike dare open his eyes? He didn't want to break away from this place, for he knew that it was a dimension where he was only a visitor. He didn't want to be snapped back to the hotel room until he was ready. The voice of the great white angel continued.

"It's simply another state of altered reality. Which one is the most real to you now, Michael?"

"White!" Mike spoke out loud.

"Yes, Michael."

"It's so good to hear you!" Mike was very excited. He almost shouted, "White! It wasn't a dream! I knew it!"

"*It wasn't a dream, Michael.*"

"What happened? Why am I not in heaven? Was there a mistake?" Mike felt so pleased to again speak with his spiritual friend!

"*Open your eyes, Michael. We have company.*"

Mike did as he was told, and gradually opened his eyes. The interdimensional portal remained stable, and Mike was not removed from his meditative state. He was floating in the lotus position in a space of incredible whiteness. It reminded Mike of the white place where he had originally met the great white angel of love. Below, but around him, were seven entities taking form in a circle. As he watched, seven hazy color groupings began to evolve. Each group was like a cloud of faint color, slowly filling itself out and gradually gaining form. He knew what was happening, and his heart jumped with joy!

Below him the seven clouds of subtle hues intensified in color and eventually glowed brightly as their real brilliant selves. There was Blue, Orange, Green, Violet, Red, White, and even GOLD! Evenly spaced, the small clouds gradually grew and became the solid angelic forms that he had met and spent time with seemingly only yesterday. Mike was overjoyed to see them. His friends were here! He was careful not to break the spiritual tether that still connected him to his humanness in the hotel room. Mike was again in two places at once.

The seven angelic entities in Mike's sanctuary remained for some moments, hands raised upward toward Mike in ceremony around the center. Mike celebrated with them. He felt an incredible feeling of sacredness around the circle, and honored it by not speaking. It was the Golden One who spoke first.

"Michael Thomas of Pure Intent, we greet you!"

"And I, you," said a grateful and peaceful Mike.

"What is it you wish to know, Michael?" The golden one was almost laughing. He knew what Mike knew, and therefore knew that Mike was beside himself with the desire to understand what had gone wrong. *Why was he on Earth again?*" It was White who spoke next, in answer to Mike's thought question.

"Perhaps you wish to review your original request, Michael?" Mike didn't know what White meant, but he was quiet while the great angel continued. Like a tape recording, Mike was suddenly presented with a verbatim playback of another point in time, a time when Mike had earlier verbalized to White what he felt HOME was. Mike listened to his own voice with the others.

"I want to be loved and around love. I want to feel peaceful in my existence. I don't want concerns and trials from the interactions of those around me. I don't want to worry about money. I want to feel RELEASE. I'm tired of being alone! I want to mean something to other entities in the Universe. I want to know that I exist for a reason, and do my part— to be a correct and appropriate part of God's plan. I don't really want to be a human as I have been. I want to be like you!"

It was Mike's description of his expectations of HOME. These were the words he had used when the great white angel had asked him to define HOME!

It was the voice of Blue who spoke next.

"Behold your life, Michael Thomas. You have the intuitive map that will allow a peaceful existence, since you understand the currentness of the way Spirit works." Mike realized that Blue was right. He was not concerned about getting work tomorrow. He had his "map," and it would help him navigate to the correct place.

The voice of the orange angel came next.

"And the gifts and tools of your high vibration on the planet will keep you balanced and out of the drama of those around you if you choose. And in the process, you have the power to slay any negative thing that should ever try and get in your way!" Mike knew Orange was telling the truth. Mike was not concerned at all about any former drama in his life. The Shirley incident was gone from his consciousness, as if it had never existed.

The voice of Green followed. It was filled with humor and was unmistakable.

"Your biology will give you the release you need, Michael. It is now filled with wisdom and knowledge." Mike had never felt better, and he knew how to keep himself fit. Green's teachings had been paramount!

It was now Violet's turn. Her voice was mellifluous and floated to Mike's ears.

"You are now part of God's plan, Michael, with purpose and responsibility. You create your own reality, and there never needs to be a moment of worry again. The family surrounds you!" Mike knew she was right. He indeed would create his future, without worry. He knew the family was there to support him, and he would always be in the right place at the right time.

Red's voice spoke up.

"You will never again be a human as you were, Michael. You have been changed forever by your own intent." Right again! Mike could never retreat backwards. He was not the same man. His apartment belonged to an old pitiful person, and even the clothes would have to be given away. Mike was new!

Then, the spectacular voice of White sounded again.

"You are a correct and appropriate part of the plan of Love, Michael. You are loved without measure, and you have the ability to give the same love to others. You have yet to realize the gift that is before you!" *What did that mean? Why was White always the one with the statement that created a question?*

And, finally, the voice of the golden one, so large and potent, so sacred, yet so soft.

"You wanted to be like an angel, Michael? What is it you learned in my house? You are a wonderful piece of God, walking the planet in a very high vibration. An angel in disguise, one of the few who even know it, and anointed of God." Indeed, Mike had asked to be like the angels, never knowing that he really was one.

Suddenly, they seemed to speak as one, as they all presented a thought to Mike's ears simultaneously.

"This IS home, Michael Thomas. You are here because you asked to be. It is the place where you belong and can make a difference for the planet. Each item you asked for is now in place. You are a warrior of the light. Like Mary, your human counterpart, you resound with the vibration of God. You have slain the giant, accepted the golden one, and have the wisdom of the ages!"

There was more, and Michael Thomas knew it was coming. The angelic beings lost their form once again, and seven small clouds of brilliant hue melded together into one vibrating area of brilliant diamondlike light! The iridescence and sparkle of the cloud was spectacular beyond words. The angels were having a meeting. Mike intuitively knew it. After some time, he again heard them speak as one."

"Michael Thomas, we give you a new entity designation today. As you walked the path, you were known as Michael Thomas of Pure Intent. You stand today as a graduate, a high vibrating entity who is neither fully human or fully angelic. Instead, you are now MICHAEL THE CURRENT. It represents the vibration of the "now" and is one of the highest compliments we can bestow."

Mike thought this was very funny, but knew that the angels were serious in their honoring of his new vibration. The spectacular diamond cloud slowly became a diamond shape and seemed to rise up from below and flow over him, encompassing the entire space he was in with a diamond light. He was washed in love, and again felt overwhelmed by the presence of God. Each cell celebrated, and his biology responded with a welling-up of feeling and appropriate thanks. The feeling permeated every pore of Mike's body, and he knew it was time to return to the hotel chair. The angels had one more message, and as Mike was again returned to his meditative chair, the words of their collective energies rang in his ears.

"Michael the Current, YOU ARE DEARLY LOVED."

Mike sat for some time in the hotel chair, coming down off his "high" of meditative realization. Everything he had experienced in the houses of spiritual training was real! All the teachings were accurate and valid, and all the knowledge and power was still his, as he sat in that Los Angeles hotel room. He reeled at the concept and wondered how many others like him there were.

Mike was exhausted. He almost fell asleep in the shower, but he finally made it to bed. He was too tired to think about what was next. He had to sleep, and he did—very well.

Mike was ready for life the next day. He went out on the balcony of the hotel and surveyed the area. There was no limit to what he could do. He would indeed make a difference wherever he walked.

Mike knew that much was in store for him and that he would have much to work out and learn about, especially how to integrate his new vibration while being around the older vibration of the other humans. He wasn't worried. He had the love and understanding wisdom of the ages within his soul. The angel inside him would take care of it, and he would always know what to do with every situation.

The new job was even easier to get than Mike had thought. Big companies need good sales people with integrity, and Mike exuded who he was with every word and step. He had purchased a new wardrobe and had set his goals high. He walked into the largest company that needed his expertise, past the sign that said "No help needed." He had his job in minutes and left the building ready to hold yet another ceremony focusing on how humans can create their own reality.

Mike had been preoccupied with the newness of who he was. The fact that this was HOME was finally starting to become part of his consciousness. His new job was secure, and he was beginning to look for a place to live. Three days had passed, when in the shower one morning, a realization hit him like a ton of bricks.

What had White said that Mike had not understood? *Michael, you have yet to realize the gift that is before you!* Michael's eyes filled with tears of understanding. The gift was the greatest one of all. It only could have been given to him as a human, and it had successfully hidden from him in all the spectacular events of the past days on earth. It was profound in its implications, and Mike knelt while still in the bathroom and gave thanks for the truth of the revelation. He shook with the potential of it, and searched his memory for the information he needed. His heart pounded as he thought about what it all meant.

WE LEAVE MICHAEL THOMAS at this point in the story. Michael has a quest. Because of his new intuitive tools and gifts, Michael knows that he is not complete. His map will guide him in the right direction, and his internal Sword of Truth will be his light in the darkness, a vibrating heart frequency that will sound the *F* note and sing his joy at the right time. Mike has a clear picture from the House of White etched into the tenderest cells of his heart and mind.

Nothing will stop "Michael the Current" from finding a sacred gift that is waiting for him in the sea of humanity around him. His smile is as big as any human being can muster in the absolute knowledge that his quest will be successfully completed—all he has to do is begin it.

Mike realized that he had been given the gift of a second chance to find a precious one, the love of his life, a contract so potent that it would be like a magnet for them both, unable to continue apart on the same planet.

Mike is in search of a beautiful red-haired woman with skin like ivory and eyes like emeralds. He doesn't know her Earth name, but it doesn't matter. The energy of Anolee will be like a beacon in the darkness to his soul.

He thought of the unborn children, and it fanned his resolve to find this flower of his life.

There was electricity in the air that crackled with the energy of spiritual purpose and love, ready to be fulfilled and kept precious. The smell of victory was aromatic. The only scheduled rose in Mike's life was about to be found, admired, and loved for its beauty. Its fragrance would be appreciated for a lifetime—held and adored for its perfect beauty and natural elegance.

She was out there somewhere, and Mike was going to find her.

The angels smiled and knew that Michael would achieve his goal.

Michael Thomas indeed was HOME.

AFTERWORD

Within the pages of this tale of Michael Thomas and the seven angels, there are many hidden metaphors and New Age spiritual truths. From the number of chapters, to the numerology of the spiritual names, there are many more lessons to be gleaned for those who wish to find them.

The colors also have known energies, and they give further insight into what is actually being presented—far more than the text would have you believe.

Here are some study questions that might be fun to pose within a group:

(1)   What was the real message behind the strange map given to Michael Thomas in the blue house? How can you apply it to everyday life?

(2)   What was meant by the rotting food on the road? What is the "food of Spirit," and why can't it exist beyond the plate it is served on?

(3)   Why didn't any of the angels argue with Michael or make him behave when they knew he was headed for trouble?

(4)   Where is the real lesson behind the "WE" of our biology?

(5)   Does the vibrational increase for a human really create a challenge? Where else have you seen this fact given?

(6)   Why were the old energy weapons of Michael Thomas needed in a spiritual venue? Why did they call him a "warrior" of the light? Isn't that an old energy concept?

(7)   Who really was IT? What is the dark side?

I have a confession. The true metaphysical attribute that this story represents is never mentioned in this book. It is one word that does not exist in the text. Can you guess it?

Finally a fun thing: Take a good look at the cover of this book.

(1)   Who is really with Michael Thomas?

(2)   Who is actually wearing the wings?

As you close this book, ask yourself, "Am I HOME like Michael Thomas?"

It is my great wish that each of you finds this place.

— LEE CARROLL

P.S.: This book was written in hotel rooms all over the United States and Canada. My thanks to the energies of Chicago; Washington, DC; Mesa, Arizona; Houston; Gainesville and Orlando, Florida; Indianapolis; Montreal; Milwaukee; Seattle; Atlanta; Tucson; and Kansas City—and all the states I flew over while writing on my trusty laptop on the airplane.

$\mathscr{A}$BOUT THE AUTHOR

After graduating with a business and economics degree from California Western University in California, **Lee Carroll** started a business in San Diego that has flourished for 27 years.

Where do parables and angelic stories fit into all this? As Lee tells it, God had to hit him "between the eyes" to prove that his spiritual experience was real. The year 1989 was the turning point, when the first psychic told him about Kryon—and then three years later when the second unrelated psychic told him the same thing (spelling the name KRYON in session)!

Timidly, the first Kryon writings were presented to the metaphysical community in Del Mar, California, and the rest is history—with a total of six metaphysical books being released in a four-year span. There are now over a quarter of a million books in print in over seven languages worldwide.

Lee and his partner, Jan, started the Kryon light groups in Del Mar in 1991, and quickly moved from a living room setting to a Del Mar church. Now they are hosting meetings all over the globe, with audiences of up to 1,000 people. Kryon has the largest consistent New Age folder in the history of America Online, and attracts many more electronic browsers on his dual web sites: (www.kryon.com) and (www.kryon.org). The national *Kryon Quarterly* magazine was started in 1995. This New Age full-color 40-page periodical, without any advertising, now has over 3,500 subscribers in over 12 countries.

In 1995, Lee was asked to present his work at the United Nations (U.N.) before a U.N.–chartered group known as the Society for Enlightenment and Transformation (S.E.A.T.). The meeting was so well accepted that he was brought back for a second New York visit in 1996.

The connection with Hay House is a strong one and promises more to come! Lee continues to write inspired stories and parables from his home in San Diego.

✤ NOTES ✤

❦ NOTES ❦

✦ NOTES ✦

✤ NOTES ✤

❧ NOTES ❧

✦ NOTES ✦

❖ ❖ ❖

We hope you enjoyed this Hay House book.
If you would like to receive a free catalog featuring additional
Hay House books and products, or if you would like information
about the Hay Foundation, please contact:

Hay House, Inc.
P.O. Box 5100
Carlsbad, CA 92018-5100

(760) 431-7695 or **(800) 654-5126**
(760) 431-6948 (fax) or **(800) 650-5115 (fax)**

Please visit the Hay House Website at: **www.hayhouse.com**

❖ ❖ ❖